NINE MEN PLUS

NINE MEN PLUS

SUPREME COURT OPINIONS ON FREE SPEECH AND FREE PRESS

AN ACADEMIC GAME-SIMULATION

created by
William I. Gorden
Kent State University

WM. C. BROWN COMPANY PUBLISHERS Dubuque, Iowa

Copyright © 1971 by
Wm. C. Brown Company Publishers

ISBN 0–697–04113–1

Second Printing, 1973

Printed in the United States of America

Dedicated to those families whose peace and security have suffered because one of their members struggled to realize the First Amendment.

"I'll tell you what frightens me. The violence of your students. The throwing of objects at enforcement men. The burning of buildings. The total disregard for other people's rights, while they are yelling for their rights. The arsenal of weapons found at Kent State in dorms.

"Who is putting these riotous ideas into the students' heads? Can you give me a sensible answer to that?"

AN OHIO TAXPAYER
MAY 28, 1970

"Every idea is an incitement."

JUSTICES OLIVER WENDELL HOLMES
AND LOUIS D. BRANDEIS
JUNE 8, 1925

Contents

Preface

Let us consider for a moment how long each of us would hesitate if asked some of the following questions by a probing reporter from one of the leading networks. Remember that time is money, and the networks cannot afford many 20-second pauses. As the camera zooms in on that room in our dorm, apartment, or home, what will be our answers to the following?

1. In view of the destructiveness which has accompanied so many student demonstrations, isn't it about time we ban large gatherings of students?
2. Do you defend filthy speech?
3. Shouldn't we protect our children from violence and perverted sex in modern films?
4. Are you opposed to laws which protect the flag?
5. What's wrong with prayer in the school?
6. Should a public official have to put up with demonstrators picketing outside his home?
7. Does a United States citizen have the right to travel to any country he chooses?
8. How can we balance the public's "right to know" against being "tried in the press"?
9. Why shouldn't we require government employees, policemen, firemen, and teachers to sign loyalty oaths?
10. Should demonstrations be permitted on the grounds of a courthouse or jail?
11. Should radicals who advocate that youth "kill their parents" be arrested?
12. What does freedom of speech and freedom of press mean to you personally?

If any of us are inarticulate in our answers, there are good reasons for being so. They are complex questions. Undoubtedly our hesitancies result, in part, from very limited opportunities to look a fellow human being in the eye while trying to give a sensible answer to tough questions, and being good at almost anything tough takes training and practice. People who rarely talk about free speech and free press, obviously, will find that unfamiliar words and ideas are put together with difficulty. In short, they will not speak freely about free speech. Our schools should be one place which provides an environment where students can think through, talk about, and argue out their opinions about freedom. *Nine Men Plus* is designed to meet such a need. It is the first and only attempt that I know of to create an environment where student will face student to talk about free speech and free press.

The format of this text is dialogue—dialogue which involves formulating answers to the above "on-the-spot" kind of questions about free speech and free press which have worked their way up to the highest court in the land. It differs from other texts about free speech and free press because *Nine Men Plus* is an academic game-simulation. It is meant to be played rather than read. Small clusters of students within a classroom can "play" together in their simulation of the Court's decision-making process after minimal directions from the instructor. Or the large class, in a more formal fashion, can debate and simulate a large jury. Most texts about High Court decisions are long on explanation and short on references to the justices' own words. If this book errs, it errs in the opposite direction, because the heart and mind of this text are the words of the justices who wrote the majority and dissenting opinions to the First Amendment cases. These opinions can stand in their own right, and they will earn respect and provoke ample explication by the participants in the simulation.

Instructors in the disciplines of political science, law, journalism, and speech communication assisted in the selection of these cases. Traditionally, the study of the High Court's decisions has been the province of the political science department and law schools; however, in more recent years the departments of journalism, mass communication, and rhetoric have demonstrated a vigorous interest in introducing their students to the landmark free speech-free press cases and the reasoning of the great minds of the Court which has led to these decisions.

These fields so intimately involved with the written and the spoken word most assuredly have a stake in First Amendment guarantees. From the days of Milton's attack upon the control of the press by licensing to this past decade's heavy sentences and fines on the purveyors of pornography, the press has had a vital stake in the law. The high school and the college student's concern for these matters is not just theoretical, but rather is motivated by real conflicts about censorship and control of the school newspaper and literary magazines. The dramatic arts, likewise, know what controversy is. They have been driven to an interest in the legal definitions of obscenity as they have witnessed the emotional reactions to nudity and the drama of absurdity, occasionally resulting in the closing down of a show. Similarly, those who enter the radio and television fields must soon learn what their responsibilities are under the FCC doctrines of fairness and balanced programming. Finally, scholars and students of rhetoric also have been forced to learn what are the legal parameters of their art because of the spokesmen who lead demonstrations, organize boycotts and picketing, who are intemperate and sometimes advocate violence. Naturally concerned about how man relates to man, indignant about injustice and abridgment of freedoms, and repelled by regimentation and docility, these are the disciplines which must help politically conscious students to find ways of working both inside and outside of channels for realization of the social contract.

I have found that the materials herein have ready acceptance on a number of levels. *Nine Men Plus* may serve as the major text in a course which might be entitled "Legal and Constitutional Issues of Free Speech and Free Press" or "Historic and Contemporary Problems in the Freedom of Speech and Freedom of Press." Colleagues have told me that they find the text a useful central instrument to teach a two- or three-week unit on free speech in the basic speech-communication course. The text design certainly lends itself to speech-communication experiences so important to development of an articulate public self. That is to say, the student who plays becomes more conversant with the language of great deliberative minds seeking to balance that "free play of the Spirit" against the preservation of the state. In the simulation, students have frequent opportunities to vocalize their own opinions and to trade ideas with their peers. This game differs from so many other simulations in that it fits into the normal fifty-minute period and in that it may be either completed within that period or continued.

The cases within each division are chronologically arranged under one of six categories: I. Academic Freedom, II. Censorship, III. Defamation and Libel, IV. Political Dissent, V. Privacy, and VI. Provocation and Demonstration. Each case is briefly summarized and has ten exact quotations from the opinions of the justices who heard it. The authorship of *only* one or two of the quotations is provided in order not to disclose which way the case was decided.

The cases included date from World War I to today. The majority of them are drawn from the past two decades because only in more recent times have the justices fully explained their decisions for the consumption of the general public. Modern students attend to the present. Their concerns for freedom of speech, press, and assembly are now concerns. The High Court's most recent deliberations consequently are of greatest interest.

The title *Nine Men Plus* is an obvious reference to the nine justices on the High Court. The title of an academic game-simulation should provide some hint that a novel kind of educational experience is offered. The caption begs the question: plus what? I will not answer *what* in such a way as to make it a problem of simple addition (9 + x =   ), but I do suggest that those of us who will study the opinions of the nine men who address each other as "brother" may discover an awakening kinship with them.

That is to say, there is a *plus* factor in this text if there is information-gain which facilitates dialogue about civil liberties; it is plus if participants become less passive and more vigorous defenders of human dignity; and it is plus if students come to be more interested in joining that aristocratic tradition which exalts knowledge over ignorance, and competence over mediocrity.

The idea for a game-simulation in free speech and free press came to me during a term of post-doctoral study at Northwestern University while taking a course taught by Franklyn Haiman. My first trial games took place later during that same year while studying with Theodore Clevenger at Florida State University. I am grateful to both of these excellent teachers who particularly have awakened for me and others the conscience of our discipline. Students who played *Nine Men Plus* at the following universities helped greatly in the debugging process: The University of North Carolina at Greensboro, thanks to Tom Tedford; Denver University, thanks to Alvin Goldberg; Purdue University, thanks to L. David Schuelke; and at Kent State University, thanks to my colleagues in the Division of Rhetoric and Communication. In addition, I wish to acknowledge the counsel of Robert Hunter of the Law College at Akron University and William Fisher, Professor in the School of Journalism at Kent State, whose students, like my own, have spent many hours reading from the *United States Supreme Court Reports.*

William I. Gorden

Introduction

At 7 A.M., Friday, May 1, 1970, Steven Sharoff, a graduate student in history at Kent State University and a son of a retired police chief, talked with Chris Plant, a colleague, about his anguish over President Nixon's announcement that previous night to expand the war into Cambodia. Early in the morning, these friends made up a name for an organization—World Historians Opposed to Racism and Exploitation (WHORE). They hurriedly printed leaflets announcing their organization and a noon rally.

About 500 persons gathered on the hillside of the commons facing the victory bell to listen to the "world historians." That noon a veteran who had won the Silver Star in Vietnam with the 101st Airborne burned his discharge papers. A few minutes later a copy of the Constitution torn from a sixth-grade textbook was buried in a shallow grave. One bushy-haired student tried to prevent the funeral by shouting, "Stop them. Once you bury the Bill of Rights you have no rights." But the ceremony was completed and the assembly dispersed peacefully. In the weekend which followed, fifty windows of stores were broken. The ROTC building was burned while a crowd cheered, and the National Guard was ordered onto the campus: tanks into the streets, bands of guardsmen posted at every campus entrance. The throbbing pulsations from helicopters overhead and the odor of tear gas were continuing reminders of their presence.

Better Than Bullets

On Sunday, Allison Krause bravely, arrogantly, foolishly or lovingly (who knows why) placed a blossom into the gun barrel of one of the National Guardsmen. She told the guardsman that "Flowers are better than bullets." On Monday, under a blue spring sky, Allison and three other students were shot dead and ten more were wounded by a savage barrage from the guardsmen. Until that moment the atmosphere was almost carnival with the tossing to and fro of the tear gas canisters. Today a nation grieves because students assembled on the commons would not disperse, and the green is stained with red.

But not all grieved; tens of thousands put their names on petitions in support of the actions of the guard. The campus was evacuated; entrances became checkpoints, and special identification credentials determined ingress and egress. For weeks any assembly was at the mayor's discretion. Even a memorial service was forbidden for a month. Dorms were searched without a warrant, some faculty members were stopped from distributing handbills informing students about their rights, persons gathering names on an antiwar petition were detained by the police, and the Federal Bureau of Investigation interrogated students, not only about the shootings, but also to ask if certain of their teachers "ever said anything against the government."

To me, the First Amendment had never before seemed so fragile, and still the embodiment of what should be the most indestructible tenets of a free society:

> Congress shall make no law respecting an establishment of religion or prohibiting the free exercise thereof; or abridging the freedom of speech; or of the press; or the right of the people peaceably to assemble, and to petition the Government for a redress of grievances.

1

These rights are not to be submitted to a vote—to all for free speech and free press to shout aye or nay—but are part of the agreement of birth in this nation. The English barons more than 750 years ago had to demand that King John sign the Magna Charta. The security of private property and of person, the right to judgment by one's peers, the right to seek redress of grievances from the sovereign, and the right to due process—all these basic assumptions of our citizenship earned by others before us are the principles to which we turn when lawlessness threatens. To look elsewhere is to put one's fate in the hands of the anarchists, the vigilantes, or the military. The constructive alternative at Kent, whether one defends the shootings by the guard or accuses the guard of reckless slaughter, is through the courts and through public debate.

The Kent tragedy joins those many other events in our national history in which the line between words and actions has blurred, where the freedom to differ and defy has proved intolerable. That troublesome person Roger Williams, to escape exportation to England by officials of Massachusetts Bay Colony in 1636, fled to the wilderness of Rhode Island. Not long after the adoption in 1791 of the Bill of Rights, the Alien and Sedition Acts gave the President authority to banish or imprison persons who, by writing or speaking, or in any other way, tried to arouse discontent with the government. In 1837, a mob gathered to destroy the presses of an antislavery newspaper in Alton, Illinois. Elijah Lovejoy, the editor, was killed trying to stop them. During the last half of the nineteenth century, Anthony Comstock carried his crusade against immorality into national legislation, and as a nation we are not yet completely free to make our own choice about what we shall read or see.

In the wake of the Russian revolution and World War I, the Espionage and Sedition Acts convicted Shenck, Abrams, and Debs for speeches and writings against United States military policy. Red flag laws and syndicalism statutes in the twenties were enacted in many states. The *ex parte* injunction was widely used to prevent assembly and picketing by organizing labor. Dirk De Jonge, both a Communist and a labor leader, was arrested under the Oregon Syndicalism Act in 1934 for speaking at a meeting in protest of conditions in the county jail, strike-breaking action by the police, raids on their Communist headquarters, and the shooting of striking longshoremen by Portland police. During this same period, but ten years earlier, John T. Scopes was fired and tried for teaching evolution in a biology class.

In the thirties, the High Court took up the right of a city to stop a scandal sheet prior to its publication and distribution. The forties witnessed the internment of persons of Japanese heritage. That decade also saw many cases involving the use of discretionary municipal power to grant or prohibit permits to speak, distribute literature, solicit, or use loudspeakers in the streets and in public places. To date, over fifty cases involving such issues have been brought to the Supreme Court by members of the Jehovah's Witnesses sect.

In the fifties, during the McCarthy hysteria, the issues centered about investigations, loyalty oaths, and censorship of obscene literature and films. Scarcely were the fifties past before the sit-ins, kneel-ins, wade-ins, the demonstrations, shootings, nightsticks, cattle prods, fire hoses, and police dogs, served up nightly on dinner-time television, once again forced the public and the courts to debate the boundaries of "speech plus." Prayer and religious exercises in the schools and loyalty of teachers continued to be at issue, but such problems were soon dimmed in comparison with the new militancy of youth in protest. So much has happened so fast: occupation of buildings, mass rallies, superfluous use of obscenities, desecration of sacred symbols, and rejection in dress and posture by the young of those over thirty, and on top of all this, ridicule of the police and courtroom decorum.

The polarization between black and white, between young and old, now brings to the courts the most serious questions any people can face about freedom of speech, press, and assembly: How far must be the distance between expression and action, between desecration and destruction, between conspiracy and acts of violence? Judge Learned Hand, in *The Spirit of Liberty*, said:

> Liberty lies in the hearts of men and women; when it dies there, no constitution, no law, no court, can save it; no constitution, no law, no court can even do much to help it. While it lies there it needs no constitution, no law, no court to save it.*

*Learned Hand, *The Spirit of Liberty* (New York: Random House, Inc., Vintage Books, 1960), p. 190.

I do not believe that revolution is around the corner or that the spirit of liberty is near death in our land; rather it seems evident to me that our youth as never before in our history are demanding not only to be heard but to have a say in their immediate future.

At last the vote for eighteen-year-olds has been signed into law and has been found constitutional by the Supreme Court when applied to national elections. Young people do not want to be sent to war before they have a say in declaring or not declaring that war. They have a very real interest in the ideals of American patriots and the realization of these ideals over poverty, racial prejudice, pollution, and militarism. Because demonstrations and disruptions have landed so many of their number in the courts, there is natural self-interest in the way these ideals are spelled out through the legal system. They may long for the Woodstock nation in the flower children age, but a dream-for-community cannot be until youth and their plain-spoken antagonists can engage in a dialogue about their fears, hates, and ideals. With no taint of intellectual elitism those who love books must meet with those who live by television. The Bill of Rights must be reasoned out in answers sensible to the businessman and rephrased into the argot of the construction worker. Who won a particular Supreme Court case matters little to most students and probably not at all to most nonstudents. What does matter are the reasons that lie behind the interpretations of our Constitutional rights and responsibilities.

A Small and Distinctive Body

No other small group of men in our government outside the Supreme Court can lay claim to participation in so long a dialogue about freedom. No other government body, perhaps because no other men are appointed for the rest of their working lives to such a continuing decision-making group, has had to learn to work intimately with its members though their opinions may sharply sound again and again from opposite sides of questions of personal and societal values.

They have made mistakes which have lasted for years. Their about-faces, occasionally, have been rationalized by precedents which have been outrageously dredged up or construed to fit. The Court has had to endure pressures from high places, to hear their decisions, even in the Senate Chamber, labeled smut, to tolerate shouts of impeachment, and to hear the Chief of the FBI, among others, assail some of their number for being soft on criminals and communists.

Libertarians have been far from pleased with the High Court. A number of the Court's decisions have tilted the scales of justice to the side of the state when a "clear and present danger" was difficult to discern. The bookseller, theater manager, broadcaster, and artist have had cause to realize that art, even when in the hands of the High Court, is a chancy profession. Moreover, the Court has sometimes refused to rule on cases vital to our national welfare, such as conscription in an undeclared war, tax exemption of religious institutions, and even the rights of topless go-go girls.

But the Court has made its mark upon our speech, although it has occasionally refused to speak to every facet of our behavior. Think for a moment about just a few of the many phrases which have become a part of our language because of the Court: "clear and present danger," "prior restraint," "knowing membership," "utterly without redeeming social importance," "pure speech," "with reckless disregard," and "the right of privacy." These are the weighted words by which educated men interpret the social contract spelled out in the Constitution and in the Bill of Rights.

The Lesson of the Game

There is something very *a propos* in a game-simulation of a court. The lessons of the courtroom have much in common with the lessons we learn from games. Games are instruments which help children to organize equitable relationships within a small span of time and a limited space. A child learns to manage within that temporary environment the basic principles of fairness, and he may also taste of the injustice of chance. He learns to follow explicit rules and to base present judgments on agreed-upon past behaviors or arrangements. By game activities those parameters which seem fair are routinized and those which are unfair are modified or abandoned. The necessity of narrowly drawn rules becomes evident.

The playing of games thus contributes to learning to abide by the rules of the social order and to governing behavior which is antisocial. Similarly, the Supreme Court is the highest agency for clarifying the rules we live by and the social contract we live under.

In the larger environment the rules are not always so explicitly stated or agreed upon, and so we have the courts. Take, for example, the assumption that life ought to be valued more highly than property which is challenged by the order of a mayor to shoot to kill looters, or the historic right to privacy in one's household which is abridged by the wiretap and modern technological snooping. Changing patterns of living, technological invention, such as the telephone, and oral contraceptives are the kinds of new input which call for new interpretations of the old truths. Precedent and the Court serve as the stabilizing factor in times of changing perspectives.

The courtroom is an environment within the larger environment. The real world is shut off from the witnesses; the jury is sequestered; and retribution is forestalled for a time. There are the facts of the case presented to members of the jury, but there are also the perceptions of these data which may be colored differently according to each peculiar background. The jurors' varied assumptions about the value of life and property, about freedom of expression, and about clear and present danger make it very obvious that individual decisions may differ. The verdict is based upon consensus or, in the case of the "nine old men" on the Supreme Court, upon majority rule. Coming to a decision is frequently not an easy task. The deliberations involve the weighing of evidence, the analyses of cause and effect, the consideration of motives, and even the degree of "liking" of and respect for one's fellow juror or justice.

Nine Men Plus is a game-simulation where all these elements of the decision-making process are squeezed into a limited time-space environment. As was mentioned in the preface, the simulation fits into the usual class hour. Consequently, much that goes into the long, often tedious, process of the legal decision-making process is necessarily omitted. Of course, to lengthen the game and to make its decision binding upon certain parties after the game is over would move measurably toward more realism. Were it possible for this game to include motion pictures of the alleged crime and live persons playing the role of witnesses, prosecutor, counsel for the defense, the judge and jurors, the optimum in simulation learning experiences would be reached, short of the real experience itself.

Obviously realism is sacrificed and admittedly suffers from the synopses of cases. To select some words of the justices over other words is incomplete and unfair, just as in playing *Monopoly* the purchase of a property certainly is an unfair representation of the total negotiation and costs involved in the purchase of real estate. Within these limitations, then, *Nine Men Plus* provides a relatively painless, even pleasurable, way of acquainting students with some of the legal issues of our day. It operates under the assumption that a more articulate, a more informed people are the *sine qua non* of this noble experiment of government. The game thus attempts to bring alive the conviction-persuasive environment integral to the jury room and to the conversation of intelligent people. Only a few Americans ever sit on a jury, and only a very select number ever become court justices, but since we live by law and its interpretations, it indeed seems fitting that young citizens study the decision-making process of the Highest Court in the land by simulation of that process.

Using This Text

In my course entitled "Free Speech Colloquium" I have discovered what I believe to be a healthy balance between individual assignments and group activities. The usual pattern of each unit includes (a) individual assignments to study background cases, (b) followed by small-group participation in the simulations of the more recent cases, and (c) topped off by guest lecturers who have been involved in a free speech or a free press controversy.

For example, in the Censorship Unit, *Near* v. *Minnesota*, *Roth* v. *US*, and *Times* v. *Chicago* were first assigned for individual study. Next the class participated in several rounds of the simulation in which they became acquainted with Freedman, Memoirs, and Ginzburg. Following this we were fortunate to be able to bring into the classroom Nico Jacobellis, the Cleveland Heights theater manager in whose case the "national community standard" criterion was argued.

Academic Solitaire

This text is inductive in that reading the case summary and selected quotations becomes a step-by-step process of inquiry. The student is not given the outcome of a case at the onset. Only after he has made an effort to understand the facts and rationale stated in the justices' own words is he then expected to check *his answer* with the *Decision* (contained in Appendix A in the back of the text).

I would advise the student, even when working alone, to fill in the ballots. This forces him to make an educated guess about which party won the case, Phase I; about which justices sided for the majority or dissented, Phase II; and he must put into writing how he would decide the case if he were a justice, Phase III. It is a form of Academic Solitaire which may heighten the desire for involvement and may reinforce memory, both features very much needed to make productive self-study. Hopefully a few students, as a result of examining the selected quotations, will discover certain cases they would like to read in full. Thus *Nine Men Plus*, with its summaries, selected quotations, and verdicts, serves as an annotated guide which may lead one into the law library. This is to suggest that the *Nine Men Plus* simulation, even when studied alone, is a stimulating, convenient guide to primary materials.

Developing New Cases

One feature of self-study which should not be overlooked involves adding new cases. My students have taken special pride in developing cases which each of them has researched. In *Nine Men Plus* the teacher has a vehicle and a format. How does this work? A number of important cases are not included in this text because of the author's oversight, his preference, or space limitation. In addition, during each month in which the Supreme Court is in session, there are new decisions published which should be examined as they arise. The up-to-date instructor, therefore, may request that an individual student, or perhaps a team of students, research a particular current case. Such an assignment may accomplish more "learning" if the student has a pattern to follow as is provided in this text: making a summary, selecting ten representative quotations from the Court's opinions, and, finally, preparing the Decision with brief rationale. The student-developed case may then be *played* as are the other cases in this text. Extra forms and ballots are provided for this purpose.

Developing new cases promotes a constructive pattern of involvement with each other's research and holds the attraction of an economical division of energies. I find this kind of co-scholarship a delightful, exciting, and comfortable pattern of pedagogy. There is system and order here; there is the delight of individual discovery allied to the satisfactions of cooperative and competitive involvement with that discovery. There is comfort in that the posture of the instructor is like that of the student. His stance is not one of preaching or teaching, but of participating. This kind of use of the game-simulation in the classroom provides a very natural way to share tasks of leadership and scholarship between student and teacher.

Rules of the Game-Simulation

Overview of Procedure for Playing NINE MEN PLUS in Small Groups

STEPS

1. Select a case. Tear out a ballot from the back of the book. Write the parties on the ballot.

2. Players number off and divide up quotations. *MASK OVER* all quotations not assigned to you.

3. Player number one reads aloud the case summary and serves as chairman. The chairman also keeps time for each stage and calls for the votes. After the summary has been read, two minutes' time is set aside for each player to silently examine his quotation(s).

4. Information Exchange—ten-minute limit. Players take turns reading aloud or paraphrasing their quotations. They ask each other questions and generally try to discover *who won* the case and *which way* two of the justices voted. The chairman serves as a facilitator during this period.

5. Vote Phase I, *Who Won*. Each player secretly circles the party whom he believes the Court decided for and in Phase II, *Which Way Justice* (optional), writes in one or two justices under majority or dissenting positions.

6. Conviction-Persuasion Exchange—ten-minute limit. (If there are more than eight players, 15 minutes.) Each player makes a brief statement of his position. All players are then open to question, to debate, and to attempt to persuade each other. The more players persuaded to vote alike, the higher is their score for those on the majority side. The chairman serves as a chief justice, joins in the discussion, encourages interaction, and occasionally serves as an arbiter should the need arise.

7. Vote Phase III, *If I Were Justice Today*. Each player secretly writes in the party who *he believes should* have won the case. His vote is made independent of how the case actually was decided.

8. Check Decision to determine points in Phases I and II as is explained on ballots. The Decisions are alphabetically arranged in the Appendix A.

9. Now total votes in Phase III to determine points as explained on ballots.

10. Repeat on a second and a third case.

Complete Instructions for
NINE MEN PLUS

An Academic Game-Simulation

GOALS: To acquire the highest total points by making correct judgments concerning who won, which way certain justices voted, and by persuading others to your viewpoint concerning Supreme Court Cases. Of course, the long-range goals are to become better acquainted with selected cases where the freedom of speech and freedom of press were at stake and to become a more articulate person concerning the rights and responsibilities of Free Speech and Free Press.

Game Procedure

1. TO BEGIN. See that all players have the *Nine Men Plus* text. *Do not* turn ahead to the *Decision* which is located in the Appendixes, but do examine the ballot and scoring rules if the game is new to you. Tear out a ballot. Select a case from the collection in an area which interests the players involved or which is suggested by the instructor. Then print in the blanks on the ballot under Phase I the parties of the case chosen for play. Next, all players number off. Up to ten persons may play. The players divide up the quotations. If there are fewer than ten players, some players should have more than one quotation assigned to them. Take turns in future rounds to permit others to have this slight advantage. When a second quotation is assigned to a player, both of his quotations should be on the same page to facilitate masking. If there are only three players, each player takes a complete page. The game is more interesting, however, if six to ten persons play. MASK OVER those quotations not assigned to you. Player number one reads aloud the summary statement. (The ten quotations are representative evidence and reasoning from the opinions of the justices. Only two of the quotations are identified by the authoring justice.) After the summary has been read, two minutes' time is set aside for each player to silently examine his quotation(s).

2. INFORMATION EXCHANGE PERIOD (Ten-minute limit). The player who read the summary statement keeps time and serves as chairman. Some quotations will be easy to understand immediately; others may not take on meaning until later, like some hard-to-fit pieces of a jigsaw which do not seem to belong until nearly all other pieces are in place. Quotations may be paraphrased or read in part or in full during this period. All information exchanges must be *oral*. Players may pose questions; they may add background information known about this case or related cases. Each player may exchange as little or as much information as he wishes, keeping in mind that he is trying to discover which party won the case, which way two of the justices voted, and that he later will want to persuade his fellow players to side with him in Phase III. In short, he wants to gather enough information to make correct judgments and enough goodwill to have his own viewpoint respectfully considered. At the close of the Information Exchange, each player privately fills out the *Who Won—*Phase I and *Which Way Justice—*Phase II on his ballot.

The purpose of Phase II—*Which Way Justice* is to interest the player in the viewpoint of particular justices. In addition to gradually getting to know the positions taken, say by Warren on obscenity, one is constantly reminded that these words were words of different men—men who were obligated by the nature of their positions to record the reasoning of their decisions. Phase II also provides a bit more risk and adventure to the game.

If sometime before the ten minutes allotted for the Information Exchange Period it becomes apparent that each player has formed his opinion and is prepared to vote in Phase I and Phase II, any player may make a motion to end the exchange and to vote. To do so, however, the vote must be unanimous.

3. The CONVICTION-PERSUASION PERIOD comes next. (Ten-minute limit. If there are more than eight players, 15 minutes.) During this period each player plays the role of a justice and does his best to persuade the other players to side with him in the *If I Were Justice Today*—Phase III. By playing a role of a justice it is not intended that a player act out a particular Court justice, but rather that he represent his own convictions in a role of a justice. Each player should be given the opportunity for at least one statement in favor of his own position, but this need not be done in rigid order. Players may speak more than once and may freely question and respond to each other as long as time permits. They may come to an open agreement upon how they will vote in Phase III, or they may refuse to stipulate which way their votes will be cast. When the time is up, each player votes in secret in Phase III, and he may change his vote in Phase I or Phase II if he has changed his mind.

4. SCORING. When all ballots have been completed for all three phases, player number one turns to the Decision and reads it aloud. Each player then scores his own Phase I and Phase II.

Phase I—*Who Won:* Players with a correct answer get 100 points each.

Phase II—*Which Way Justice:* Players who correctly place one justice receive 10 points; if two justices are correctly placed, the players receive 20 points each. Each justice misplaced subtracts 10 points from a player's score. No more than two justices may be so placed.

Phase III—*If I Were Justice Today:* The player serving as chairman asks each player to state the side for which he voted in Phase III. The vote is scored as follows:

—If the vote is unanimous in Phase III, all players get 100 points each.

—If there is no unanimity but a majority of more than one, each of those players gets 75 points.

—If the majority is simple, that is, only one more than half, each of those players gets 50 points.

—The players who are in a minority of more than one get 25 points each.

—A tie vote gets 0 points.

—A one-man minority gets 0 points.

EQUALIZING RULE FOR PHASE III. The Equalizing Rule applies *only* to Phase III when playing a second or third case. The purpose of this rule is to help insure that all players will vote their convictions and that no player, because of his more conservative or liberal point of view, is penalized for a consistently low minority score. When the votes are tallied in Phase III in the second case, should the pattern of voting be identical to that in Phase III of Case 1, the score in Phase III of Case 2 is equalized to that of the majority. For example, if a four-man majority received 75 points each and a two-man minority received only 25 points in the Phase III, Case 1, then in the second case where the voting was identical, each minority player would receive 100 additional points in order to equalize all players' scores so that their totals for the Phase III for Case 1 and Case 2 would be 150 points each. If the voting pattern for Case 3, Phase III, is again identical, the Equalizing Rule is again applied. The Equalizing Rule applies to Phase III only and is used only when a pattern emerges.

PLAYERS SHOULD REMEMBER THAT MOST BEGINNING PLAYERS MUST PLAY A GAME OR TWO OF BASEBALL OR BRIDGE OR NINE MEN PLUS BEFORE THEY UNDERSTAND ALL THE RULES OR THEIR REASON FOR BEING. SO LET'S BEGIN.

* * *

Modifying Rules

The rules for a game about freedom of speech and freedom of press should not be unchangeable. Time limits, for example, occasionally might be extended by two-thirds vote or general agreement. Ballots might be abandoned altogether if the players want to allot an entire period to discussion of particularly provocative issues such as symbolic speech and flag desecration. Feel free to modify these rules.

*   *   *

Time Needed

Once the game is understood, two cases can easily be completed in 45 to 50 minutes; three cases may be played in 60 to 70 minutes. If only one or two cases can be completed within a particular time period, either let that score determine the winner or, better still, save the Score Sheets until the next period and continue play.

*   *   *

Playing Alone

An individual player follows the same rules with the exception that he does not exchange information; rather, he carefully studies the summary statement and quotations from the justices. Then he votes in Phase I and Phase II and immediately checks the Decision. Obviously, when playing alone Phase III cannot be played competitively. Nevertheless, the solitaire player may wish to write in his opinion. This manner of play serves as an excellent way to study and to test one's own opinion against that of the Supreme Court.

*   *   *

In the Large Classroom

Even large classes may play if a teacher or a student leader serves as chairman to conduct the Information Exchange and the Conviction-Persuasion Periods and to assist in tallying votes, particularly in Phase III. For example, if there are fifty students in the room, every fifth person may number off one to ten and may take the correspondingly numbered quotation. All other persons in the class close their texts and must listen as the ten class members participate in the information exchange. It should be stressed here that participants should be expected to paraphrase rather than read their quotations. At first the exchange may seem a bit awkward, but given a little encouragement and patience, even naturally hesitant students can be encouraged to share their information and ideas about who won the case. If the desks cannot be arranged in a circle, students should be urged to stand and be recognized when they speak. During the Conviction Phase all players may participate in arguing their positions as well as in the voting. All members of the class, however, vote in all three phases. Yet another way to play is to divide the class into teams who cast their votes as units. Or, small groups of five to eight may prefer to play in different parts of the room and later have a play-off of their winners. A class and instructor should feel free to adapt the rules to their particular situation.

*   *   *

Replayable

The simulation is well suited to a replay of cases by simply reshuffling the players. When the personnel changes, obviously it is a new ball game.

Academic Freedom

*This case might also be categorized in the unit on Political Heresy. Since so many of the cases might obviously fit equally well in more than one unit, no attempt will be made to alert the reader to this overlapping.

WEST VIRGINIA STATE BOARD OF EDUCATION et al.

v.

BARNETTE et al.

319 US 649   June 14, 1943

SUMMARY: The West Virginia flag salute regulation reads, in part, "Whereas, the West Virginia Board of Education holds that national unity is the basis of national security; that the flag of our Nation is the symbol of our national unity . . . refusal to salute the flag shall be regarded as an act of insubordination. . . ." Barnette, a member of the Jehovah's Witnesses sect, believed that to salute the flag was to "make a graven image, or any likeness" and therefore forbade his children to salute the U.S. flag.

Justices: OWEN J. ROBERTS	FELIX FRANKFURTER	FRANK MURPHY
HUGO L. BLACK	HARLAN F. STONE	ROBERT H. JACKSON
STANLEY REED	WILLIAM O. DOUGLAS	WILEY RUTLEDGE

West Virginia   1

West Virginia   2

"I cannot bring my mind to believe that 'liberty' secured by the Due Process Clause gives this Court authority to deny to the State of West Virginia the attainment of that which we all recognize as a legitimate legislative end, namely, the promotion of good citizenship, by employment of that means here chosen."

—FRANKFURTER

". . . the refusal of these persons to participate in the ceremony does not interfere with or deny the rights of others to do so. Nor is there any question in this case that their behavior is peaceful and orderly. The sole conflict is between authority and rights of the individual."

West Virginia   3   **West Virginia**   4

"It is now a commonplace that censorship or suppression of expression of opinion is tolerated by our Constitution only when the expression presents a clear and present danger of action. . . ."

"To sustain the compulsory flag statute we are required to say that a Bill of Rights which guards the individual's right to speak his own mind left it open to public authorities to compel him to utter what is not in his mind."

—ROBERTS

West Virginia   5   **West Virginia**   6

"But West Virginia does not compel the attendance at its public schools of the children here concerned. West Virginia does not compel, for it cannot. This court denied the right of a state to require its children to attend public schools. Pierce v. Society of Sisters, 268 US 510. . . . Parents have the privilege of choosing which schools they wish their children to attend. Barnette may send his children to a parochial school."

"In Hamilton v. Regents, 293 US 245, this Court unanimously held that one attending a state-maintained university cannot refuse attendance on courses that offend his religious scruples."

"The subjection of dissidents to the general requirement of saluting the flag, as a measure conducive to the training of children in good citizenship, is very far from being the first instance of exacting obedience to general laws that have offended deep religious scruples. Compulsory vaccination, see Jacobson v. Massachusetts, food inspection regulations, see Sharpiro v. Lyle, the obligation to bear arms, see Hamilton v. Regents. . . ."

"Over a decade ago Chief Justice Hughes led this Court in holding that the display of a red flag as a symbol of opposition by peaceful and legal means to organized government was protected by the free speech guaranties of the constitution.
Stromberg v. California Constitution, 283 US 359. . . ."

"Not so long ago we were admonished that the only check upon our own exercise of power is our own sense of self-restraint. For the removal of unwise laws from the statute books appeal lies not to the courts but to the ballot and the processes of democratic government. U.S. v. Butler, 352 US 380. . . ."

"Children of this faith have been expelled from school and are threatened with exclusion for no other cause. Officials threaten to send them to reformatories maintained for criminally inclined juveniles. Parents of such children have been prosecuted and are threatened with prosecution for causing delinquency."

SCHOOL DISTRICT OF ABINGTON TOWNSHIP, PENNSYLVANIA et al., Appellants

v.

EDWARD LEWIS SCHEMPP et al.

———

WILLIAM J. MURRAY III, etc., et al., Petitioners

v.

JOHN N. CURLETT et al.

374 US 203   June 17, 1963

SUMMARY: A Pennsylvania law required that "at least ten verses shall be read, without comment, at the opening of each public school on each school day. Any child shall be excused from such Bible reading or attending such Bible reading, upon the written request of his parent or guardian." The Schempp family, husband and wife and two of their three children, of Unitarian faith, brought suit to enjoin the enforcement of the statute. In a separate action, Madalyn Murray and her son, both professed atheists, filed in a Maryland state court a petition for mandamus to compel rescission of a similar rule of the Baltimore school board.

Justices: EARL WARREN   TOM C. CLARK   POTTER STEWART
              HUGO L. BLACK   JOHN M. HARLAN   BYRON R. WHITE
              WILLIAM O. DOUGLAS   WILLIAM J. BRENNAN, JR.   ARTHUR J. GOLDBERG

Abington   1   **Abington**   2

"Spending federal funds to employ chaplains for the armed forces might be said to violate the Establishment Clause. Yet a lonely soldier stationed at some faraway outpost could surely complain that a government which did not provide him the opportunity for pastoral guidance was affirmatively prohibiting the free exercise of his religion."

—STEWART

"As a matter of history, the First Amendment was adopted solely as a limitation upon the newly created National Government. The events leading to its adoption strongly suggest that the Establishment Clause was primarily an attempt to insure the Congress not only would be powerless to establish a national church, but would also be unable to interfere with existing state establishments. Each state was left free to go its own way and pursue its own policy with respect to religion. Thus Virginia from the beginning pursued a policy of disestablishmentarianism. Massachusetts, by contrast, had an established church until well into the nineteenth century."

Abington   **3**   **Abington**   **4**

"It might be argued here that parents who wanted their children to be exposed to religious influences in school could, under Pierce, send their children to private or parochial schools. But the consideration which renders this contention too facile to be determinative has already been recognized by the Court: 'Freedom of speech, freedom of the press, freedom of religion are available to all, not merely to those who can pay their own way.' Murdock v. Pennsylvania, 319 US 105, 111."

"Our decisions make clear that there is no constitutional bar to the use of government property for religious purposes."

Abington   **5**   **Abington**   **6**

"And a refusal to permit religious exercises thus is seen, not as the realization of state neutrality, but rather as the establishment of a religion of secularism, or at the least, as government support of the beliefs of those who think that religious exercise should be conducted in private."

"On each school day at the Abington High School between 8:15 and 8:30 A.M., while the pupils are attending their homerooms or advisory sections, opening exercises are conducted pursuant to the statute. The exercises are broadcast into each room through an intercommunications system and are now conducted under the supervision of a teacher by students attending the school's radio and television workshop. . . . The exercises are closed with the flag salute and such pertinent announcements as are in the interest of the students."

Abington   7   **Abington**   8

"The student reading the verses from the Bible may select the passages and read from any version he chooses, although the only copies furnished by the school are the King James Version, copies of which were circulated to each teacher by the school district. During the period in which the exercises have been conducted, the King James, the Douay and the Revised Standard Versions of the Bible have been used, as well as the Jewish Holy Scriptures."

"The vice of all such arrangements under the Establishment Clause is that the state is lending its assistance to a church's effort to gain and keep adherents."

Abington   9   **Abington**   10

"That is to say that to withstand the strictures of the Establishment Clause there must be a secular legislative purpose and a primary effect that neither advances nor inhibits religion.

". . . applying the Establishment Clause principles to the cases at bar we find that the States are requiring the selection and reading at the opening of the school day of verses from the Holy Bible and the recitation of the Lord's Prayer by the students in unison. These exercises are prescribed as part of the curricular activities of students who are required by laws to attend school."

—CLARK

"Also opposite is the answer given more than 70 years ago by the Supreme Court of Wisconsin to the argument that an excusal provision saved a public school devotional exercise from constitutional invalidation: '. . . the excluded pupil loses caste with his fellows, and is liable to be regarded with aversion, and subjected to reproach and insult.'"

HARRY KEYISHIAN et al., Appellants

v.

BOARD OF REGENTS OF THE UNIVERSITY OF THE STATE OF NEW YORK et al.
385 US 589   January 23, 1967

SUMMARY: Keyishian, an instructor in English, in addition to four other faculty members of the University of the State of New York at Buffalo, refused to sign a certificate that he was not a Communist and that if he had ever been a Communist, he would so communicate this fact to the president of the university. Keyishian's one-year contract was not renewed and the other faculty suffered either loss of their jobs or would be liable to when their contracts expired. The Board of Regents was directed under the Feinburg Law and other related state laws to disqualify and remove such persons from public schools and also to make a list of "subversive" organizations. Keyishian brought action for a declaratory judgment as to the constitutionality of the law and for injunctive relief.

Justices:		
EARL WARREN	TOM C. CLARK	POTTER STEWART
HUGO BLACK	JOHN M. HARLAN	BYRON R. WHITE
WILLIAM O. DOUGLAS	WILLIAM J. BRENNAN, JR.	ABE FORTAS

Keyishian   1

Keyishian   2

"In Elfbrandt v. Russell, 384 US 11 . . . we said, 'Those who join an organization but do not share its unlawful purposes and who do not participate in its unlawful activities surely pose no threat, either as citizens or as public employees.' "

"Our Nation is deeply committed to safeguarding academic freedom, which is of transcendent value to all of us and not merely to the teachers concerned. That freedom is therefore a special concern of the First Amendment which does not tolerate laws that cast a pall of orthodoxy over the classroom."

". . . In Lerner v. Casey, 357 US 468 . . . our Brother Harlan again upheld the severance of a public employer for his refusal to answer questions concerning his loyalty."

"In Addler v. Board of Education 1952, our late Brother Minton wrote for the Court: 'A teacher works in a sensitive area in a school-room. There he shapes the attitude of young minds toward the society in which they live. In this, the state has a vital concern. It must preserve the integrity of the schools. That the school authorities have the right and the duty to screen the officials, teachers, and employees as to their fitness to maintain the integrity of the schools as a part of an ordered society, cannot be doubted.'"

"The result must be to stifle 'that free play of the spirit which all teachers ought especially to cultivate and practice. . . .' That probability is enhanced by the provisions requiring an annual review of every teacher to determine whether any utterance or act of his, inside the classroom or out, came within the sanctions of the laws."

". . . the appellants have neither exhausted their administrative remedies, nor pursued the remedy of judicial review of agency action as provided. . . . In short they have not gone through the channels to state why they will not comply with the loyalty laws, before they asked for injunctive action."

Keyishian 7

"The issue here is a narrow one. It is not freedom of speech, freedom of press, freedom of thought, freedom of assembly, or of association, even in the Communist Party. It is simply this: May the State provide that one who, after a hearing with full judicial review, is found to willfully advocate, advise, or teach that our Government should be overthrown by force or violence or other unlawful means; or to have willfully and deliberately printed, published, etc., any book or paper that so advocated *and to have personally* advocated such doctrine himself; or who willfully and deliberately becomes a member of an organization who advocates such doctrine, is prima facie disqualified from teaching in its university? My answer in keeping with all of our court cases up until today, is 'Yes!' "

—CLARK

Keyishian 8

"And again in 1958 Beilan v. Board of Education, supra. There our late brother Burton wrote for the Courts: 'By engaging in teaching in the public schools the petitioner did not give up his right to freedom of belief, speech or association. He did, however, undertake obligations of frankness, candor and cooperation in answering inquiries made of him by his employing Board examining into his fitness to serve it as a public school teacher.' "

Keyishian 9

"In Sweezy v. N.H., 354 US 243 . . . we said: 'The essentiality of freedom in the community of American universities is almost self-evident. No one should underestimate the vital role in a democracy that is played by those who guide and train our youth. To impose any straitjacket upon the intellectual leaders in our colleges and universities would imperil the future of our Nation.' "

—BRENNAN

Keyishian 10

"Our experience under the Sedition Act of 1798, 1 Stat 596, taught us that dangers fatal to First Amendment freedoms inhere in the word 'seditions.' See New York Times Co. v. Sullivan. . . . And the word 'treasonable,' if left undefined, is no less dangerously uncertain."

MARVIN L. PICKERING, Appellant

v.

BOARD OF EDUCATION OF TOWNSHIP HIGH SCHOOL
District 205, Will County, Illinois
391 US 563 June 3, 1968

SUMMARY: Pickering, a high school teacher, wrote a letter to the editor of a local newspaper criticizing the way in which the board of education and the superintendent of schools had handled past proposals to raise new revenue and the allocations of funds. Pickering, after a full hearing before the school board, was dismissed because the board determined that his letter was detrimental to the efficient operation and administration of the schools.

Justices:	EARL WARREN	JOHN M. HARLAN	BYRON R. WHITE
	HUGO BLACK	WILLIAM J. BRENNAN, JR.	ABE FORTAS
	WILLIAM O. DOUGLAS	POTTER STEWART	THURGOOD MARSHALL

Pickering   1   **Pickering**   2

". . . it cannot be gainsaid that the State has interests as an employer in regulating the speech of its employees that differ significantly from those it possesses in connection with regulation of the speech of the citizenry in general. The problem in any case is to arrive at a balance between the interests of the teacher, as a citizen, in commenting upon matters of public concern and the interests of the State, as an employer, in promoting the efficiency of the public services it performs through its employees."

". . . the Handbook for Teachers of the district specifically stated at that time that material submitted to local papers should be checked with the building principal and submitted in triplicate to the publicity coordinator."

Pickering 3

Pickering 4

"As I see it, a teacher may be fired without violation of the First Amendment for knowingly or recklessly making false statements regardless of their impact on the school."

—White

"As I see it, the bond issue is a fight between the Board of Education that is trying to push tax-supported athletics down our throats with education, and a public that has mixed emotions about both of these items because they feel they are already paying enough taxes, and simply don't know whom to trust with any money. I must sign this letter as a citizen, taxpayer and voter, not as a teacher, since that freedom has been taken from the teachers by the administration. Do you really know what goes on behind those stone walls at the high school?

Respectfully,
Marvin L. Pickering"

Pickering 5

Pickering 6

"Pursuant to Illinois law, the Board was required to hold a hearing on the dismissal. At the hearing the Board charged that numerous statements in the letter were false and that the publication of the statements unjustifiably impugned the 'motives and honesty, integrity, truthfulness, responsibility and competency' of both the Board and the school administration. The Board also charged that the false statements damaged the professional reputations of its members and of the school administration, would be disruptive of faculty discipline, and would tend to foment 'controversy, conflict and dissension' among teachers, administrators, the Board of Education, and the residents of the district."

". . . four statements challenged by the Board are factually incorrect in varying degrees.
. . . (6) Appellant claimed that the Board had been spending $200,000 a year on athletics while neglecting the wants of teachers. This claim is incorrect in that the $200,000 per year figure included over $130,000 of nonrecurring capital expenditures. (7) Appellant also claimed that the Board had been spending $50,000 a year on transportation for athletes. This claim is completely false in that the expenditures on travel for athletes per year were $10,000."

Pickering 7

"The public interest in having free and un-hindered debate on matters of public importance—the core value of the Free Speech Clause of the First Amendment is so great that it has been held that a State cannot authorize the recovery of damages by a public official for defamatory statements directed at him except when such statements are shown to have been made either with knowledge of their falsity or with reckless disregard for their truth or falsity. New York Times Co. v. Sullivan, 376 US 254. . . ."

—Marshall

Pickering 8

Quotation from Pickering's letter to the newspaper:
"Did you know that those letters had to have the approval of the superintendent before they could go in the paper? That's the kind of to-talitarianism teachers live in at the high school, and your children go to school in."

Pickering 9

"If Pickering's false statements were either knowingly or recklessly made, injury to the school system becomes irrelevant, and the First Amendment would not prevent his discharge."

Pickering 10

"The Board contends that 'the teacher by virtue of his public employment has a duty of loyalty to support his superiors in attaining the generally accepted goals of education, and that, if he must speak out publicly he should do so factually and accurately commensurate with his education and experience.'"

JOHN F. TINKER and Mary Beth Tinker, Minors, etc., et al., Petitioners

v.

DES MOINES INDEPENDENT COMMUNITY SCHOOL DISTRICT et al.

393 US 503   February 24, 1969

SUMMARY: In December, 1965, a group of adults and students in Des Moines determined to publicize their objections to the hostilities in Vietnam by wearing black armbands during the holiday season and by fasting. The principals of the Des Moines schools, upon learning of these plans, adopted a policy that any student wearing an armband would be suspended if he failed to remove it when requested to do so. The children who wore the armbands were suspended, and the District Court dismissed their requests for an injunction restraining the school officials from disciplining the children and held that the school authorities' action was reasonable in order to prevent disturbance of school discipline.

Justices:	EARL WARREN	POTTER STEWART	BYRON R. WHITE
	HUGO L. BLACK	JOHN M. HARLAN	ABE FORTAS
	WILLIAM O. DOUGLAS	WILLIAM J. BRENNAN, JR.	THURGOOD MARSHALL

Tinker   1

"Only a few of the 18,000 students in the school system wore the black armbands. Only five students were suspended for wearing them. There is no indication that the work of the schools or any class was disrupted. Outside the classrooms, a few students made hostile remarks to the children wearing armbands, but there were no threats or acts of violence on school premises. The District Court concluded that the action of the school authorities was reasonable because it was based upon their fear of a disturbance from the wearing of the armbands. But, in our system, undifferentiated fear or apprehension of disturbance is not enough to overcome the right to freedom of expression."

Tinker   2

"It is also relevant that the school authorities did not purport to prohibit the wearing of all symbols of political or controversial significance. The record shows that students in some of the schools wore buttons relating to national political campaigns, and some even wore the Iron Cross, traditionally a symbol of Nazism. The order prohibiting the wearing of armbands did not extend to these. Instead, a particular symbol—black armbands worn to exhibit opposition to this Nation's involvement in Vietnam—was singled out for prohibition.

—FORTAS

Tinker   **3**   **Tinker**   **4**

"Ordered to refrain from wearing the armbands in school by the elected school officials and the teachers vested with state authority to do so, apparently only seven out of the school system's 18,000 pupils deliberately refused to obey the order. One defying pupil was Paul Tinker, 8 years old, who was in the second grade; another, Hope Tinker, was 11 years old and in the fifth grade; a third member of the Tinker family was 13, in the eighth grade; and a fourth member of the same family was John Tinker, 15 years old, an 11th-grade high school pupil. Their father, a Methodist minister without a church, is paid a salary by the American Friends Service Committee. Another student who defied the school order and insisted on wearing an armband in school was Chris John Eckhardt, an 11th-grade pupil and a petitioner in this case. His mother is an official in the Women's International League for Peace and Freedom."

"While the record does not show that any of these armband students shouted, used profane language, or were violent in any manner, detailed testimony by some of them shows their armbands caused comments, warnings by other students, the poking of fun at them, and a warning by an older football player that other nonprotesting students had better let them alone. There is also evidence that a teacher of mathematics had his lesson period practically 'wrecked' chiefly by disputes with Mary Beth Tinker, who wore her armband for her 'demonstration.'"

Tinker   **5**   **Tinker**   **6**

"While the absence of obscene remarks or boisterous and loud disorder perhaps justifies the Court's statement that the few armband students did not actually 'disrupt' the classwork, I think the record overwhelmingly shows that the armbands did exactly what the elected school officials and principals foresaw they would, that is, took the students' minds off their classwork and diverted them to thoughts about the highly emotional subject of the Vietnam war. And I repeat that if the time has come when pupils of state-supported schools, kindergartens, grammar schools, or high school, can defy and flout orders of school officials to keep their minds on their own schoolwork, it is the beginning of a new revolutionary era of permissiveness in this country fostered by the judiciary."

"The truth is that a teacher of kindergarten, grammar school, or high school pupils no more carries into a school with him a complete right to freedom of speech and expression than an anti-Catholic or anti-Semite carries with him a complete freedom of speech and religion into a Catholic church or Jewish synagogue. Nor does a person carry with him into the United States Senate or House, or into the Supreme Court, or any other court, a complete constitutional right to go into those places contrary to their rules and speak his mind on any subject he pleases. It is a myth to say that any person has a constitutional right to say what he pleases, where he pleases, and when he pleases. Our Court has decided precisely the opposite."

—BLACK

Tinker 7

"Nor are public school students sent to the schools at public expense to broadcast political or any other views to educate and inform the public. The original idea of school, which I do not believe is yet abandoned as worthless or out of date, was that children had not yet reached the point of experience and wisdom which enabled them to teach all of their elders. It may be that the Nation has outworn the old-fashioned slogan that 'children are to be seen not heard,' but one may, I hope, be permitted to harbor the thought that taxpayers send children to school on the premise that at their age they need to learn, not teach."

Tinker 8

"First Amendment rights, applied in light of the special characteristics of the school environment, are available to teachers and students. It can hardly be argued that either students or teachers shed their constitutional rights to freedom of speech or expression at the schoolhouse gate. This has been the unmistakable holding of this Court for almost 50 years. . . . The problem posed by the present case does not relate to regulation of the length of skirts or the type of clothing, to hair style, or deportment. . . . It does not concern aggressive, disruptive action or even group demonstrations. Our problem involves direct, primary First Amendment rights akin to 'pure speech.' "

Tinker 9

"Turned loose with lawsuits for damages and injunctions against their teachers as they are here, it is nothing but wishful thinking to imagine that young, immature students will not soon believe it is their right to control the schools rather than the right of the States that collect the taxes to hire the teachers for the benefit of the pupils. This case, therefore, wholly without constitutional reasons in my judgment, subjects all the public schools in the country to the whims and caprices of their loudest-mouthed, but maybe not their brightest, students. I, for one, am not fully persuaded that school pupils are wise enough, even with this Court's expert help from Washington, to run the 23,390 public school systems in our 50 states."

Tinker 10

"We cannot close our eyes to the fact that some of the country's greatest problems are crimes committed by the youth, too many of school age. School discipline, like parental discipline, is an integral and important part of training our children to be good citizens—to be better citizens. Here a very small number of students have crisply and summarily refused to obey a school order designed to give pupils who want to learn the opportunity to do so. One does not need to be a prophet or the son of a prophet to know that after the Court's holding today some students in Iowa schools and indeed in all schools will be ready, able, and willing to defy their teachers on practically all orders. This is the more unfortunate for the schools since groups of students all over the land are already running loose, conducting break-ins, sit-ins, lie-ins, and smash-ins."

QUESTIONS FOR DISCUSSION

Students should be better able to answer these questions after participating in this unit. They are based upon real situations and are not limited to the clues found in the specific cases in this section. Some of the questions move out and beyond that which has yet come before the High Court.

1. In a private school does a coach have the right to kick off the team a player who refuses to stand during the flag salute ceremony prior to the start of a school basketball game?

2. If you were a parent of a kindergarten youngster, would you have a justifiable objection if before milk and cookies the teacher leads the children in the following verse?

> "Thank you for the world so sweet,
> Thank you for the food we eat,
> Thank you for the birds that sing,
> Thank you, God, for everything"

3. Should a school board require as a condition for employment that an employee sign an oath of loyalty to the state and nation?

4. May a teacher be dismissed for writing a letter critical of his school's administration?

5. May students be suspended for refusing to remove political buttons and distributing leaflets?

6. May nonschool organizations and individuals be prohibited from distributing literature on school grounds?

7. What control should the school administrators have over the editors of school newspapers?

8. What limits, if any, should govern books and periodicals contained in the school library?

9. What should be the guidelines for what the teacher might say in the classroom outside his discipline?

10. What should the teacher do about a student who habitually uses "dirty" words?

11. Should the drama teacher have to abide by certain rules concerning choice of plays?

Censorship

MUTUAL FILM CORPORATION

v.

INDUSTRIAL COMMISSION OF OHIO

236 US 230   February 23, 1915

SUMMARY: The State of Ohio, in 1913, enacted a law which established a State board of censors of motion picture films. Mutual Film Corporation, which had a profitable business, $300,000 annually, and a stock of 2,500 reels, argued that the law abridged freedom of speech and press, was costly, and was so vaguely worded that it placed undue power in a board.

Justices: EDWARD D. WHITE   WILLIS VAN DEVANTER   JOSEPH MCKENNA
            JAMES C. MCREYNOLDS   JOSEPH R. LAMAR   OLIVER W. HOLMES, JR.
            MAHLON PITNEY   CHARLES E. HUGHES   WILLIAM R. DAY

Mutual   1

"It attempts to give the board of censors legislative power, which is vested only in the General Assembly of the State, subject to a referendum vote of the people, in that it gives to the board the power to determine the application of the statute without fixing any standard by which the board shall be guided in its determination, and places it in the power of the board, acting with similar boards in other States, to reject, upon any whim or caprice, any film which may be presented, and power to determine the legal status of the foreign board or boards, in conjunction with which it is empowered to act."

Mutual   2

"The film consists of a series of instantaneous photographs or positive prints of action upon the stage or in the open. By being projected upon a screen with great rapidity there appears to the eye an illusion of motion. They depict dramatizations of standard novels, exhibiting many subjects of scientific interest, the properties of matter, the growth of the various forms of animal and plant life, and explorations and travels; also events of historical and current interest—the same events which are described in words and by photographs in newspapers, weekly periodicals, magazines and other publications, of which photographs are promptly secured a few days after the events which they depict happen; thus regularly furnishing and publishing news through the medium of motion pictures under the name of 'Mutual Weekly.' Nothing is depicted of a harmful or immoral character."

Mutual   **3**   **Mutual**   **4**

"Are moving pictures within the principle [free speech], as it is contended they are? They, indeed, may be mediums of thought, but so are many things. So is the theater, the circus, and all other shows and spectacles, and their performances may be thus brought by the like reasoning under the same immunity from repression or supervision as the public press— made the same agencies of civil liberty."

"Section 4. 'Only such films as are in the judgment and discretion of the board of censors of a moral, educational or amusing and harmless character shall be passed and approved by such board.' The films are required to be stamped or designated in a proper manner.

"Section 5. The board may work in conjunction with censor boards of other States as a censor congress, and the action of such congress in approving or rejecting films shall be considered as the action of the state board, and all flims passed, approved, stamped and numbered by such congress, when the fees therefor are paid shall be considered approved by the board."

Mutual   **5**   **Mutual**   **6**

"The board has demanded of complainant that it submit its films to censorship and threatens, unless complainant complies with the demand, to arrest any and all persons who seek to place on exhibition any film not so censored or approved by the censor congress on and after November 4, 1913, the date to which the act was extended. It is physically impossible to comply with such demand and physically impossible for the board to censor the films with such rapidity as to enable complainant to proceed with its business, and the delay consequent upon such examination would cause great and irreparable injury to such business and would involve a multiplicity of suits."

"An affidavit was filed made by the 'general secretary of the national board of censorship of motion pictures, whose office is at No. 50 Madison Avenue, New York City.' The 'national board,' it is averred, 'is an organization maintained by voluntary contributions, whose object is to improve the moral quality of motion pictures.' Attached to the affidavit was a list of subjects submitted to the board which are 'classified according to the nature of said subjects into scenic, geographic, historical, classic, educational and propagandistic.'"

"Appellants' motion pictures constitute part of 'the press' of Ohio within the comprehensive meaning of that term. They play an increasingly important part in the spreading of knowledge and the molding of public opinion upon every kind of political, educational, religious, economic and social question. The regular publication of new films under the name of 'Mutual Weekly' is clearly a press enterprise. "See 11, Art I, Ohio constitution, providing that 'Every citizen may freely speak, write and publish his sentiments on all subjects, being responsible for the abuse of the right; and no law shall be passed to restrain or abridge the liberty of speech, or of the press.'"

"But they [films] may be used for evil, and against that possibility the statute was enacted. Their power of amusement and, it may be, education, the audiences they assemble, not of women alone nor of men alone, but together, not of adults only, but of children, make them the more insidious in corruption by a pretense of worthy purpose or if they should degenerate from worthy purpose. Indeed, we may go beyond that possibility. They take their attraction from the general interest, eager and wholesome it may be, in their subjects, but a prurient interest may be excited and appealed to. Besides, there are some things which should not have pictorial representation in public places and to all audiences."

"It cannot be put out of view that the exhibition of moving pictures is a business pure and simple, originated and conducted for profit, like other spectacles not to be regarded, nor intended to be regarded by the Ohio constitution, we think, as part of the press of the country or as organs of public opinion. They are mere representations of events, of ideas and sentiments published and known, vivid, useful and entertaining no doubt, but, as we have said, capable of evil, having power for it, the greater because of their attractiveness and manner of exhibition."

—McKENNA

"The objection to the statute is that it furnishes no standard of what is educational, moral, amusing or harmless and hence leaves decision to arbitrary judgment, whim and caprice; or, aside from those extremes, leaving it to the different views which might be entertained of the effect of the pictures, permitting the 'personal equation' to enter, resulting 'in unjust discrimination against some propagandist film,' while others might be approved without question. But the statute by its provisions guards against such variant judgments, and its terms, like other general terms, get precision from the sense and experience of men and become certain and useful guides in reasoning and conduct. The exact specification of the instances of their application would be as impossible as the attempt would be futile."

JOSEPH BURSTYN, Inc., Appellant

v.

LEWIS A. WILSON, Commissioner of Education of the State of New York et al.

343 US 495   May 26, 1952

SUMMARY: The Italian-made film "The Miracle," directed by Roberto Rossellini, tells the story of a simple-minded girl who while tending her goats on a mountainside one day meets a bearded stranger. She thinks he is St. Joseph, her favorite saint. The bearded stranger plies the girl with wine and apparently has intercourse with her, although this scene is only briefly implied. When later this girl finds she is pregnant, she will not do menial work. Some humor her, but most mock. She gives birth within a church and murmurs "My son! My love! My flesh!" New York State first licensed it and then rescinded the license on the grounds that the picture was "sacrilegious."

Justices:	FRED M. VINSON	FELIX FRANKFURTER	HAROLD H. BURTON
	HUGO L. BLACK	WILLIAM O. DOUGLAS	TOM C. CLARK
	STANLEY REED	ROBERT H. JACKSON	SHERMAN MINTON

Burstyn   1

"It cannot be doubted that motion pictures are a significant medium for the communication of ideas. They may affect public attitudes and behavior in a variety of ways, ranging from direct espousal of a political or social doctrine to the subtle shaping of thought which characterizes all artistic expression. The importance of motion pictures as an organ of public opinion is not lessened by the fact that they are designed to entertain as well as to inform."

Burstyn   2

"That books, newspapers, and magazines are published and sold for profit does not prevent them from being a form of expression whose liberty is safeguarded by the First Amendment. We fail to see why operation for profit should have any different effect in the case of motion pictures.

"It is further urged that motion pictures possess a greater capacity for evil, particularly among the youth of a community, than other modes of expression. Even if one were to accept this hypothesis, it does not follow that motion pictures should be disqualified from First Amendment protection. If there be capacity for evil it may be relevant in determining the permissible scope of community control, but it does not authorize substantially unbridled censorship such as we have here."

—CLARK

"To hold that liberty of expression by means of motion pictures is guaranteed by the First and Fourteenth Amendments, however, is not the end of our problem. It does not follow that the Constitution requires absolute freedom to exhibit every motion picture of every kind at all times and all places. That much is evident from the series of decisions of this Court with respect to other media of communication of ideas. Nor does it follow that motion pictures are necessarily subject to the precise rules governing any other particular method of expression. Each method tends to present its own peculiar problems."

"Application of the 'sacrilegious' test, in these or other respects, might raise substantial questions under the First Amendment's guaranty of separate church and state with freedom of worship for all. However, from the standpoint of freedom of speech and the press, it is enough to point out that the state has no legitimate interest in protecting any or all religions from views distasteful to them which is sufficient to justify prior restraints upon the expression of those views. It is not the business of government in our nation to suppress real or imagined attacks upon a particular religious doctrine, whether they appear in publications, speeches, or motion pictures."

"In October, 1948, a month after the Rome premiere of 'The Miracle,' the Vatican's censorship agency, the Catholic Cinematographic Centre, declared that the picture 'constitutes in effect an abominable profanation from religious and moral viewpoints.' By the Lateran agreements and the Italian Constitution the Italian Government is bound to bar whatever may offend the Catholic religion. However, the Catholic Cinematographic Centre did not invoke any governmental sanction thereby afforded. The Italian Government's censorship agency gave 'The Miracle' the regular nulla osta clearance. The film was freely shown throughout Italy, but was not a great success. Italian movie critics divided in opinion."

"Upon the failure of the License Commissioner's effort to cut off showings of 'The Miracle,' the controversy took a new turn. On Sunday, January 7, 1951, a statement of His Eminence, Francis Cardinal Spellman, condemning the picture and calling on 'all right thinking citizens' to unite to tighten censorship laws, was read at all masses in St. Patrick's Cathedral.

"The views of Cardinal Spellman aroused dissent among other devout Christians. Protestant clergymen, representing various denominations, after seeing the picture, found in it nothing 'sacrilegious or immoral to the views held by Christian men and women,' and with a few exceptions agreed that the film was 'unquestionably one of unusual artistic merit.'"

Burstyn 7

"William P. Clancy, a teacher at the University of Notre Dame, wrote in The Commonweal, the well-known Catholic weekly, that 'the film is not *obviously* blasphemous or obscene, either in its intention or execution.' The Commonweal itself questioned the wisdom of transforming Church dogma which Catholics may obey as 'a free act' into state-enforced censorship for all. Allen Tate, the well-known Catholic poet and critic, wrote: 'The picture seems to me to be superior in acting and photography but inferior dramatically. . . . In the long run what Cardinal Spellman will have succeeded in doing is insulting the intelligence and faith of American Catholics with the assumption that a second-rate motion picture could in any way undermine their morals or shake their faith.' "

Burstyn 8

"It would startle Madison and Jefferson and George Mason, could they adjust themselves to our day, to be told that the freedom of speech which they espoused in the Bill of Rights authorizes a showing of 'The Miracle' from windows facing St. Patrick's Cathedral in the forenoon of Easter Sunday, just as it would startle them to be told that any picture, whatever its theme and its expression, could be barred from being commercially exhibited. The general principle of free speech, expressed in the First Amendment as to encroachments by Congress, and included as it is in the Fourteenth Amendment, binding on the States, must be placed in its historical and legal contexts. The Constitution, we cannot recall too often, is an organism, not merely a literary composition."

—BURTON

Burstyn 9

"The New York Court of Appeals' statement that the dictionary 'furnishes a clear definition,' justifying the vague scope it gave to 'sacrilegious,' surely was made without regard to the lexicographic history of the term. As a matter of fact, the definition from Funk & Wagnalls' used by the Court of Appeals is taken straight from 18th-century dictionaries, particularly Doctor Johnson's. In light of that history it would seem that the Funk & Wagnalls' definition uses 'sacrilege' in its historically restricted meaning, which was not and could hardly have been, the basis for condemning 'The Miracle.' If the New York court reads the Funk & Wagnalls' definition in a broader sense, in a sense for which history and experience provide no gloss, it inevitably left the censor free to judge by whatever dogma he deems 'sacred' and to ban whatever motion pictures he may assume would 'profane' religious doctrine widely enough held to arouse protest."

Burstyn 10

"Which is 'sacrilegious'? The doctrine of transubstantiation, and the veneration of relics or particular stone and wood embodiments of saints or divinity, both sacred to Catholics, are offensive to a great many Protestants, and therefore for them sacrilegious in the view of the New York court. Is a picture treating either subject, whether sympathetically, unsympathetically, or neutrally, 'sacrilegious'? It is not a sufficient answer to say that 'sacrilegious' is definite, because all subjects that in any way might be interpreted as offending the religious beliefs of any one of the 300 sects of the United States are banned in New York. To allow such vague, undefinable powers of censorship to be exercised is bound to have stultifying consequences on the creative process of literature and art—for the films are derived largely from literature. History does not encourage reliance on the wisdom and moderation of the censor as a safeguard in the exercise of such drastic power over the minds of men."

SAMUEL ROTH, Petitioner

v.

THE UNITED STATES OF AMERICA

———

DAVID S. ALBERTS

v.

STATE OF CALIFORNIA

354 US 476   June 24, 1957

SUMMARY: Roth, a bookseller in New York, was convicted for mailing obscene circulars and a book in violation of a federal obscenity statute. Alberts conducted a mail-order business in Los Angeles and was convicted for a like offense under the California Penal Code.

Justices: EARL WARREN   WILLIAM O. DOUGLAS   JOHN M. HARLAN
              HUGO L. BLACK   HAROLD H. BURTON   WILLIAM J. BRENNAN, JR.
              FELIX FRANKFURTER   TOM C. CLARK   CHARLES E. WHITTAKER

Roth   1   **Roth**   2

"The tests by which these convictions were obtained require only the arousing of sexual thoughts. Yet the arousing of sexual thoughts and desires happens every day in normal life in dozens of ways."

"Any test that turns on what is offensive to the community's standards is too loose, too capricious, too destructive of freedom of expression to be squared with the First Amendment. Under that test, juries can censor, suppress, and punish what they don't like, provided the matter relates to 'sexual impurity' or has a tendency 'to excite lustful thoughts.' This is community censorship in its worst forms. It creates a regime where in the battles between the literati and the Philistines, the Philistines are certain to win."

—DOUGLAS

Roth 3

Roth 4

"The guaranties of freedom of expression in effect in 10 of the 14 States which by 1792 had ratified the Constitution gave no absolute protection for every utterance. Thirteen of the 14 States provided for the prosecution of libel, and all of those States made either blasphemy or profanity, or both, statutory crimes."

"As a people, we cannot afford to relax that standard. For the test that suppresses a cheap tract today can suppress a literary gem tomorrow. All it need do is to incite a lascivious thought or arouse a lustful desire. The list of books that judges or juries can place in that category is endless.

"I would give the broad sweep of the First Amendment full support. I have the same confidence in the ability of our people to reject noxious literature as I have in their capacity to sort out the true from the false in theology, economics, politics or any other field."

Roth 5

Roth 6

"As early as 1712, Massachusetts made it criminal to publish 'any filthy, obscene, or profane song, pamphlet, libel or mock sermon' in imitation or mimicking of religious services. Acts and Laws of the Province of Mass. Bay, c. CV §8 (1712), Mass. Bay Colony Charter and Laws 399 (1814). Thus, profanity and obscenity are related offenses.

"In light of history it is apparent that the unconditional phrasing of the First Amendment was not intended to protect every utterance."

"All ideas having even the slightest redeeming social importance—unorthodox ideas, controversial ideas, even ideas hateful to the prevailing climate of opinion—have the full protection of the guaranties, unless excludable because they encroach upon the limited area of more important interests. But implicit in the history of the First Amendment is the rejection of obscenity as utterly without redeeming social importance. This rejection for that reason is mirrored in the universal judgement that obscenity should be restrained, reflected in the international agreement of over 50 nations, in the obscenity laws of all 48 states, and in the 20 obscenity laws enacted by the Congress from 1842 to 1956."

—Brennan

"The early leading standard of obscenity allowed material to be judged merely by the effect of an isolated excerpt upon particularly susceptible persons. Regina v. Hicklin [1868] LR3QB360. Some American courts adopted this standard but later decisions have rejected it and substituted this test: whether to the average person, applying contemporary community standards, the dominant theme of the material taken as a whole appeals to prurient interest."

"The defendants in both cases were engaged in the business of purveying textual or graphic matter openly advertised to appeal to the erotic interest of their customers. They were plainly engaged in the commercial exploitation of the morbid and shameful craving for materials with prurient effect. I believe that State and Federal Governments can Constitutionally punish such conduct."

"I assume there is nothing in the Constitution which forbids Congress from using its power over the mails to proscribe *conduct* on the grounds of good morals. No one would suggest that the First Amendment permits nudity in public places, adultery, and other phases of sexual misconduct.

"I can understand (and at times even sympathize) with programs of civic groups and church groups to protect and defend the existing moral standards of the community. I can understand the motives of the Anthony Comstocks who would impose Victorian standards on the community. When speech alone is involved, I do not think that government, consistently with the First Amendment, can become the sponsor of any of these movements."

"The absence of dependable information on the effect of obscene literature on human conduct should make us wary. It should put us on the side of protecting society's interest in literature, except and unless it can be said that the particular publication has an impact on action that the government can control."

TIMES FILM CORP.

v.

CITY OF CHICAGO et al.

365 US 43   January 23, 1961

SUMMARY: Times Film applied for a permit to show a film known as "Don Juan," and tendered the required license fee, but refused to submit the film for examination as required by the city. The city's censorship statute forbade exhibition unless a film met certain standards. The issue at stake was "prior restraint," in short, prior review and thereafter granting or withholding permission to exhibit.

Justices: EARL WARREN   WILLIAM O. DOUGLAS   WILLIAM J. BRENNAN, JR.
              HUGO L. BLACK   TOM C. CLARK   CHARLES E. WHITTAKER
              FELIX FRANKFURTER JOHN M. HARLAN   POTTER STEWART

Times   1   **Times**   2

"And as if to emphasize the point involved here, we added that 'The phrase "prior restraint" is not a self-wielding sword. Nor can it serve as a talismanic test.' Even as recently as our last Term we again observed the principle, albeit in an allied area, that the State possesses some measure of power 'to prevent the distribution of obscene matter.'"

—CLARK

". . . Chief Justice Hughes, in discussing the classic statements concerning the immunity of the press from censorship, observed that the principle forbidding previous restraint 'is stated too broadly, even if such restraint is deemed to be prohibited.'"

City of Chicago Code Sec 155-4:
"If a picture or series of pictures, for the showing or exhibition of which an application for a permit is made, is immoral, or obscene, or portrays depravity, criminality, or lack of virtue of a class of citizens of any race, color, creed or religion and exposes them to contempt, derision, or obloquy, or tends to produce breach of the peace or riots, or purports to represent any hanging, lynching, or burning of a human being, it shall be the duty of the commissioner of police to refuse such permit, otherwise it shall be his duty to grant such permit."

"Petitioner claims that the nature of the film is irrelevant, and that even if this film contains the basest type of pornography, or incitement to riot, or forceful overthrow of the orderly government, it may nonetheless be shown without prior submission for examination. The challenge here is to the censor's basic authority; . . ."

". . . in Joseph Burstyn, Inc. v. Wilson, supra, we found motion pictures to be within the guarantees of the First and Fourteenth Amendments, but we added that this was 'not the end of our problem. It does not follow that the Constitution requires absolute freedom to exhibit every motion picture of every kind at all times and all places.'"

"The regime of censorship is deadening. One who writes cannot afford entanglements with the man whose pencil can keep his production from market. The result is a pattern of conformity."

Times   7   **Times**   8

"Atlanta barred *Lost Boundaries,* the story of a Negro physician . . . who 'passed' for white. . . . *Scarface,* thought by some as the best of the gangster films, was held up for months; then it was so badly mutilated that retakes costing a hundred thousand dollars were required to preserve its continuity.

". . . from *Joan of Arc* the Maryland board eliminated: 'Oh, God, why hast thou forsaken me?' "

"A statute authorizing previous restraint upon the exercise of the guaranteed freedom by judicial decision after trial is as obnoxious to the Constitution as one providing for like restraint by administrative order."

Times   9   **Times**   10

"The First Amendment was designed to enlarge, not to limit, freedom in literature, and in the arts as well as in politics, economics, law and other fields."

"To me, this case clearly presents the question of our approval of unlimited censorship of motion pictures before exhibition through a system of administrative licensing. Moreover, the decision presents a real danger of eventual censorship for every form of communication."

—WARREN

MANUAL ENTERPRISES, Inc., et al., Petitioners

v.

J. EDWARD DAY, Postmaster General of the United States
370 US 478   June 25, 1962

SUMMARY: The Alexander, Virginia, postmaster withheld delivery of 405 copies of three magazines titled *MANual*, *Trim*, and *Grecian Guild Pictorial*. The Post Office Judicial Officer, after a hearing, determined the magazines had no literary, scientific, or other merit, that they were read almost entirely by homosexuals, that they appealed to the prurient interest of homosexuals. He also stated that the magazines provided information as to where, how, and from whom to obtain obscene materials. For these reasons he ruled the magazines nonmailable matter.

Justices:	EARL WARREN	WILLIAM O. DOUGLAS	WILLIAM J. BRENNAN, JR.
	HUGO L. BLACK	TOM C. CLARK	POTTER STEWART
	FELIX FRANKFURTER	JOHN M. HARLAN	BYRON R. WHITE

Manual Enterprises 1

"Womack had also suggested to the photographers that they exchange customer names with the hope of compiling a master list of homosexuals. He himself had been convicted of selling obscene photographs via the mails. Womack v. United States, 111 App DC 8, 294 F2d 204 (1961). More recently he has pleaded not guilty by reason of insanity to like charges. Washington Post, Feb. 1, 1962, p. D-3. Furthermore, he was warned in March, April, and July of 1959 that a number of his photographer advertisers were being prosecuted for mailing obscene matter and that he might be violating the law in transmitting through the mails their advertisements."

Manual Enterprises 2

"Turning to Womack, the president and directing force of all three corporate publishers, it is even clearer that we are not dealing here with a 'Jack and Jill' operation. Mr. Womack admitted that the magazines were planned for homosexuals, designed to appeal to and stimulate their erotic interests. To improve on this effect, he made suggestions to photographers as to the type of pictures he wanted. For example, he informed one of the studios listed in his publications that 'physique fans' want their 'truck driver types' already cleaned up, showered, and ready for bed . . . [and] it is absolutely essential that the models have pretty faces and a personality not totally unrelated to sex appeal.' "

"The advertisements and photographer lists in such magazines were quite naturally 'designed so as to attract the male homosexual and to furnish him with names and addresses where nude male pictures in poses and conditions which would appeal to his prurient interest may be obtained.' Moreover, the advertisements themselves could leave no more doubt in the publishers' minds than in those of the solicited purchasers. To illustrate: some captioned a picture of a nude or scantily attired young man with the legend 'perfectly proportioned, handsome, male models, age 18-26.' Others featured a photograph of a nude male with the area around the privates obviously retouched so as to cover the genitals and part of the pubic hair and offered to furnish an 'original print of this photo.'"

"The magazines have no social, educational, or entertainment qualities but are designed solely as sex stimulants for homosexuals. They 'consist almost entirely of photographs of young men in nude or practically nude poses handled in such a manner as to focus attention on their genitals or buttocks or to emphasize these parts. . . .' Because of this content the magazines do 'not appeal to the ordinary male adult, . . . [who] would have no interest in them and would not buy them under ordinary circumstances and . . . [therefore] the readers of these publications consist almost entirely of male homosexuals and possibly a few adolescent males. . . .' The publishers freely admit that the magazines are published to appeal to the male homosexual group."

"Section 1461 explicitly provides that:
'Every obscene, lewd, lascivious, indecent, filthy or vile article, matter, thing, device, or substance; and . . . [e]very written or printed card, letter, circular, book, pamphlet, advertisement, or notice of any kind giving information, directly or indirectly, where, or how, or from whom, or by what means any of such mentioned matters, articles, or things may be obtained . . . [i]s declared to be nonmailable matter and shall not be conveyed in the mails or delivered from any post office or by any letter carrier.'" (Emphasis supplied.)

"However, it is enough to dispose of this case that Congress has not, in Section 1461, authorized the Postmaster General to employ any process of his own to close the mails to matter which, in his view, falls within the ban of that section. 'The provisions . . . would have to be far more explicit for us to assume that Congress made such a radical departure from our traditions and undertook to clothe the Postmaster General with the power to supervise the taste of the reading public of the country.' Hannegan v. Esquire, Inc., 327 US at 156, 90 L ed 586, 66 S Ct 456."

—BRENNAN

"Obscenity under the federal statute thus requires proof of two distinct elements: (1) patent offensiveness; and (2) 'prurient interest' appeal. Both must conjoin before challenged material can be found 'obscene' under section 1461. In most obscenity cases, to be sure, the two elements tend to coalesce, for that which is patently offensive will also usually carry the requisite 'prurient interest' appeal. It is only in the unusual instance where, as here, the 'prurient interest' appeal of the material is found limited to a particular class of persons that occasion arises for a truly independent inquiry into the questions whether or not the material is patently offensive."

"Petitioners are three corporations respectively engaged in publishing magazines titled *MANual, Trim,* and *Grecian Guild Pictorial.* They have offices at the same address in Washington, D. C., and a common president, one Herman L. Womack. The magazines consist largely of photographs of nude, or near-nude, male models and give the names of each model and the photographer, together with the address of the latter. They also contain a number of advertisements by independent photographers offering nudist photographs for sale."

"On the issue of obscenity, as distinguished from unlawful advertisting, the case comes to us with the following administrative findings, which are supported by substantial evidence and which we, and indeed the parties, for the most part, themselves, accept: (1) the magazines are not, as asserted by petitioners, physical culture or 'body-building' publications, but are composed primarily, if not exclusively, for homosexuals, and have no literary, scientific or other merit, (2) they would appeal to the 'prurient interest' of such sexual deviates, but would not have any interest for sexually normal individuals; and (3) the magazines are read almost entirely by homosexuals, and possibly a few adolescent males; the ordinary male adult would not normally buy them."

"How one can fail to see the obvious in this record is beyond my comprehension. In the words of Milton: 'O dark, dark, dark amid the blaze of noon.' For one to conclude that the above undisputed facts and findings are insufficient to show the required scienter, however stringently it may be defined, is in effect to repeal the advertising provisions of section 1461. To condition nonmailability on proof that the sender actually saw the material being sold by his advertisers is to portray the Congress as the 'mother' in the jingle, 'Mother may I go out to swim? Yes, my darling daughter. Hang your clothes on a hickory limb and don't go near the water.'"

—Clark

NICO JACOBELLIS, Appellant

v.

OHIO

378 US 184   June 22, 1964

SUMMARY: "The Lovers" is a French film about an unhappy marriage and the wife's affair with a young archaeologist. The last reel depicts an explicit love scene. Nico Jacobellis, manager of a motion picture theater in Cleveland Heights, Ohio, was convicted for exhibiting the film. He was fined $500 on possession, $2000 for exhibition, and "sentenced to the workhouse if the fines were not paid."

Justices: EARL WARREN   TOM C. CLARK   POTTER STEWART
              HUGO L. BLACK   JOHN M. HARLAN   BYRON R. WHITE
              WILLIAM O. DOUGLAS   WILLIAM J. BRENNAN, JR. ARTHUR J. GOLDBERG

Jacobellis   1   **Jacobellis**   2

"Nor may the constitutional status of the material be made to turn on a 'weighing' of its social importance against its prurient appeal, for a work cannot be proscribed unless it is 'utterly' without social importance. See Zeitlin v. Arnebergh, 59 Cal 2d 901, 920."

"It has been suggested that the 'contemporary community standards' aspect of the Roth test implies a determination of the constitutional question of obscenity in each case by the standards of the particular local community from which the case arises. This is an incorrect reading of Roth."

—BRENNAN

Jacobellis 3

"It is my belief that when the Court said in Roth that obscenity is to be defined by reference to 'community standards,' it meant community standards—not a national standard, as is sometimes argued. I believe that there is no provable 'national standard,' and perhaps there should be none. At all events, this Court has not been able to enunciate one, and it would be unreasonable to expect local courts to divine one. It is said that such a 'community' approach may well result in material being proscribed as obscene in one community and not in another, and in all probability, that is true. But communities throughout the Nation are in fact diverse, and it must be remembered that, in cases such as this one, the Court is confronted with the task of reconciling conflicting rights of the diverse communities within our society and of individuals."

—WARREN

Jacobellis 4

"In judging alleged obscenity the Court is no more 'censoring' expression than it has in other cases 'censored' criticism of judges and public officials, advocacy of governmental overthrow, or speech alleged to constitute a breach of the peace. Use of an opprobrious label can neither obscure nor impugn the Court's performance of its obligation to test challenged judgments against the guarantees of the First and Fourteenth Amendments and, in doing so, to delineate the scope of constitutionally protected speech. Hence we reaffirm the principle that, in 'obscenity' cases as in all others involving rights derived from the First Amendment guarantees of free expression, this Court cannot avoid making an independent constitutional judgment on the facts of the case as to whether the material involved is constitutionally protected."

Jacobellis 5

"Material is obscene and not constitutionally protected against regulation and proscription if 'to the average person, applying contemporary community standards, the dominant theme of the material taken as a whole appeals to prurient interests.'"

Jacobellis 6

"There is an explicit love scene in the last reel of the film, and the State's objections are based almost entirely upon the scene. The film was favorably reviewed in a number of national publications, although disparaged in others, and was rated by at least two critics of national stature among the best films of the year in which it was produced. It was shown in approximately 100 of the larger cities in the United States, including Columbus and Toledo, Ohio."

Jacobellis 7

"... the use to which various materials are put—not just the words and pictures themselves—must be considered in determining whether or not the materials are obscene. A technical or legal treatise on pornography may well be inoffensive under most circumstances, but at the same time, 'obscene' in the extreme when sold or displayed to children."

Jacobellis 8

"Recognizing that the test for obscenity enunciated there—'whether to the average person, applying contemporary community standards, the dominant theme of the material taken as a whole appeals to prurient interests,' 354 US at 489 1 L ed 2d at 1509—is not perfect, we think any substitute would raise equally difficult problems, and we therefore adhere to that standard."

Jacobellis 9

"It can hardly be assumed that all patrons of a particular library, bookstand, or motion picture theater are residents of the smallest local 'community' that can be drawn around the establishment. Furthermore, to sustain the suppression of a particular book or film in one locality would deter its dissemination in other localities where it might be held not obscene, since sellers and exhibitors would be reluctant to risk criminal conviction in testing the variation between the two places. It would be a hardy person who would sell a book or exhibit a film anywhere in the land after this Court had sustained the judgment of one 'community' holding it to be outside the constitutional protection."

Jacobellis 10

"I have viewed the film and I wish merely to add to my Brother Brennan's description that the love scene deemed objectionable is so fragmentary and fleeting that only a censor's alert would make an audience conscious that something 'questionable' is being portrayed. Except for this rapid sequence, the film concerns itself with the history of an ill-matched and unhappy marriage, a familiar subject in old and new novels and in current television soap operas."

RONALD L. FREEDMAN, Appellant,

v.

STATE OF MARYLAND

380 US 51 March 1, 1965

SUMMARY: Freedman exhibited the film "Revenge at Daybreak" at his Baltimore theater without first submitting the picture to the State Board of Censors as was required by law. The state conceded that the picture did not violate the statutory standards and would have received a license if properly submitted.

Justices:	EARL WARREN	TOM C. CLARK	POTTER STEWART
	HUGO L. BLACK	JOHN M. HARLAN	BYRON R. WHITE
	WILLIAM O. DOUGLAS	WILLIAM J. BRENNAN, JR.	ARTHUR J. GOLDBERG

Freedman   1

"Any authority to obtain a temporary injunction gives the State 'the paralyzing power of a censor.' . . . I would put an end to all forms and types of censorship and give full literal meaning to the command of the First Amendment."

Freedman   2

"For the reasons there stated, I do not believe any form of censorship—no matter how speedy or prolonged it may be—is permissible. As I see it, a pictorial presentation occupies as preferred a position as any other form of expression. If censors are banned from the publishing business, from the pulpit, from the public platform—as they are—they should be banned from the theater."

—DOUGLAS

Freedman   3   **Freedman**   4

"The requirement of prior submission to a censor sustained in Times Film is consistent with our recognition that films differ from other forms of expression. Similarly, we think that the nature of the motion picture industry may suggest different time limits for a judicial determination. . . . One possible scheme would be to allow the exhibitor or distributor to submit his film early enough to ensure an orderly final disposition of the case before the scheduled exhibition date—far enough in advance so that the exhibitor could safely advertise the opening on a normal basis.

—BRENNAN

"On several occasions I have indicated my view that movies are entitled to the same degree and kind of protection under the First Amendment as other forms of expression."

Freedman   5   **Freedman**   6

"How or whether Maryland is to incorporate the required procedural safeguards in the statutory scheme is, of course, for the State to decide. But a model is not lacking: In Kingsley Books Inc. v. Brown, 354 US 436 . . . , we upheld a New York injunctive procedure designed to prevent the sale of obscene books."

"First, the burden of proving that the film is unprotected expression must rest on the censor."

"Risk of delay is built into the Maryland procedure, as is borne out by experience; in the only reported case indicating the length of time required to complete an appeal, the initial judicial determination has taken four months and final vindication of the film on appellate review six months."

"In the area of freedom of expression it is well established that one has standing to challenge a statute on the ground that it delegates overly broad licensing discretion to an administrative office, whether or not his conduct could be proscribed by a properly drawn statute, and whether or not he applied for a license."

"Under the statute, the exhibitor is required to submit the film to the Board for examination, but no time limit is imposed for completion of Board action."

"In Times Film Corp. v. City of Chicago, 365 US 43 . . . , we considered and upheld a requirement of submission of motion pictures in advance of exhibition."

A BOOK NAMED "JOHN CLELAND'S MEMOIRS OF A WOMAN
OF PLEASURE" et al., Appellant

v.

ATTORNEY GENERAL OF THE COMMONWEALTH OF MASSACHUSETTS

383 US 413   March 21, 1966

SUMMARY: The book commonly known as *Fanny Hill,* written by John Cleland about 1750 concerning the adventures of a prostitute, was declared obscene by Massachusetts courts. G. P. Putnam's Sons was the publisher involved.

Justices:	EARL WARREN	ABE FORTAS	JOHN M. HARLAN
	HUGO L. BLACK	WILLIAM O. DOUGLAS	WILLIAM J. BRENNAN, JR.
	POTTER STEWART	TOM C. CLARK	BYRON R. WHITE

Cleland   1

"These scenes run the gamut of possible sexual experience such as lesbianism, female masturbation, homosexuality between young boys, the destruction of a maidenhead with consequent gory descriptions, the seduction of a young virgin boy, the flagellation of male by female. . . . In one sequence, four girls in a baudy house are required in the presence of another to relate the lurid details of their loss of virginity and their glorification of it. This is followed the same evening by 'public trials' in which each of the four girls engages in sexual intercourse with a different man while the others witness, with Fanny giving a detailed description of the movement and reaction of each couple. In each of the sexual scenes the exposed bodies of the participants are described in minute and individual detail. The pubic hair is often used for a background to the most vivid and precise descriptions of the response, condition, size, shape and color of the sexual organs before, during, and after orgasm. . . ."

Cleland   2

"In addition, there is persuasive evidence from criminologists and police officials. Inspector Herbert Case of the Detroit Police Department contends that sex murder cases are invariably tied to some form of obscene literature. And the Director of the Federal Bureau of Investigation, J. Edgar Hoover, has repeatedly emphasized that pornography is associated with an overwhelmingly large number of sex crimes."

Cleland   **3**   **Cleland**   **4**

"Psychological and physiological studies clearly indicate that many persons become sexually aroused from reading obscene material. While erotic stimulation caused by pornography may be legally insignificant in itself, there are medical experts who believe that such stimulation frequently manifests itself in criminal behavior or other antisocial conduct. For example, Dr. George W. Henry of Cornell University has expressed the opinion that obscenity, with its exaggerated and morbid emphasis on sex, particularly abnormal and perverted practices, and its unrealistic presentation of sexual behavior and attitudes, may induce antisocial conduct by the average person."

"To say that Fanny is an 'intellectual' is an insult to those who travel under that tag. She was nothing but a harlot—a sensualist—exploiting her sexual attractions which she sold for fun, for money, for lodging and keep, for an inheritance, and finally for a husband. If she was curious about life, her curiosity extended only to the pursuit of sexual delight wherever she found it."

Cleland   **5**   **Cleland**   **6**

"However, the public should know of the continuous flow of pornographic material reaching this Court and the increasing problem States have in controlling it. *Memoirs of a Woman of Pleasure,* the book involved here, is typical. I have 'stomached' past cases for almost 10 years without much outcry. Though I am not known to be a purist—or shrinking violet—this book is too much even for me. . . . in order to give my remarks the proper setting, I have been obliged to portray the book's contents, which causes me embarrassment."

—CLARK

"The book relates the adventures of a young girl who becomes a prostitute in London. At the end, she abandons that life and marries her first lover, observing:

'Thus at length, I got snug into port, where, in the bosom of virtue, I gather'd the only uncorrupt sweets: where looking back on the course of vice I had run, and comparing its infamous banishments with the infinitely superior joys of innocence, I could not help pitying, even in point of taste, those who are immersed in gross sensuality, are insensible to the so delicate charms of VIRTUE, than which even PLEASURE has not a greater friend, nor VICE a greater enemy.'"

"Every time an obscenity case is to be argued here, my office is flooded with letters and postal cards urging me to protect the community or the Nation by striking down the publication. The messages are often identical even down to commas and semicolons. The inference is irresistible that they were all copied from a school or church blackboard. Dozens of postal cards are often mailed from the same precinct. The drives are incessant and the pressures are great. Happily we do not have to bow to them. I mention them only to emphasize the lack of popular understanding of our constitutional system. Publications and utterances were made immune from majorial control by the First Amendment, applicable to the States by the Fourteenth. No exceptions were made, not even for obscenity."

"All possible uses of the book must therefore be considered, and the mere risk that the book might be exploited by panderers because it so pervasively treats sexual matters cannot alter the fact—given the view of the Massachusetts Court attributing to *Memoirs* a modicum of literary and historical value—that the book will have redeeming social importance in the hands of those who publish or distribute it on the basis of that value."

—Brennan, Jr.

"Perhaps the most frequently assigned justification for censorship is the belief that erotica produce antisocial sexual conduct. But that relationship has yet to be proven. Indeed, if one were to make judgments on the basis of speculation, one might guess that literature of the most pornographic sort would, in many cases, provide a substitute—not a stimulus—for antisocial sexual conduct. See Murphy, The Value of Pornography, 10 Wayne L Rev 655, 661, and n. 19 (1964)."

"We are not judges, not literary experts or historians or philosophers. We are not competent to render an independent judgment as to the worth of this book or any book, except in our capacity as private citizens."

RALPH GINZBURG et al., Petitioners

v.

UNITED STATES

383 US 436   March 21, 1966

SUMMARY: Ginzburg, and three corporations controlled by him, used the mail for distributing allegedly obscene literature, namely the magazine *Eros*, containing articles and photos on sex and love; a biweekly newsletter, dedicated to "keeping sex an art and preventing it from becoming a science"; and the *Housewives' Handbook on Selective Promiscuity.* The prosecution charged that the materials in themselves might not be obscene, but in the context of the advertising, publicity, and sale they had become so. Commercial exploitation was charged. Mailing privileges were sought by Ginzburg from Intercourse and Blue Ball, Pennsylvania, and were finally obtained from Middlesex, New Jersey.

Justices: EARL WARREN   TOM C. CLARK   POTTER STEWART
              HUGO L. BLACK   JOHN M. HARLAN   BYRON R. WHITE
              WILLIAM O. DOUGLAS   WILLIAM J. BRENNAN, JR.   ABE FORTAS

Ginzburg   1   **Ginzburg**   2

"In U.S. v. Rebhuhn, . . . the defendants had indiscriminately flooded the mails with advertisements, plainly designed merely to catch the prurient, though under the guise of distributing works of scientific or literary merit."

"The 'leer of the sensualist' . . . permeates the advertising for the three publications. . . . The deliberate representation of petitioners' publications as erotically arousing, for example, stimulated the reader to accept them as prurient, he looks for titillation, not for saving intellectual content."

Ginzburg   **3**   Ginzburg   **4**

"I cannot imagine of any promotional effort that would make Chapters 7 and 8 of the Song of Solomon any the less or any more worthy of First Amendment protection than does their unostentatious inclusion in the average edition of the Bible."

            —DOUGLAS

". . . questionable publications are obscene in a context which brands them as obscene as that term is defined in Roth—a use inconsistent with any claim to the shelter of the First Amendment."

Ginzburg   **5**   Ginzburg   **6**

". . . to determine whether Ginzburg or anyone else can be punished as a common criminal for publishing or circulating obscene material are so vague and meaningless that they practically leave the fate of a person charged with violating censorship statutes to the unbridled discretion, whim and caprice of the judge or jury which tries him."

"The Rev. George VonHelsheimer III,* a Baptist minister, testified that he used *The Wife's Handbook on Selective Promiscuity* 'in my pastoral counseling and my formal psychological counseling.' "

*Consultant to President Kennedy's Study Group on National Voluntary Services.

Ginzburg   7

"I believe the Federal Government is without any power whatever under the Constitution to put any type of burden on speech and expression of ideas of any kind (as distinguished from conduct)."

Ginzburg   8

"Man was not made in a fixed mold. If a publication caters to the idiosyncrasy of a minority, why does it not have some 'social importance'? Each of us is a very temporary transient with likes and dislikes that cover the spectrum. However plebeian my taste may be, who am I to say that others' tastes must be so limited and that other tastes have no social importance?"

Ginzburg   9

"Censorship reflects a society's lack of confidence in itself. It is a hallmark of an authoritarian regime. Long ago those who wrote our First Amendment charted a different course."

Ginzburg   10

"When an exploitation of interests in titillation by pornography is shown with respect to material lending itself to such exploitation through persuasive treatment or description of sexual matters, such evidence may support the determination that the material is obscene even though in other contexts the material would escape such condemnation."

—WARREN

SAM GINSBERG, Appellant

v.

STATE OF NEW YORK

390 US 629   April 22, 1968

SUMMARY: Ginsberg was convicted for selling "girlie" magazines to a minor under the age of seventeen years. A state statute prohibited a person from knowingly selling certain material "harmful to minors." Harmful was defined as any description or representation of nudity, sexual conduct, etc., when it (1) predominantly appeals to the prurient interest of minors, (2) is patently offensive to prevailing standards in the adult community as a whole with respect to what is suitable material for minors, and (3) is utterly without redeeming social importance for minors.

Justices:	EARL WARREN	WILLIAM O. DOUGLAS	BYRON R. WHITE
	HUGO L. BLACK	WILLIAM J. BRENNAN, JR.	ABE FORTAS
	JOHN M. HARLAN	POTTER STEWART	THURGOOD MARSHALL

Ginsberg, Sam 1   **Ginsberg, Sam** 2

"Appellant and his wife operate 'Sam's Stationery and Luncheonette' in Bellmore, Long Island. They have a lunch counter and, among other things, also sell magazines including some so-called 'girlie' magazines. Appellant was prosecuted under two informations, each in two counts, which charged that he personally sold a 16-year-old boy two 'girlie' magazines on each of two dates in October, 1965, in violation of §484-h of the New York Penal Code."

"I think a State may permissibly determine that, at least in some precisely delineated areas, a child—like someone in a captive audience— is not possessed of that full capacity for individual choice which is the presupposition of First Amendment guarantees."

—STEWART

Ginsberg, Sam 3

"While the supervision of children's reading may best be left to their parents, the knowledge that parental control or guidance cannot always be provided and society's transcendent interest in protecting the welfare of children justify reasonable regulation of the sale of material to them."

Ginsberg, Sam 4

"A doctrinaire, knee-jerk application of the First Amendment would, of course, dictate the nullification of this New York statute. But that result is not required, I think, if we bear in mind what it is that the First Amendment protects.
"The First Amendment guarantees liberty of human expression in order to preserve in our Nation what Mr. Justice Holmes called a 'free trade of ideas.' To that end, the Constitution protects more than just a man's freedom to say or write or publish what he wants. It seems as well the liberty of each man to decide for himself what he will read and to what he will listen. The Constitution guarantees, in short, a society of free choice. Such a society presupposes the capacity of its members to choose."

Ginsberg, Sam 5

"APPENDIX A, New York Penal Law §484-h . . . (b) 'nudity' means the showing of the human male or female genitals, pubic area or buttocks with less than a full opaque covering, or the showing of the female breast with less than a fully opaque covering of any portion thereof below the top of the nipple, or the depiction of covered male genitals in a discernibly turgid state."

Ginsberg, Sam 6

"But obscenity is not protected expression and may be suppressed without a showing of the circumstances which lie behind the phrase 'clear and present danger' in its application to protected speech."

Ginsberg, Sam   7

"Today this Court sits as the Nation's board of Censors. With all respect, I do not know of any group in the country less qualified first, to know what obscenity is when they see it, and second to have any considered judgment as to what the deleterious or beneficial impact of a particular publication may have on minds either young or old.

"I would await a constitutional amendment that authorized the modern Anthony Comstocks to censor literature before publishers, authors, or distributors can be fined or jailed for what they print or sell."

—DOUGLAS

Ginsberg, Sam   8

"The conviction of Ginsberg on the present facts is a serious invasion of freedom. To sustain the conviction without inquiry as to whether the material is 'obscene' and without any evidence of pushing or pandering, in face of this Court's asserted solicitude for First Amendment values, is to give the State a role in the rearing of children which is contrary to our traditions and to our conception of family responsibility."

Ginsberg, Sam   9

"There is a view held by many that the so-called 'obscene' book or tract or magazine has a deleterious effect upon the young, although I seriously doubt the wisdom of trying by law to put the fresh, evanescent, natural blossoming of sex in the category of 'sin.'

"That, however, was the view of our preceptor in this field, Anthony Comstock, who waged his war against 'obscenity' from the year 1872 until his death in 1915."

Ginsberg, Sam   10

"The two magazines that the 16-year-old boy selected are vulgar 'girlie' periodicals. However tasteless and tawdry they may be, we have ruled (as the Court acknowledges) that magazines indistinguishable from them in content and offensiveness are not 'obscene' within the constitutional standards heretofore applied."

INTERSTATE CIRCUIT INC., Appellant

v.

CITY OF DALLAS

UNITED ARTISTS CORPORATION, Appellant

v.

CITY OF DALLAS

390 US 676   April 22, 1968

SUMMARY: A Dallas ordinance, adopted in 1965, required that a film exhibitor, before any showing of a film, file with the City Motion Picture Classification Board a proposed classification of the film together with a summary of its plot. If the Board is then displeased with the proposed classification, the film must be exhibited before five or more members of the Board. The Interstate Circuit exhibitor was enjoined from showing "Viva Maria" without the "Not Suitable for Young Persons" classification.

Justices: EARL WARREN   JOHN M. HARLAN   BYRON R. WHITE
              HUGO L. BLACK   WILLIAM J. BRENNAN, JR. ABE FORTAS
              WILLIAM O. DOUGLAS POTTER STEWART   THURGOOD MARSHALL

Interstate   1

"If he is unable to determine what the ordinance means, he runs the risk of being foreclosed, in practical effect, from a significant portion of the movie-going public. Rather than running the risk, he might choose nothing but the innocuous, perhaps save for the so-called 'adult' pictures. Moreover, a local exhibitor who cannot afford the risk of losing the youthful audience when a film may be of marginal interest to adults—perhaps a 'Viva Maria'—may contract to show only the totally inane. The vast wasteland that some have described in reference to another medium might be a verdant paradise in comparison."

—MARSHALL

Interstate   2

"The vice of vagueness is particularly pronounced where expression is sought to be subjected to licensing. It may be unlikely that what Dallas does in respect to the licensing of motion pictures would have a significant effect upon film makers in Hollywood or Europe. But what Dallas may constitutionally do, so may other cities and States."

Interstate   **3**

"... we have indicated more generally that because of its strong and abiding interest in youth, a State may regulate the dissemination to juveniles of, and their access to, materials objectionable as to them, but which a State could not regulate to adults. Ginsberg v. New York. 390 US 676" [20 L Ed 2d 195]

Interstate   **4**

"Five members of the Board viewed 'Viva Maria.' Eight members voted to classify it as 'not suitable for young persons,' the ninth member not voting. The Board gave no reasons for its determination. . . . Two Board members, a clergyman and a lawyer, testified at the hearing. Each adverted to several scenes in the film which, in their opinion, portrayed male-female relationships in a way contrary to 'acceptable and approved behavior.' Each acknowledged, in reference to scenes in which clergymen were involved in violence, most of which was farcical, that 'sacrilege' might have entered into the Board's determination. And both conceded that the asserted portrayal of 'sexual promiscuity' was implicit rather than explicit, i.e., that it was a product of inference by, and imagination of, the viewer."

Interstate   **5**

"It is difficult to see how the Court could suppose that its Memoirs formula offers more precise warnings to filmmakers than does the Dallas ordinance. Surely the Court cannot now believe that 'redeeming social value,' 'patent offensiveness,' and 'prurient interest' are, particularly as modified so as to apply to children, terms of common understanding and clarity."

Interstate   **6**

"In my opinion, the ordinance does not fail either to give adequate notice of the films that are to be restricted or to provide sufficiently defined standards for its administration."

Interstate 7

"I believe that no improvement in this chaotic state of affairs is likely to come until it is recognized that this whole problem is primarily one of state concern, and that the Constitution tolerates much wider authority and discretion in the States to control the dissemination of obscene materials than it does in the Federal Government."

—HARLAN

Interstate 8

Chapter 46A of the 1960 Revised Code of Civil and Criminal Ordinances of the City of Dallas, as amended, provides: "A film shall be considered 'likely to invite or encourage' crime, delinquency or sexual promiscuity on the part of young persons, if, in the judgment of the Board, there is a substantial probability that it will create the impression on young persons that such conduct is profitable, desirable, acceptable, respectable, praiseworthy or commonly accepted. A film shall be considered as appealing to prurient interests of young persons, if in the judgment of the Board, its calculated or dominant effect on young persons is substantially to arouse sexual desire. In determining whether a film is 'not suitable for young persons,' the Board shall consider the films as a whole, rather than isolated portions, and shall determine whether its harmful effects outweigh artistic or educational values such film may have for young persons."

Interstate 9

"Most of the present Justices who believe that 'obscenity' is not beyond the pale of governmental control seemingly consider that the Roth-Memoirs-Ginzburg test permits suppression of material that falls short of so-called 'hard core pornography,' on equal terms as between federal and state authority. Another view is that only 'hard core pornography may be suppressed, whether by federal or state authority. And still another view, that of this writer, is that, only 'hard core pornography' may be suppressed by the Federal Government, whereas under the Fourteenth Amendment States are permitted wider authority to deal with obnoxious matter than might be justifiable under a strict application of the Roth-Memoirs-Ginzburg rules."

Interstate 10

". . . Two members of the Court steadfastly maintain that the First and Fourteenth Amendments render society powerless to protect itself against the dissemination of even the filthiest materials."

QUESTIONS FOR DISCUSSION

1. Should a city ban films which are extremely offensive to certain religious or racial groups?

2. What is the legal definition of obscenity?

3. Are publishers of obscene materials lawbreakers?

4. May cities prevent the exhibition of certain films?

5. When is an advertisement obscene?

6. What power does the post office have over obscene materials?

7. Can a merchant be convicted for selling a "girlie" magazine to minors?

8. Should censorship standards be different for adults and children?

9. Can a city legally stop suggestive acts and nudity in its theaters, restaurants, and nightclubs?

10. What is the relationship between obscene literature and speech and criminal acts?

Defamation and Libel

J. M. NEAR, Appellant

v.

STATE OF MINNESOTA EX. REL. FLOYD OLSON

283 US 697   June 1, 1931

SUMMARY: Near, publisher of *The Saturday Press,* ran a series of articles making accusations against public figures in Minneapolis. The city secured a temporary injunction restraining future publications of the newspaper. He was convicted of a "malicious, scandalous, and defamatory newspaper. . . ." Near then invoked the protection of the Fourteenth Amendment and charged that the statute was unconstitutional because it limited his freedom of the press.

Justices: CHARLES E. HUGHES   JAMES C. McREYNOLDS   PIERCE BUTLER
OLIVER W. HOLMES   LOUIS D. BRANDEIS   HARLAN F. STONE
WILLIS VAN DEVANTER   GEORGE SUTHERLAND   OWEN J. ROBERTS

Near   1   **Near**   2

"The record shows and it is conceded that defendants' regular business was the publication of malicious, scandalous and defamatory articles concerning the principal public officers, leading newspapers of the city and many private persons and the Jewish race. It also shows that it was their purpose at all hazards to continue to carry on the business. In every edition slanderous and defamatory matter predominates to the practical exclusion of all else. Many of the articles are so highly improbable as to compel a finding that they are false. The articles themselves show malice."

". . . the articles charged in substance that a Jewish gangster was in control of gambling, bootlegging and racketeering in Minneapolis, and that law enforcing officers and agencies were not energetically performing their duties. Most of the charges were directed against the chief of police; he was charged with gross neglect of duty, illicit relations with gangsters, and with participation in graft."

Near 3

"Public officers, whose character and conduct remain open to debate and free discussion in the press, find their remedies for false accusations in actions under libel laws . . . and not in proceedings to restrain the publication of newspapers and periodicals."

Near 4

"At the beginning of the action on November 22, 1927, and upon the verified complaint, an order was made directing the defendants to show cause why a temporary injunction should not issue and meanwhile forbidding the defendants to publish, circulate or have in their possession any editions of the periodical from September 24, 1927, to November 19, 1927, inclusive, and from publishing, circulating, or having in their possession 'any future editions of said The Saturday Press. . . .' "

Near 5

"The statute is not aimed at the redress of individual or private wrongs. Remedies for libel remain available and unaffected. The statute, said the Court, 'is not directed to threaten libel but at existing business which, generally speaking, involved more than libel.' It is directed against scandalous matter as 'detrimental to public morals and to the general welfare,' tending 'to disturb the peace of the community' and 'to provoke assaults and the commission of crime.' "

Near 6

". . . for approximately one hundred and fifty years there has been almost an entire absence of attempts to impose previous restraints upon publications. . . . The fact that the liberty of the press may be abused by miscreant purveyors of scandal does not make any the less necessary the immunity of the press from previous restraint in dealing with official misconduct."

—HUGHES

"The Minnesota statute does not operate as a *previous* restraint on publication within the proper meaning of that phrase. It does not authorize administrative control in advance . . . but prescribes a remedy to be enforced by a suit in equity, i.e. . . . *from further committing, conducting, or maintaining any such nuisance.*"

"Confessedly, the Federal Constitution prior to 1868, when the 14th Amendment was adopted, did not protect the right of free speech or press against state action. . . . This court was not called on until 1925 to decide whether the 'liberty' protected by the 14th Amendment includes the right of free speech and press. That question was decided in the affirmative."

"The following articles appear in the last edition published, dated November 19, 1927:

'FACTS NOT THEORIES'

"'I am a bosom friend of Mr. Olson,' snorted a gentleman of Yiddish blood . . . 'I am not taking orders from men of Barnett faith, at least right now. There have been too many men in this city and especially those in official life, who HAVE been taking orders and suggestions from JEW GANGSTERS, therefore we HAVE Jew Gangsters, practically ruling Minneapolis. 'It was buzzards of the Barnett stripe who shot down my buddy. . . . It was Jew thugs who have "pulled" practically every robbery in this ctiy.'"

". . . Constant and protracted false and malicious assaults of any insolvent publisher may have purpose and sufficient capacity to contrive and put into effect a scheme or program for oppression, blackmail, or extortion."

—BUTLER

JOSEPH BEAUHARNAIS, Petitioner

v.

PEOPLE OF THE STATE OF ILLINOIS

343 US 250   April 28, 1952

SUMMARY: Beauharnais distributed a leaflet entitled "Preserve and Protect White Neighborhoods," and it ended with an application for a 1950 membership to the White Circle League of America, Inc. He was indicted on a charge that he published lithographs portraying "depravity, criminality, unchastity, or lack of virtue" of citizens of the Negro race and exposed them to "contempt, derision, or obloquy," in violation of an Illinois statute which prohibited publications so attacking "citizens of any race, color, creed, or religion."

Justices: FRED M. VINSON   FELIX FRANKFURTER   HAROLD H. BURTON
              HUGO L. BLACK   WILLIAM O. DOUGLAS   TOM C. CLARK
              STANLEY REED   ROBERT H. JACKSON   SHERMAN MINTON

Beauharnais   1   **Beauharnais**   2

"Moreover, the same kind of state law that makes Beauharnais a criminal for advocating segregation in Illinois can be utilized to send people to jail in other states for advocating equality and nonsegregation. What Beauharnais said in his leaflet is mild compared with usual arguments on both sides of racial controversies."

"Punishment of printed words, based on their *tendency* either to cause breach of the peace or injury to persons or groups, in my opinion, is justifiable only if the prosecution survives the 'clear and present danger' test."

—JACKSON

Beauharnais 3

"Hitler and his Nazis showed a conspiracy could be that which was aimed at destroying a race by exposing it to contempt, derision and obloquy. I would be willing to concede that such conduct directed at a race or group in this country could be made an indictable offense. For such a project would be more than the exercise of free speech.

"I would also be willing to concede that even without the element of conspiracy there might be times and occasions when the legislative or executive branch might call a halt to inflammatory talk, such as the shouting of 'fire' in a school or a theater.

"My view is that if in any case other public interests are to override the plain command of the First Amendment, the peril of speech must be clear and present, leaving no room for argument, raising no doubts as to the necessity of curbing speech in order to prevent disaster."

Beauharnais 4

"Libel of any individual was a common-law crime, and thus criminal in the colonies. Indeed, at common law, truth or good motives was no defense. In the first decades after the adoption of the Constitution, this was changed by judicial decision, statute or constitution in most states, but nowhere was there any suggestion that the crime of libel be abolished."

Beauharnais 5

"Below was a call for 'One million self-respecting white people in Chicago to unite. . . .' with the statement added that 'if persuasion and the need to prevent the white race from becoming mongrelized by the Negro will not unite us, the aggressions . . . rapes, robberies, knives, guns and marijuana of the Negro surely will.'"

Beauharnais 6

"No one will gainsay that it is libelous falsity to charge another with being a rapist, robber, carrier of knives and guns, and user of marijuana."

—Frankfurter

Beauharnais   **7**   **Beauharnais**   **8**

"It is suggested that while it was clearly within the constitutional power of Illinois to punish this utterance if the proceeding were properly safeguarded, in this particular case Illinois denied the defendant rights which the Due Process Clause commands."

"Freedom of petition, assembly, speech and press could be greatly abridged by a practice of meticulously scrutinizing every editorial, sermon or other printed matter to extract two or three naughty words on which to hang charges of 'group libel.'"

Beauharnais   **9**   **Beauharnais**   **10**

"The testimony at the trial was substantially undisputed. From it the jury could find that Beauharnais was president of the White Circle League; that, at a meeting on January 6, 1950, he passed out bundles of the lithographs in question, together with other literature, to volunteers for distribution to downtown Chicago street corners the following day. . . ."

"From the murder of the abolitionist Lovejoy in 1837 to the Cicero riots in 1951, Illinois has been the scene of exacerbated tension between races, often flaring into violence and destruction. In many of these outbreaks, utterances of the character here in question, so the Illinois legislature could conclude, played a significant part."

MANUEL D. TALLEY, Petitioner

v.

CALIFORNIA

362 US 60   March 7, 1960

SUMMARY: Manuel Talley was convicted in Los Angeles Municipal Court for violating an ordinance which made it a criminal offense to distribute "any hand-bill in any place under any circumstances," unless it had printed on it the names and addresses of the persons who prepared, distributed, and sponsored it. The handbills at issue urged a boycott against certain listed merchants and businessmen who carried products of manufacturers who did not offer equal employment opportunities to Negroes, Mexicans, and Orientals.

Justices: EARL WARREN	WILLIAM O. DOUGLAS	WILLIAM J. BRENNAN, JR.
HUGO L. BLACK	TOM C. CLARK	CHARLES E. WHITTAKER
FELIX FRANKFURTER	JOHN M. HARLAN	POTTER STEWART

Talley   1

"The ordinance, 28.06 of the Municipal Code of the City of Los Angeles, provides:

'No person shall distribute any hand-bill in any place under any circumstances, which does not have printed on the cover, or the face thereof, the name and address of the following:

(a) The person who printed, wrote, compiled or manufactured the same.

(b) The person who caused the same to be distributed; provided, however, that in the case of a fictitious person or club, in addition to such fictitious name, the true names and addresses of the owner, managers or agents of the person sponsoring said hand-bill shall also appear thereon.' "

Talley   2

"It was stipulated that the petitioner had distributed handbills in Los Angeles, and two of them were presented in evidence. Each had printed on it the following:

National Consumers Mobilization,
Box 6533
Los Angeles 55, Calif.
PLeasant 9-1576

The handbills urged readers to help the organization carry on a boycott against certain merchants and businessmen, whose names were given, on the ground that, as one set of handbills said, they carried products of 'manufacturers who will not offer equal employment opportunities to Negroes, Mexicans, and Orientals.' "

Talley   3   **Talley**   4

"Anonymous pamphlets, leaflets, brochures, and even books have played an important role in the progress of mankind. Persecuted groups and sects from time to time throughout history have been able to criticize oppressive practices and laws either anonymously or not at all. The obnoxious press licensing law of England, which was also enforced on the Colonies, was due in part to the knowledge that exposure of the names of printers, writers and distributors would lessen the circulation of literature critical of the government. The old seditious libel cases in England show the lengths to which government had to go to find out who was responsible for books that were obnoxious to the rulers. John Lilburne was whipped, pilloried and fined for refusing to answer questions designed to get evidence to convict him or someone else for the secret distribution of books in England."

"Two Puritan Ministers, John Penry and John Udal, were sentenced to death on charges that they were responsible for writing, printing or publishing books. Before the Revolutionary War colonial patriots frequently had to conceal their authorship or distribution of literature that easily could have brought down on them prosecutions by English-controlled courts. Along about that time the Letters of Junius were written and the identity of their author is unknown to this day. Even the Federalist Papers, written in favor of the adoption of our Constitution, were published under fictitious names. It is plain that anonymity has sometimes been assumed for the most constructive purposes."

Talley   5   **Talley**   6

"We have recently had occasion to hold in two cases that there are times and circumstances when States may not compel members of groups engaged in the dissemination of ideas to be publicly identified. Bates v. Little Rock, 361 US 516, 4 L ed 2d 480, 80 S Ct 412; National Asso. for Advancement of Colored People v. Alabama, 357 US 449, 462, 2 L ed 2d 1488, 1499, 78 S Ct 1163. The reason for those holdings was that identification and fear of reprisal might deter perfectly peaceful discussions of public matters of importance. This broad Los Angeles ordinance is subject to the same infirmity."

"At oral argument, the City's chief law enforcement officer stated that the ordinance was originally suggested in 1931 by the Los Angeles Chamber of Commerce in a complaint to the City Council urging it to 'do something about these handbills and advertising matters which were false and misleading.' Upon inquiry by the Council, he said, the matter was referred to his office, and the Council was advised that such an ordinance as the present one would be valid. He further stated that this ordinance, relating to the original inquiry of the Chamber of Commerce, was thereafter drafted and submitted to the Council. It was adopted in 1932."

Talley 7

"Talley makes no showing whatever to support his contention that a restraint upon his freedom of speech will result from the enforcement of the ordinance. The existence of such a restraint is necessary before we can strike the ordinance down."

Talley 8

"But even if the State had this burden, which it does not, the substantiality of Los Angeles' interest in the enforcement of the ordinance sustains its validity. Its chief law enforcement officer says that the enforcement of the ordinance prevents 'fraud, deceit, false advertising, negligent use of words, obscenity, and libel,' and, as we have said, that such was its purpose. In the absence of any showing to the contrary by Talley, this appears to me entirely sufficient."

Talley 9

"All that Los Angeles requires is that one who exercises his right of free speech through writing or distributing handbills identify himself just as does one who speaks from the platform. The ordinance makes for the responsibility in writing that is present in public utterance. When and if the application of such an ordinance in a given case encroaches on First Amendment freedoms, then will be soon enough to strike that application down. But no such restraint has been shown here."

—CLARK

Talley 10

"Contrary to petitioner's contention, the ordinance as applied does not arbitrarily deprive him of equal protection of the law. He complains that handbills are singled out, while other printed media—books, magazines and newspapers — remain unrestrained. However, '[t]he problem of legislative classification is a perennial one, admitting of no doctrinaire definition. Evils in the same field may be of different dimensions and proportions, requiring different remedies. . . . Or the reform may take one step at a time, addressing itself to the phase of the problem which seems most acute to the legislative mind. . . . The prohibition of the Equal Protection Clause goes no further than the invidious discrimination.' "

NEW YORK TIMES COMPANY, Petitioner

v.

L. B. SULLIVAN

———

RALPH D. ABERNATHY et al., Petitioner

v.

L. B. SULLIVAN

376 US 54   March 9, 1964

SUMMARY: The Alabama Courts awarded Sullivan damages of $500,000 from four Negro Clergymen and the *New York Times* because of a paid advertisement in that paper which had accused the city of Montgomery of mistreatment of Negroes. The ad was titled "Heed Their Rising Voices."

Justices:	EARL WARREN	TOM C. CLARK	POTTER STEWART
	HUGO L. BLACK	JOHN M. HARLAN	BYRON R. WHITE
	WILLIAM O. DOUGLAS	WILLIAM J. BRENNAN, JR.	ARTHUR J. GOLDBERG

N. Y. Times   1   **N. Y. Times**   2

"In Beauharnais v. Illinois, 343 US 250, the Court sustained an Illinois criminal libel statute as applied to a publication held to be both defamatory of a racial group and 'liable to cause violence and disorder.'"

"Finally there is evidence that the Times published the advertisement without checking its accuracy against the news stories in the Times' own files."

N. Y. Times   3   **N. Y. Times**   4

"Like 'insurrection,' contempt, advocacy of unlawful acts, breach of the peace, obscenity,
solicitation of legal business, and the various
other formulae for the repression of expression that have been challenged in this Court,
libel can claim no talismanic immunity from
constitutional limitations."

"The Times' failure to retract upon respondent's demand although it later retracted upon
the demand of Governor Patterson, is likewise not adequate evidence of malice for constitutional purposes."

N. Y. Times   5   **N. Y. Times**   6

"It is uncontroverted that some of the statements contained in the two paragraphs were
not accurate description of events which occurred in Montgomery."

"The half-million-dollar verdict does give dramatic proof, however, that state libel laws
threaten the very existence of an American
press virile enough to publish unpopular views
on public affairs and bold enough to criticize
the conduct of public officials."

N. Y. Times   7   **N. Y. Times**   8

"The statements were false only in that the police had been 'deployed near' the campus but had not actually 'ringed' it and had not gone there in connection with the state demonstration, and in that Dr. King had been arrested only four times."

"A rule compelling the critic of official conduct to guarantee the truth of all his factual assertions—and to do so on pain of libel judgments virtually unlimited in amount—leads to a comparable 'self-censorship.'"

—BRENNAN

N. Y. Times   9   **N. Y. Times**   10

The 3rd paragraph of an advertisement in the New York Times.

"In Montgomery, Alabama, after students sang 'My Country 'Tis of Thee' on the State Capitol steps, their leaders were expelled from school, and truckloads of police armed with shotguns and tear-gas ringed the Alabama College Campus. When the entire student body protested to state authorities by refusing to reregister, their dining hall was padlocked in an attempt to starve them into submission."

The 6th paragraph.

"Again and again the Southern violators have answered Dr. King's peaceful protests with intimidation and violence. They have bombed his home almost killing his wife and child. They have assaulted his person. They have arrested him seven times—for 'speeding,' 'loitering,' and similar 'offenses.' And now they have charged him with 'perjury'—a *felony* under which they would imprison him for *ten years*."

"Justice Brandeis correctly observed, 'sunlight, is the most powerful of all disinfectants.'

"For these reasons, I strongly believe that the Constitution accords citizens and press an unconditional freedom to criticize official conduct."

—BLACK

JIM GARRISON, Appellant

v.

STATE OF LOUISIANA

379 US 64   November 23, 1964

SUMMARY: The District Attorney of Orleans Parish, Garrison, at a press conference accused eight state court judges of laziness, excessively long vacations, inefficiency, and of hampering his efforts by refusing to authorize funds for undercover investigations. He said, in part, "This raises interesting questions about the racketeer influence on our eight vacation-minded judges." Garrison was convicted of defamation, and the Louisiana Supreme Court affirmed the conviction.

Justices:	EARL WARREN	TOM C. CLARK	POTTER STEWART
	HUGO L. BLACK	JOHN M. HARLAN	BYRON R. WHITE
	WILLIAM O. DOUGLAS	WILLIAM J. BRENNAN, JR.	ARTHUR J. GOLDBERG

Garrison 1

"Why does 'the freedom of speech' that the Court is willing to protect turn out to be so pale and tame? It is because, as my Brother Black has said, the Bill of Rights is constantly watered down through judicial 'balancing' of what the Constitution says and what judges think is needed for a well-ordered society."

—DOUGLAS

Garrison 2

"In N. Y. Times Co. v. Sullivan we held that . . . a false statement must be 'made with "actual malice"—that is, with knowledge that it was false or with reckless disregard of whether it was false or not.'"

Garrison 3

Garrison 4

". . . erroneous statement is inevitable in free debate . . . it must be protected if the freedoms of expression are to have 'breathing space.' . . . only those false statements made with the high degree of awareness of their probable falsity demanded by the N. Y. Times may be subject of either civil or criminal sanctions."

". . . the use of the words 'racketeer influences' when applied to anyone suggests and imputes that he has been influenced to practice fraud, deceit, trickery, cheating, and dishonesty."

Garrison 5

Garrison 6

"The dispute between appellant (Garrison) and the judges arose over disbursement from a Fines and Fees Fund. . . . The eight judges . . . adopted a rule that no further disbursements . . . from the Fund would be approved except with the concurrence of five of the eight judges . . . and turned down disbursements to pay appellant's undercover investigations of commercial vice in the Burbon and Coral Street districts."

Louisiana's Libel Law
Louisiana Revised Statute. 1950 Tit14
Defamation: in part
"To expose any person to hatred, contempt, or ridicule, or to deprive him of the benefit of public confidence . . . shall be fined not more than three thousand dollars, or imprisoned for not more than one year or both."

Garrison 7

"As the Louisiana Supreme Court viewed the statement, it constituted an attack upon the personal integrity of the judges, rather than on official conduct."

Garrison 8

"I believe that the First Amendment, made applicable to the States by the Fourteenth, protects every person from having a state or the federal government fine, imprison or assess damage against him when he has been guilty of no conduct . . . other than expressing an opinion, even though others may believe that his views are unwholesome, unpatriotic, stupid or dangerous."

—WARREN

Garrison 9

"Under a rule like the Louisiana defamation statute permitting the finding of malice based on an intent to inflict harm through falsehood, it becomes a hazardous matter to speak out against a popular politician, with the result that the dishonest and incompetent will be shielded."

Garrison 10

"The expression that eight judges have enjoyed 300 days' vacation out of 19 months suggests and connotes a violation of the 'Deadhead' statute. . . . The expressions charged contain personal attack upon the integrity and honesty of the eight judges. . . ."

WILLIAM C. LINN, Petitioner

v.

UNITED PLANT GUARD WORKERS OF AMERICA, Local 114, et al.

383 US 53   February 21, 1966

SUMMARY: Linn, an assistant manager of the Pinkerton National Detective Agency, Inc., filed a one-million-dollar libel suit against the union alleging that statements in a leaflet were "wholly false, defamatory and untrue" as the union well knew. The leaflet charged that the Pinkerton agency had a large volume of work in Saginaw, Michigan, employing fifty-two men and that these men "were deprived of their *right to vote* in three NLRB elections." The lower courts dismissed the complaint.

Justices:	EARL WARREN	TOM C. CLARK	POTTER STEWART
	HUGO L. BLACK	JOHN M. HARLAN	BYRON R. WHITE
	WILLIAM O. DOUGLAS	WILLIAM J. BRENNAN, JR.	ABE FORTAS

Linn   1

"The complaint alleged that, during a campaign to organize Pinkerton's employees in Detroit, the respondents had circulated among the employees leaflets which stated inter alia:

'(7) Now we find out that Pinkerton's has had a large volume of work in Saginaw.

'United Plant Guard Workers now has evidence they have had it for years.

'A. That Pinkerton has 10 jobs in Saginaw, Michigan.

'B. Employing 52 men.

'C. Some of these jobs are 10 yrs. old!

'(8) Make you feel kind of sick and foolish.

'(9) The men in Saginaw were deprived of their *right to vote* in three N.L.R.B. elections. Their names were not summitted [sic]. These guards were voted into the Union in 1959! These Pinkerton guards were *robbed* of pay increases. The Pinkerton manegers [sic] were *lying* to us—all the time the contract was in effect. No doubt the Saginaw men will file criminal charges. Somebody may go to Jail!' "

Linn   2

"Although libelous statements cannot serve as the predicate for an unfair labor practice charge, like any other misleading statement they may in certain circumstances induce the NLRB to set aside the results of an election. See Bok, The Regulation of Campaign Tactics in Representation Elections Under the National Labor Relations Act, 78 Harv L Rev 38, 82-84 (1964)."

Linn   3   **Linn**   4

"For example, Congress has provided that an unfair labor practice charge may not be based on the 'expressing of any views, argument, or opinion . . . if such expression contains no threat of reprisal or force or promise of benefit.' 29 USC sec. 158 (c) (1964 ed). And one of its statutes, 29 USC sec. 411 (a) (2) (1964 ed), has been construed to prevent unions from disciplining members who utter defamatory statements during the course of internal union disputes."

"The foregoing considerations do not apply to the extent that the use of verbal weapons during labor disputes is not confined to any issue in the dispute, or involves a person who is neither party to nor agent of a party to the dispute. In such instances, perhaps the courts ought to be free to redress whatever private wrong has been suffered."

Linn   5   **Linn**   6

"In my judgment, the structure provided by Congress for the handling of labor-management controversies precludes any court from entertaining a libel suit between parties to a labor dispute or their agents where the allegedly defamatory statement is confined to matters which are part of the fabric of the dispute. The present controversy is just such a case."

"When Congress passed the National Labor Relations Act, it must have known, as almost all people do, that in labor disputes both sides are masters of the arts of vilification, invective and exaggeration. In passing this law Congress indicated no purpose to try to purify the language of labor disputes or force the disputants to say nice things about one another. Nor do I believe Congress intended to leave participants free to sue one another for libel for insults they hurl at one another in the heat of battle. The object of the National Labor Relations Act was to bring about agreements by collective bargaining, not to add fuel to the fire by encouraging libel suits with their inevitable irritations, and dispute-prolonging tendencies."

—BLACK

"In United Automobile Workers v. Russell, 356 US 634, 2 L ed 2d 1030, 78 S Ct 932 (1958), we again upheld state jurisdiction to entertain a compensatory and punitive damage action by an employee for malicious interference with his lawful occupation. In each of these cases the 'type of conduct' involved, i.e., 'intimidation and threats of violence,' affected such compelling state interests as to permit the exercise of state jurisdiction. Garmon, supra, at 248, 3 L ed 2d at 785. We similarly conclude that a State's concern with redressing malicious libel is 'so deeply rooted in local feeling and responsibility' that it fits within the exception specifically carved out by Garmon."

"Likewise, in a number of cases, the Board has concluded that epithets such as 'scab,' 'unfair,' and 'liar' are commonplace in these struggles and not so indefensible as to remove them from the protection of 7, even though the statements are erroneous and defame one of the parties to the dispute. Yet the Board indicated that its decisions would have been different had the statements been uttered with actual malice, 'a deliberate intention to falsify' or 'a malevolent desire to injure.' E.g., Bettcher Mfg. Corp. 76 NLRB 526 (1948); Atlantic Towing Co. 75 NLRB 1169, 1170-1173 (1948)."

"We note that the Board has given frequent consideration to the type of statements circulated during labor controversies, and that it has allowed wide latitude to the competing parties. It is clear that the Board does not 'police or censor propaganda used in the elections it conducts, but rather leaves to the good sense of the voters the appraisal of such matters, and to opposing parties the task of correcting inaccurate and untruthful statements.' Stewart-Warner Corp. 102 N.L.R.B. 1153, 1158 (1953). It will set aside an election only where a material fact has been misrepresented in the representation campaign; opportunity for reply has been lacking; and the misrepresentation has had an impact on the free choice of the employees participating in the election."

"Labor disputes are ordinarily heated affairs; the language that is commonplace there might well be deemed actionable per se in some state jurisdictions. Indeed, representation campaigns are frequently characterized by bitter and extreme charges, countercharges, unfounded rumors, vituperations, personal accusations, misrepresentations and distortions. Both labor and management often speak bluntly and recklessly, embellishing their respective positions with imprecatory language. Cafeteria Union v. Angelos, 320 US 293, 295, 88 L ed 58, 59, 64 S Ct 126 (1943). It is therefore necessary to determine whether libel actions in such circumstances might interfere with the national labor party."

—CLARK

CURTIS PUBLISHING COMPANY

v.

WALLACE BUTTS

388 US 130

ASSOCIATED PRESS

v.

EDWIN A. WALKER*

388 US 889

June 12, 1967

SUMMARY: *The Saturday Evening Post* published an article which accused "Wally" Butts, the football coach of the University of Georgia, of giving details of his game plan to the University of Alabama coach, Paul Bryant. The Georgia jury returned a verdict for $60,000 in general damages and $3,000,000 in punitive damages for Butts.

The second case arose out of an eyewitness account of events on the campus of the University of Mississippi on the night of September 30, 1962, when a massive riot erupted because of federal efforts to enforce enrollment of a Negro, James Meredith. The AP dispatch stated that General Edwin Walker, retired, encouraged rioters to use violence. The Texas Court awarded Walker a verdict of $500,000 compensatory damages and $300,000 punitive damages.

Justices: EARL WARREN	TOM C. CLARK	POTTER STEWART
HUGO L. BLACK	JOHN M. HARLAN	BYRON R. WHITE
WILLIAM O. DOUGLAS	WILLIAM J. BRENNAN, JR.	ABE FORTAS

*Each case should be entered separately on the ballot.

Curtis   1   **Curtis**   2

"It said, for example, that '[a] publication may be so extravagant in its denunciation and so vituperative in its character as to justify an inference of malice,' and that 'proof that the plaintiff did demand a retraction but that the defendant failed to retract the article may be considered by you on the question of punitive damages.' But '[d]ebate on public issues will not be uninhibited if the speaker must run the risk that it will be proved in court that he spoke out of hatred; even if he did speak out of hatred, utterances honestly believed contribute to the free interchange of ideas and the ascertainment of truth.'"

"It strikes me that the Court is getting itself in the same quagmire in the field of libel in which it is now helplessly struggling in the field of obscenity. No one, including this Court, can know what is and what is not constitutionally obscene or libelous under this Court's rulings."

—BLACK

Curtis 3

"Apparently because of declining advertising revenues, an editorial decision was made to 'change the image' of the Saturday Evening Post with the hope that circulation and advertising revenues would thereby be increased. The starting point for this change of image was an announcement that the magazine would embark upon a program of 'sophisticated muckraking,' designed to 'provoke people, make them mad.' "

Curtis 4

"In contrast to the Butts article, the dispatch which concerns us in Walker was news which required immediate dissemination. The Associated Press received the information from a correspondent who was present at the scene of the events and gave every indication of being trustworthy and competent. His dispatches in this instance, with one minor exception, were internally consistent and would not have seemed unreasonable to one familiar with General Walker's prior publicized statements on the underlying controversy. Considering the necessity for rapid dissemination, nothing in this series of events gives the slightest hint of a severe departure from accepted publishing standards."

Curtis 5

"The evidence showed that the Butts story was in no sense 'hot news' and the editors of the magazine recognized the need for a thorough investigation of the serious charges. Elementary precautions were, nevertheless, ignored. The Saturday Evening Post knew that Burnett had been placed on probation in connection with bad checks charges, but proceeded to publish the story on the basis of his affidavit without substantial independent support. Burnett's notes were not even viewed by any of the magazine's personnel prior to publication. John Carmichael who was supposed to have been with Burnett when the phone call was overheard was not interviewed. No attempt was made to screen the films of the game to see if Burnett's information was accurate, and no attempt was made to find out whether Alabama had adjusted its plans after the alleged divulgence of information."

Curtis 6

"The present cases involve not 'public officials,' but 'public figures' whose views and actions with respect to public issues and events are often of as much concern to the citizen as the attitudes and behavior of 'public officials' with respect to the same issues and events.

"All of us agree that the basic considerations underlying the First Amendment require that some limitations be placed on the application of state libel laws to 'public figures' as well as 'public officials.' "

—WARREN

Curtis   7

"Georgia is a state university, but Butts was employed by this Georgia Athletic Association, a private corporation, rather than by the State itself. Butts had previously served as head football coach of the University and was a well-known and respected figure in coaching ranks. He had maintained an interest in coaching and was negotiating for a position with a professional team at the time of publication."

Curtis   8

"The article was entitled 'The Story of a College Football Fix' and prefaced by a note from the editors stating: 'Not since the Chicago White Sox threw the 1919 World Series has there been a sports story as shocking as this one. . . . Before the University of Georgia's plays, defensive patterns, all the significant secrets Georgia's football team possessed.' The text revealed that one George Burnett, an Atlanta insurance salesman, had accidentally overheard, because of electronic error, a telephone conversation between Butts and the head coach of the University of Alabama, Paul Bryant, which took place approximately one week prior to the game. Burnett was said to have listened while 'Butts outlined Georgia's offensive plays . . . and told . . . how Georgia planned to defend. . . . Butts mentioned both players and plays by name.' "

Curtis   9

"At trial both sides attempted to reconstruct the stormy events on the campus of the University of Mississippi. Walker admitted his presence on the campus and conceded that he had spoken to a group of students. He claimed, however, that he had counseled restraint and peaceful protest, and exercised no control whatever over the crowd which had rejected his plea. He denied categorically taking part in any charge against the federal marshals."

Curtis   10

"Walker was a private citizen at the time of the riot and publication. He had pursued a long and honorable career in the United States Army before resigning to engage in political activity, and had, in fact, been in command of the federal troops during the school segregation confrontation at Little Rock, Arkansas, in 1957. He was acutely interested in the issue of physical federal intervention, and had made a number of strong statements against such action which had received wide publicity. Walker had his own following, the 'Friends of Walker,' and could fairly be deemed a man of some political prominence."

RED LION BROADCASTING COMPANY, INC., etc., et al., Petitioners

v.

FEDERAL COMMUNICATIONS COMMISSION et al.

395 US 367   June 9, 1969

SUMMARY: The Reverend Billy James Hargis, as part of his "Christian Crusade" series, on November 27, 1964, attacked Fred J. Cook, who had authored the paperback book titled: *Goldwater—Extremist on the Right*. Cook demanded free reply time and was denied that opportunity by the Red Lion Broadcasting Company. The Federal Communications Commission subsequently declared that Red Lion had failed to meet its obligation under the fairness doctrine.

Justices:	EARL WARREN	WILLIAM J. BRENNAN, JR.	BYRON R. WHITE
	HUGO L. BLACK	JOHN M. HARLAN	THURGOOD MARSHALL
	WILLIAM O. DOUGLAS	POTTER STEWART	

Red Lion   1

"According to the record, Hargis asserted that his broadcast included the following statement: 'Now, this paperback book by Fred J. Cook is entitled, "Goldwater—Extremist on the Right." Who is Cook? Cook was fired from the New York World Telegram after he made a false charge publicly on television against an unnamed official of the New York City government. New York publishers and Newsweek Magazine for December 7, 1959, showed that Fred Cook and his pal, Eugene Gleason, had made up the whole story and this confession was made to New York District Attorney, Frank Hogan. After losing his job, Cook went to work for the left-wing publication, The Nation, one of the most scurrilous publications of the left which has championed many communist causes over many years.'"

Red Lion   2

"The broadcasters challenge the fairness doctrine and its specific manifestations in the personal attack and political editorial rules on conventional First Amendment grounds, alleging that the rules abridge their freedom of speech and press. Their contention is that the First Amendment protects their desire to use their allotted frequencies continuously to broadcast whatever they choose, and to exclude whomever they choose from ever using that frequency. No man may be prevented from saying or publishing what he thinks, or from refusing in his speech or other utterances to give equal weight to the views of his opponents. This right, they say, applies equally to broadcasters."

"When a broadcaster grants time to a political candidate, Congress itself requires that equal time be offered to his opponents. It would exceed our competence to hold that the Commission is unauthorized by the statute to employ a similar device where personal attacks or political editorials are broadcast by a radio or television station."

The FCC rule 32 Fed Reg 10303 reads in part: "Personal attacks; political editorials.

'(a) When, during the presentation of views on a controversial issue of public importance, an attack is made upon the honesty, character, integrity or like personal qualities of an identified person or group, the licensee shall, within a reasonable time and in no event later than one week after the attack, transmit to the person or group attacked (1) notification of the date, time and identification of the broadcast; (2) a script or tape (or an accurate summary if a script or tape is not available) of the attack; and (3) an offer of a reasonable opportunity to respond over the licensee's facilities.' "

"Rather than confer frequency monopolies on a relatively small number of licensees, in a Nation of 200,000,000, the Government could surely have decreed that each frequency should be shared among all or some of those who wish to use it, each being assigned a portion of the broadcast day or the broadcast week. The ruling and regulations at issue here do not go quite so far. They assert that under specified circumstances, a licensee must offer to make available a reasonable amount of broadcast time to those who have a view different from that which has already been expressed on his station. The expression of a political endorsement, or of a personal attack while dealing with a controversial public issue, simply triggers this time-sharing."

"Before 1927, the allocation of frequencies was left entirely to the private sector, and the result was chaos. It quickly became apparent that broadcast frequencies constituted a scarce resource whose use could be regulated and rationalized only by the Government. Without government control, the medium would be of little use because of the cacaphony of competing voices, none of which could be clearly and predictably heard. Consequently, the Federal Radio Commission was established to allocate frequencies among competing applicants in a manner responsive to the public 'convenience, interest, or necessity.' "

"The litigants embellish their first amendment arguments with the contention that the regulations are so vague that their duties are impossible to discern. Of this point it is enough to say that, judging the validity of the regulations on their face as they are presented here, we cannot conclude that the FCC has been left a free hand to vindicate its own idiosyncratic conception of the public interest or of the requirements of free speech. Past adjudications by the FCC give added precision to the regulations; there was nothing vague about the FCC's specific ruling in Red Lion that Fred Cook should be provided an opportunity to reply."

—WHITE

"It is strenuously argued, however, that if political editorials or personal attacks will trigger an obligation in broadcasters to afford the opportunity for expression to speakers who need not pay for time and whose views are unpalatable to the licensees, then broadcasters will be irresistibly forced to self-censorship and their coverage of controversial public issues will be eliminated or at at least rendered wholly ineffective. Such a result would indeed be a serious matter, for should licensees actually eliminate their coverage of controversial issues, the purposes of the doctrine would be stifled."

"Licenses to broadcast do not confer ownership of designated frequencies, but only the temporary privilege of using them. 47 USC 301. Unless renewed, they expire within three years. 47 USC 307 (d). The statute mandates the issuance of licenses if the 'public convenience, interest or necessity will be served thereby.' 47 USC 307 (a). In applying this standard the Commission for 40 years has been choosing licensees based in part on their program proposals."

"13 FCC, at 1251-1252:
'In determining whether to honor specific requests for time, the station will inevitably be confronted with such questions as . . . whether there may not be other available groups or individuals who might be more appropriate spokesmen for the particular point of view than the person making the request. The latter's personal involvement in the controversy may also be a factor which must be considered, for elementary considerations of fairness may dictate that time be allocated to a person or group which has been specifically attacked over the station, where otherwise no such obligation would exist.' "

GREENBELT COOPERATIVE PUBLISHING ASSOCIATION, Inc., et al., Petitioners

v.

CHARLES S. BRESLER

398 US 6   May 18, 1970

SUMMARY: Charles Bresler, a prominent local real estate developer and a member of the Maryland House of Delegates, sued the *Greenbelt News Review* for libel. The thrust of his complaint arose from two articles which referred to the word "blackmail" which had been used several times during a City Council debate for rezoning a tract of land. A jury awarded Bresler $5,000 in compensatory damages and $12,500 in punitive damages. The Maryland Court of Appeals affirmed the judgment.

Justices:	WARREN E. BURGER	JOHN M. HARLAN	BYRON R. WHITE
	HUGO L. BLACK	WILLIAM J. BRENNAN, JR.	THURGOOD MARSHALL
	WILLIAM O. DOUGLAS	POTTER STEWART	

Greenbelt 1

"Two news articles in consecutive weekly editions of the paper stated that at the public meetings some people had characterized Bresler's negotiating position as 'blackmail.' The word appeared several times, both with and without quotation marks, and was used once as a subheading within a news story."

Greenbelt 2

"In the present case Bresler's counsel conceded in his opening statement to the jury that Bresler was a public figure in the community. This concession was clearly correct. Bresler was deeply involved in the future development of the City of Greenbelt. He had entered agreements with the city for zoning variances in the past, and was again seeking such favors to permit the construction of housing units of a type not contemplated in the original city plan. At the same time the city was trying to obtain a tract of land owned by Bresler for the purpose of building a school."

Greenbelt   **3**   **Greenbelt**   **4**

"This case involves newspaper reports of public meetings of the citizens of a community concerned with matters of local government interest and importance. The very subject matter of the news reports, therefore, is one of particular First Amendment concern. 'The maintenance of the opportunity for free political discussion to the end that government may be responsive to the will of the people and that changes may be obtained by lawful means . . . is a fundamental principle of our constitutional system.' *Stromberg v. California, supra,* at 369."

"It is not disputed that the articles published in the petitioners' newspaper were accurate and truthful reports of what had been said at the public hearings before the city council.

"The mayor of the city testified, 'Certainly nothing in here that reports the meeting any different from the way it happened. This is pretty much the way it happened. If I would say anything, it is rather conservative in presenting some of the comments.'

"The reporter who wrote one of the articles testified '[T]he people were really mad and that the word "blackmail" was used not once or twice like in my story, but over and over and over again.'

'Q. By who?

'A. By people at the meeting. And I felt if I left that out I really wouldn't be writing a truthful article.'"

Greenbelt   **5**   **Greenbelt**   **6**

"The Greenbelt News Review was performing its wholly legitimate function as a community newspaper when it published full reports of these public debates in its news columns. If the reports had been truncated or distorted in such a way as to extract the word 'blackmail' from the context in which it was used at the public meetings, this would be a different case. But the reports were accurate and full. Their headlines, 'School Site Stirs Up Council—Rezoning Deal Offer Debated' and 'Council Rejects by 4-1 High School Site Deal,' made it clear to all readers that the paper was reporting the public debates on the pending land negotiations."

"Under the law of Maryland the crime of blackmail consists in threatening to accuse any person of an indictable crime or of anything which, if true, would bring the person into contempt or disrepute, with a view to extorting money, goods, or things of value. See Maryland Code Ann. Art. 27, 561-563 (1967). There is, of course, no indication in any of the articles that Bresler had engaged in anything approaching such conduct."

—STEWART

Greenbelt   7

" 'It seems that this is a slight case of blackmail,' commented Mrs. Majorie Bergemann on Monday night, and the word was echoed by many speakers from the audience.

"Councilman David Champion, however, denied that it was 'blackmail,' explaining that he would rather 'refer to it (i.e., the negotiations—Ed.) as a two-way street.'

"Speaking from the floor, Gerald Gough commented: 'Everyone knows there's a need for a school—just walk through the halls of High Point. The developer knows there's a need and says, "we'll meet your need if you meet our need." In my opinion, it's highly unethical.' "

Greenbelt   8

Greenbelt News Review October 14, 1965. Article quoted in part:

"Among the parents who spoke was Mrs. Joseph Rosetti, who said: 'I have several children going into high school, but I would rather adhere to the Greenbelt Master Plan than overcrowd the town with dense development. I would stand for my children's discomfort, rather than give in to a blackmailing scheme.' "

Greenbelt   9

"The *New York Times* case was an effort to effectuate the policies of the First Amendment by recognizing the difficulties of ascertaining the truth of allegations about a public official whom the newspaper is investigating with an eye to publication. Absent protection for the nonreckless publication of 'facts' which subsequently prove to be false, the danger is that legitimate news and communication will be suppressed. But it is quite a different thing, not involving the same danger of self-censorship, to immunize professional communicators from liability for their use of ambiguous language and their failure to guard against the possibility that words known to carry two meanings, one of which imputes commission of a crime, might seriously damage the object of their comment in the eyes of the average reader."

—WHITE

Greenbelt   10

"In *New York Times Co. v. Sullivan*, 376 U.S. 254, we held that the Constitution permits a 'public official' to recover money damages for libel only if he can show that the defamatory publication was not only false but was uttered with 'actual malice'—that is, with knowledge that it was false or with reckless disregard of whether it was false or not.' *Id.*, at 280. In *Curtis Publishing Co. v. Butts*, 388 U.S. 130, we dealt with the constitutional restrictions upon a libel suit brought by a 'public figure.' "

QUESTIONS FOR DISCUSSION

1. Should a state prohibit published or spoken statements which defame members of certain races, creeds, classes, or organizations?

2. Is the press entitled to special privilege in statements about public officials?

3. When are derogatory statements by one public official about another libelous?

4. What are the criteria of libel for periodicals and press?

5. How does the fairness doctrine apply to personal attacks?

6. What words can injure a person's reputation?

7. What latitude in press and speech should be permitted parties in labor disputes?

8. Should school administrators require that individuals or organizations who secure permission to post materials or distribute handbills identify themselves on such materials?

Political Dissent

CHARLES E. SCHENCK, Plff. in Err.,

v.

UNITED STATES OF AMERICA

———

ELIZABETH BAER, Plff. in Err.,

v.

UNITED STATES OF AMERICA

249 US 47   March 3, 1919

SUMMARY: Schenck was charged with an act of conspiracy to violate the Espionage Act of June 15, 1917, by causing and attempting to cause insubordination in the military and naval forces of the U.S. and for obstruction of recruitment and enlistment.

Justices:	EDWARD DOUGLAS WHITE	WILLIAM R. DAY	JAMES CLARK MCREYNOLDS
	JOSEPH MCKENNA	WILLIS VAN DEVANTER	LOUIS DEMBITZ BRANDEIS
	OLIVER WENDALL HOLMES	MAHLON PITNEY	JOHN HESSIN CLARKE

Schenck 1   **Schenck** 2

"We admit that in many places and in ordinary times the defendants, in saying all that was said in the circular, would have been within their constitutional rights."

"When a nation is at war many things that might be said in time of peace are such a hindrance to its effort that their utterance will not be endured so long as men fight, and no court could regard them as protected by any constitutional right."

Schenck   **3**

"The most stringent protection of free speech would not protect a man in falsely shouting fire in a theater and causing a panic. It does not protect a man from an injunction uttering words that may have all the effects of force. Gompers v. Buck's Stove & Range Co., 221 US 418 . . ."

—Holmes

Schenck   **4**

"The question in every case is whether the words used in such a circumstance and are of such a nature as to create a clear and present danger that they will bring about the substantive evils that Congress has a right to prevent. It is a question of proximity and degree."

—Holmes

Schenck   **5**

"The document in question, upon its first printed side, recited the 1st section of the 13th Amendment, said that the idea embodied in it was violated by the Conscription Act, and that a conscript is little better than a convict. In impassioned language it intimated that conscription was despotism in its worst form and a monstrous wrong against humanity, in the interest of Wall Street's chosen few. It said: 'Do not submit to intimidation'; but in form it confined itself to peaceful measures such as petition for the repeal of the act."

Schenck   **6**

"According to the testimony, Schenck said he was the general secretary of the Socialist party and had charge of the Socialist headquarters from which the documents were sent. He identified a book found there as the minutes of the executive committee of the party. The book showed a resolution of August 13, 1917, that 15,000 leaflets should be printed on the other side of one of them in use, to be mailed to men who had passed exemption boards, and for distribution. Schenck personally attended to the printing."

"The search warrant did not issue against the defendant, but against the Socialist headquarters at 1326 Arch Street, and it would seem that the documents technically were not even in the defendant's possession."

"The Statute of 1917, in §4, punishes conspiracies to obstruct as well as actual obstruction."

"As to the defendant Baer, there was evidence that she was a member of the executive board and that the minutes of its transaction were hers."

"The second court alleges a conspiracy to commit an offense against the United States; to wit, to use the mails for the transmission of matter declared to be non-mailable by title 12, §2, of the Act of June 15, 1917, to wit, the above mentioned document with an averment of the same overt acts."

GITLOW

v.

PEOPLE OF NEW YORK
268 US 652   June 8, 1925

SUMMARY: Benjamin Gitlow, with three others, was convicted for the statutory crime of criminal anarchy. That is the doctrine that organized government should be overthrown by force or violence. Gitlow was a member of the Left Wing of the Socialist Party, organized nationally at a conference attended by ninety delegates from twenty different states. As an officer, Gitlow arranged for the printing and distribution of the Left Wing Manifesto, of which 16,000 copies were printed.

Justices: WILLIAM HOWARD TAFT   JAMES CLARK McREYNOLDS   PIERCE BUTLER
OLIVER WENDELL HOLMES   LOUIS D. BRANDEIS   EDWARD I. SANFORD
WILLIS VAN DEVANTER   GEORGE SUTHERLAND   HARLAN FISKE STONE

Gitlow   1   **Gitlow**   2

"It is said that this manifesto was more than a theory, that it was an incitement. Every idea is an incitement. It offers itself for belief and if believed it is acted on unless some other belief outweighs it or some failure of energy stifles the movement at its birth. The only difference between the expression of an opinion and an incitement in the narrower sense is the speaker's enthusiasm, for the result."

—HOLMES

"For present purposes we may and do assume that freedom of speech and of the press—which are protected by the First Amendment from abridgment by Congress—are among the fundamental personal rights and 'liberties' protected by the due process clause of the Fourteenth Amendment from impairment by the States."

Gitlow 3

"The State cannot reasonably be required to measure the danger from every such utterance in the nice balance of a jeweler's scale. A single revolutionary spark may kindle a fire that, smouldering for a time, may burst into a sweeping destructive conflagration. It cannot be said that the State is acting arbitrarily or unreasonably when in the exercise of its judgment as to the measures necessary to protect the public peace and safety, it seeks to extinguish the spark without waiting until it has enkindled the flame or blazed into the conflagration. It cannot be reasonably required to defer the adoption of measure for its own peace and safety until the revolutionary utterances lead to actual disturbances of the public peace or imminent and immediate danger of its own destruction; but it may, in the exercise of its judgment, suppress the threatened danger of its incipiency."

—SANFORD

Gitlow 4

"The manifesto, plainly, is neither the statement of abstract doctrine nor, as suggested by counsel, mere prediction that industrial disturbances and revolutionary mass strikes will result spontaneously in an inevitable process of evolution in the economic system. It advocates and urges in fervent language mass action which shall progressively foment industrial disturbances and through political mass strikes and revolutionary mass action overthrow and destroy organized parliamentary government. It concludes with a call to action in these words: 'The proletariate revolution and the Communist reconstruction of society—*the struggle for these*—is now indispensable. . . . The Communist International calls the proletariat of the world to the final struggle!' This is not the expression of philosophical abstraction, the mere prediction of future events; it is the language of direct incitement."

Gitlow 5

"If the publication of this document has been laid as an attempt to induce an uprising against government at once and not at some indefinite time in the future it would have presented a different question. The object would have been one with which the law might deal, subject to the doubt whether there was any danger that the publication could produce any result, or in other words, whether it was not futile and too remote from possible consequences. But the indictment alleges the publication and nothing more."

Gitlow 6

"We do not regard the incidental statement in *Prudential Insurance Company v. Cheek 259 US 530, 543*, that the Fourteenth Amendment imposes no restrictions on the States concerning freedom of speech, as determination of this question.

"It is a fundamental principle, long established, that the freedom of speech and of the press which is secured by the Constitution, does not confer an absolute right to speak or publish without responsibility, whatever one may choose, or an unrestricted and unbridled license that gives immunity for every possible use of language and prevents the punishment of those who abuse this freedom."

"Eloquence may set fire to reason. But whatever may be thought of the redundant discourse before us it had no chance of starting a present conflagration. If in the long run the beliefs expressed in proletarian dictatorship are destined to be accepted by the dominant forces of the community, the only meaning of free speech is that they should be given their chance and have their way."

"The Court of Appeals held that the Manifesto 'advocated the overthrow of this government by violence, or by unlawful means.' "

" 'The Left Wing Manifesto'
Issued on Authority of the Conference
by the National Council of the
Left Wing
" 'The world is in crisis. Capitalism, the prevailing system of society, is in process of disintegration and collapse. . . . Humanity can be saved from its last excesses only by the Communist Revolution. There can be only the Socialism which is one in temper and purpose with the proletarian revolutionary struggle. . . . The revolution starts with strikes of protest, developing into mass political strikes and then into revolutionary mass action for the conquest of the power of the state.' "

"There was no evidence of any effect resulting from the publication and circulation of the Manifesto."

FRED TOYOSABUBO KOREMATSU, Petitioner

v.

UNITED STATES OF AMERICA

323 US 214   December 18, 1944

SUMMARY: Korematsu, an American citizen of Japanese descent, was convicted for remaining in San Leandro, California, in defiance of the Civilian Exclusion Order No. 34 which directed that after May 9, 1942, all persons of Japanese ancestry should be excluded from that area on the West Coast. Some 112,000 persons of Japanese ancestry were living on the Pacific Coast at the time of Executive Order 9066 which declared that "the successful prosecution of the war requires every possible protection against espionage and against sabotage to national-defense material, national-defense premises, and national-defense utilities. . . ."

Justices: HARLAN F. STONE   STANLEY REED   FRANK MURPHY
OWEN J. ROBERTS   FELIX FRANKFURTER   ROBERT H. JACKSON
HUGO L. BLACK   WILLIAM O. DOUGLAS   WILEY RUTLEDGE

Korematsu   1   **Korematsu**   2

"Therefore, the validity of action under the war power must be judged wholly in the context of war."

"Moreover, there was no adequate proof that the Federal Bureau of Investigation and the military and naval intelligence services did not have the espionage and sabotage situation well in hand during this long period. Nor is there any denial of the fact that not one person of Japanese ancestry was accused or convicted of espionage or sabotage after Pearl Harbor while they were still free, a fact which is some evidence of the loyalty of the vast majority of these individuals and of the effectiveness of the established methods of combatting these evils."

Korematsu   **3**

"There was evidence of disloyalty on the part of some, the military authorities considered that the need for action was great, and time was short. We cannot—by availing ourselves of the calm perspective of hindsight—now say that at that time these actions were unjustified."

Korematsu   **4**

"Korematsu was not excluded from the military area because of hostility to him or his race. He *was* excluded because we are at war with the Japanese Empire, because the properly constituted military authorities feared an invasion of our West Coast and felt constrained to take proper security measures, because they decided that the military urgency of the situation demanded that all citizens of Japanese ancestry be segregated from the West Coast temporarily, and finally because Congress, reposing its confidence in this time of war in our military leaders—as inevitably it must—determined that they should have the power to do just this."

—BLACK

Korematsu   **5**

"Much is said of the danger to liberty from the Army program for deporting and detaining these citizens of Japanese extraction. But a judicial construction of the due process clause that will sustain this order is a far more subtle blow to liberty than the promulgation of the order itself. A military order, however unconstitutional, is not apt to last longer than the military emergency. Even during that period a succeeding commander may revoke it all. But once a judicial opinion rationalizes such an order to show that it conforms to the Constitution or rather rationalizes the Constitution to show that the Constitution sanctions such an order, the Court for all time has validated the principle of racial discrimination in criminal procedure and of transplanting of American citizens."

Korematsu   **6**

"A military commander may overstep the bounds of Constitutionality, and it is an incident. But if we review and approve, that passing incident becomes the doctrine of the Constitution. There it has a generative power of its own, and all that it creates will be in its own image."

"This is not a case of keeping people off the streets at night as was Hirabayashi v. United States 320 US 81 . . . , nor a case of temporary exclusion of a citizen from an area for his own safety or that of the community, nor a case of offering him an opportunity to go temporarily out of an area where his presence might cause danger to himself or to his fellows. On the contrary, it is the case of convicting a citizen as a punishment for not submitting to imprisonment in a concentration camp, based on his ancestry, and solely because of his ancestry, without evidence or inquiry concerning his loyalty and good disposition towards the United States."

"No one denies, of course, that there were some disloyal persons of Japanese descent on the Pacific Coast who did all in their power to aid their ancestral land. Similar disloyal activities have been engaged in by many persons of German, Italian and even more pioneer stock in our country. But to infer that examples of individual disloyalty prove group disloyalty and justify discriminatory action against the entire group is to deny that under our system of law individual guilt is the sole basis for deprivation of rights. Moreover, this inference, which is at the very heart of the evacuation orders, has been used to support the abhorrent and despicable treatment of minority groups by the dictatorial tyrannies which this nation is now pledged to destroy."

—Murphy

"Our task would be simple, our duty clear, were this a case involving the imprisonment of a loyal citizen in a concentration camp because of racial prejudice. Regardless of the true nature of the assembly and relocation centers—and we deem it unjustifiable to call them concentration camps with all the ugly connotations that term implies—we are dealing specifically with an exclusion order. To cast this case into outlines of racial prejudice, without reference to the real military dangers which were presented, merely confuses the issue."

"According to my reading of Civilian Exclusion Order No. 34, it was an offense for Korematsu to be found in Military Area No. 1, the territory wherein he was previously living, except within the bounds of the established Assembly Center of that area."

JANIUS IRVING SCALES, Petitioner

v.

UNITED STATES

367 US 203   June 5, 1961

SUMMARY: Scales was convicted under the Smith Act which makes it a felony knowingly to hold membership in any organization which advocates the overthrow of the government by force or violence. Scales was the chairman of the North and South Carolina Districts of the Communist Party. He recruited members into the Party and promoted education of selected young Party members in secret schools. In Scale's presence at the school it was alleged the students were once shown how to kill a person with a pencil, a device which might come in handy on a picket line. He was also implicated in criticism of American aggression in Korea, of Negro oppression, and statements that revolution would come within a generation. One to whom such doctrine was preached was an FBI agent who posed as someone interested in the Party.

Justices:	EARL WARREN	WILLIAM O. DOUGLAS	WILLIAM J. BRENNAN, JR.
	HUGO L. BLACK	TOM C. CLARK	CHARLES C. WHITTAKER
	FELIX FRANKFURTER	JOHN M. HARLAN	POTTER STEWART

Scales   1   **Scales**   2

"In this instance it is an organization which engages in criminal activity, and we can perceive no reason why one who actively and knowingly works in the ranks of that organization, intending to contribute to the success of those specific illegal activities, should be any more immune from prosecution than he to whom the organization has assigned the task of carrying out the substantive criminal act."

—HARLAN

"Not one single illegal act is charged to petitioner. That is why the essence of the crime covered by the indictment is merely belief—belief in the proletarian revolution, belief in Communist creed."

Scales   3   Scales   4

"Little remains to be said concerning the claims that the statute infringes First Amendment freedoms. It was settled in Dennis that the advocacy with which we are here concerned is not constitutionally protected speech, and it was further established that a combination to promote such advocacy, albeit under the aegis of what purports to be a political party, is not such association as is protected by the First Amendment."

"The petitioner was convicted under the 'Membership Clause' of the Smith Act which bears a penalty up to 20 years imprisonment and $20,000 fine. It convicts anyone who '. . . becomes or is a member of or affiliates with, any . . . society, group, or assembly of persons (who teach, advocate, or encourage the overthrow of the existing government by force or violence), knowing the purpose thereof.'"

Scales   5   Scales   6

"On January 12, 1848, Lincoln in an address before the United States House of Representatives stated: 'Any people anywhere, being inclined and having power, have the right to rise up, and shake off the existing government, and form a new one that suits them better. This is a most valuable—a most sacred—right, a right, which we hope and believe, is to liberate the world.'"

"The First Amendment absolutely forbids Congress to outlaw membership in a political party or similar association merely because one of the philosophical tenets of that group is that the existing government should be overthrown by force at some distant time in the future when circumstances may permit."

Scales 7

Scales 8

"Spinoza summed up in a sentence much of the history of the struggle of man to think and speak what he believes: 'Laws which decree what everyone must believe, and forbid utterance against this or that opinion, have too often been enacted to confirm or enlarge the power of those who dared not suffer free inquiry to be made, and have by a perversion of authority turned the superstition of the mob into violence against opponents."

"When we allow petitioner to be sentenced to prison for six years for being a 'member' of the Communist Party, we make a sharp break with traditional concepts of First Amendment's rights and make serious Mark Twain's light-hearted comment that 'It is by the goodness of God that in our country we have those unspeakable precious things: freedom of speech, freedom of conscience, and the prudence never to practice either of them.'"

—DOUGLAS

Scales 9

Scales 10

"Of course, government can move against those who take up arms against it. Of course, the constituted authority has the right of self-preservation. But we deal in this prosecution of Scales only with the legality of ideas and beliefs, not with overt acts. The Court speaks of the prevention of 'dangerous behavior' by punishing those 'who work to bring about that behavior.' That formula returns man to the dark days when government determined what behavior was 'dangerous' and then policed dissidents for telltale signs of advocacy. What is 'dangerous behavior' that must be suppressed in its talkstage has had a vivid history even on this continent."

"Since the evidence amply showed the Party leaders were continuously preaching during the indictment period the inevitability of eventual forcible overthrow, the first and basic question is a narrow one: whether the jury could permissibly infer that such preaching, in whole or in part, 'was aimed at building up a seditious group and maintaining it in readiness for action at a propitious time . . . the kind of indoctrination preparatory to action which was condemned in Dennis.' Yates, Supra (354 US at 321, 322). On this score, we think that the jury, under instructions which fully satisfied the requirements of Yates, was entitled to infer . . . that advocacy of action' was engaged in."

THEODORE R. GIBSON, Petitioner

v.

FLORIDA LEGISLATIVE INVESTIGATING COMMITTEE

372 US 539   March 25, 1963

SUMMARY: Reverend Theodore Gibson, local President of the Miami branch of the National Association of Colored People, was questioned about 14 persons whom the state believed to have affiliation with the Communist Party. He refused to produce the membership lists of his organization but did, on the basis of his personal knowledge, say that he could associate none of the 14 with the NAACP. He was sentenced to six months' imprisonment and fined $1,200.

Justices:	EARL WARREN	TOM C. CLARK	POTTER STEWART
	HUGO L. BLACK	JOHN M. HARLAN	BYRON R. WHITE
	WILLIAM O. DOUGLAS	WILLIAM J. BRENNAN, JR.	ARTHUR J. GOLDBERG

Gibson   1

"Upon being called to the stand, the petitioner admitted that he was custodian of his organization's membership records and testified that the local group had about 1,000 members, that individual membership was renewed annually, and that the only membership lists maintained were those for the then current year."

Gibson   2

"The petitioner told the Committee that he had not brought these records with him to the hearing and announced that he would not produce them for the purpose of answering questions concerning membership in the NAACP. He did, however, volunteer to answer such questions on the basis of his own personal knowledge; when given the names and shown photographs of 14 persons previously identified as Communists or members of Communist front or affiliated organizations, the petitioner said that he could associate none of them with the NAACP."

Gibson 3

"We are here called upon once again to resolve a conflict between individual rights of free speech and association and governmental interest in conducting legislative investigations. Prior decisions illumine the contending principles.

"This Court has repeatedly held that rights of association are within the ambit of the constitutional protections afforded by the First and Fourteenth Amendments. NAACP v. Alabama, 357 US 449, 2 L ed 2d 1488, 78 S Ct 1163; Bates v. Little Rock, 361 US 516, 4 L ed 2d 480, 80 S Ct 412; Shelton v. Tucker, 364 US 479, 5 L ed 2d 231, 81 S Ct 247; NAACP v. Button, 371 US 415, 9 L ed 2d 405, 83 S Ct 328."

Gibson 4

"In fact, this very record indicates that the association was and is against communism and has voluntarily taken steps to keep Communists from being members. Each year since 1950, the NAACP has adopted resolutions barring Communists from membership in the organization. Moreover, the petitioner testified that all prospective officers of the local organization are thoroughly investigated for Communist or subversive connections and, though subversive activities constitute grounds for termination of association membership, no such expulsions from the branch occurred during the five years preceding the investigation."

Gibson 5

"Can the Government demand of a publisher the names of the purchasers of his publications? Would not the spectre of a government agent then look over the shoulder of everyone who reads? Might not the purchase of a book or pamphlet today result in a subpoena tomorrow? Would not the fear of criticism go with every person into the bookstall? If the light of publicity may reach any student, any teacher, would not free inquiry be discouraged? For are there not always books and pamphlets that are critical of the administration or that preach an unpopular policy in domestic or foreign affairs or that are in disrepute in the orthodox school of thought? If the press and its readers were subject to the harassment of hearings, investigations, reports, and subpoenas, government would indeed hold a club over speech and over the press."

Gibson 6

"I would have thought that the freedom of association which is and should be entitled to constitutional protection would be promoted, not hindered, by disclosure which permits members of an organization to know with whom they are associating and affords them the opportunity to make an intelligent choice as to whether certain of their associates who are Communists should be allowed to continue their membership."

Gibson   7   **Gibson**   8

"Until such a group, chosen as an object of Communist Party action, has been effectively reduced to vassalage, legislative bodies may seek no information from the organization under attack by duty-bound Communists. When the job has been done and the legislative committee can prove it, it then has the hollow privilege of recording another victory for the Communist Party, which both Congress and this Court have found to be an organization under the direction of a foreign power, dedicated to the overthrow of the Government if necessary by force and violence."

—WHITE

"Considering the number of congressional inquiries that have been conducted in the field of 'Communist infiltration' since the close of World War II, affecting such diverse interests as 'labor, farmer, veteran, professional, youth, and motion picture groups' (Barenblatt, supra 360 US at 119), it is indeed strange to find the strength of state interest in the same type of investigation now impugned. And it is not amiss to recall that government evidence in Smith Act prosecutions has shown that the sensitive area of race relations has long been a prime target of Communist efforts at infiltration. See Scales v. United States, 367 US 203, 235, 245, 249 note 26, 251, 255, 256, 6 L ed 2d 782, 804, 810, 812, 813, 815, 816, 81 S Ct 1469."

Gibson   9   **Gibson**   10

"Where government is the Big Brother, privacy gives way to surveillance. But our commitment is otherwise. By the First Amendment we have staked our security on freedom to promote a multiplicity of ideas, to associate at will with kindred spirits, and to defy governmental intrusion into these precincts."

"History should teach us, then, that in times of high emotional excitement minority parties and groups which advocate extremely unpopular social or governmental innovations will always be typed as criminal gangs and attempts will always be made to drive them out. It was knowledge of this fact, and of its great dangers, that caused the Founders of our land to enact the First Amendment as a guarantee that neither Congress nor the people would do anything to hinder or destroy the capacity of individuals and groups to seek converts and votes for any cause, however radical or unpalatable their principles might seem under the accepted notions of the time."

—BLACK

LOUIS ZEMEL, Appellant

v.

DEAN RUSK, Secretary of State et al.

381 US 1   May 3, 1965

SUMMARY: In the year previous to this case, 2,750,000 Americans traveled abroad, more than 1,100,000 passports were issued, but Louis Zemel, holder of a valid passport, was refused permission to travel to Cuba. His request for passport validation to Cuba stated that he wished to make the trip "to satisfy my curiosity about the state of affairs in Cuba and to make me better informed."

Justices:	EARL WARREN	TOM C. CLARK	POTTER STEWART
	HUGO L. BLACK	JOHN M. HARLAN	BYRON R. WHITE
	WILLIAM O. DOUGLAS	WILLIAM J. BRENNAN, JR.	ARTHUR J. GOLDBERG

Zemel   1

"Prior to 1961, no passport was required to travel anywhere in the Western Hemisphere. On January 3 of that year, the United States broke diplomatic and consular relations with Cuba. On January 15, the Department of State eliminated Cuba from the area for which passports were not required, and declared all outstanding United States passports (except those held by persons already in Cuba) to be invalid for travel to or in Cuba 'unless specifically endorsed for such travel under the authority of the Secretary of State.'"

Zemel   2

"Cuba is the only area in the Western Hemisphere controlled by a Communist government. It is, moreover, the judgment of the State Department that a major goal of Castro regime is to export its Communist revolution to the rest of Latin America."

Zemel 3

"That the restriction which is challenged in this case is supported by weightiest considerations of national security is perhaps best pointed up by recalling that the Cuban missile crisis of October, 1962, preceded the filing of the appellant's complaint by two months."

Zemel 4

"There are few restrictions on action which could not be clothed by ingenious argument in the garb of decreased data flow. For example, the prohibition of unauthorized entry into the White House diminishes the citizen's opportunities to gather information he might find relevant to his opinion of the way the country is being run, but that does not make his entry into the White House a First Amendment right. The right to speak and publish does not carry with it the unrestricted right to gather information."

—WARREN

Zemel 5

"The United States and other members of the Organization of American States have determined that travel between Cuba and the other countries of the Western Hemisphere is an important element in the spreading of subversion, and many have, therefore, undertaken measures to discourage such travel."

Zemel 6

"The right to travel *within* the United States is, of course, also constitutionally protected, cf. Edwards v. California, 314 US 160. . . . But that freedom does not mean that areas ravaged by flood, fire or pestilence cannot be quarantined when it can be demonstrated that unlimited travel to that area would directly and materially interfere with the safety and welfare of the area of the Nation as a whole. So it is with international travel."

Zemel 7

Zemel 8

"Like my Brother Goldberg, I cannot accept the Government's argument that the President has 'inherent' power to make regulations governing the issuance and use of passports. Post, pp. 197-198. We emphatically and I think properly rejected a similar argument advanced to support a seizure of the Nation's steel companies by the President. Youngstown Sheet and Tube Co. v. Sawyer, 343 US 579."

—BLACK

"Our Constitution has ordained that laws restricting the liberty of our people can be enacted by the Congress and by the Congress only. . . . I think the 1926 Act gives the law-making power of Congress to the Secretary and the President and that it therefore violates the constitutional command that 'all' legislative power be vested in the Congress."

Zemel 9

Zemel 10

"We held in Kent v. Dulles, 357 US 116 . . . that the right to travel overseas, as well as at home, was part of the citizen's liberty under the Fifth Amendment. That conclusion was not an esoteric one drawn from the blue. It reflected a judgment as to the peripheral rights of the citizen under the First Amendment. The right to know, to converse with others, to consult with them, to observe social, physical, political and other phenomena abroad as well as at home gives meaning to and substance to freedom of expression and freedom of press. Without those contacts, First Amendment rights suffer."

"I agree that there are areas to which Congress can restrict or ban travel. Pestilence may rage in a region making it necessary to protect not only the traveler, but those he might infect on his return. A theater of war may be too dangerous for travel. Other like situations can be put. But the only so-called danger present here is the Communist regime in Cuba. The world, however, is filled with Communist thoughts; and Communist regimes are on more than one continent. They are part of the world spectrum; and if we are to know them and understand them, we must mingle with them, as Pope John said."

W.E.B. DuBOIS CLUBS OF AMERICA et al., Appellants

v.

RAMSEY CLARK, Attorney General of the United States

389 US 309   December 11, 1967

SUMMARY: The DuBois Club sued for an order declaring the Communist-front registration provisions of the Subversive Activities Control Act invalid and enjoining the Attorney General from forcing their club to register as such.

Justices:	EARL WARREN	JOHN M. HARLAN	BYRON R. WHITE
	HUGO L. BLACK	WILLIAM J. BRENNAN, JR.	ABE FORTAS
	WILLIAM O. DOUGLAS	POTTER STEWART	THURGOOD MARSHALL

DuBois 1

"Appellants rely on Dombrowski v. Pfister, 380 US 479 (1965) to support their contention that the usual rule requiring exhaustive administrative remedies should not apply in this case. In Dombrowski, however, the constitutional issues were presented in a factual context. Upon a record demonstrating a history of harassment of petitioners in connection with their exercise of First Amendment rights, the court ordered a federal district court to issue an injunction against pending criminal prosecutions under state statutes."

—BRENNAN

DuBois 2

"First Amendment values ride on what we do today. If government can investigate ideas, beliefs, and advocacy at the left end of the spectrum, I see no reason why it may not investigate any other part of the spectrum. Yet as I read the Constitution, one of its essential purposes was to take government off the backs of people and keep it off. There is a line between action on the one hand and ideas, beliefs, and advocacy on the other."

—DOUGLAS

DuBois 3

"One can think as he likes, embrace any philosophy he chooses, and select the politics that best fits his ideals or needs. That is all implicit on the First Amendment rights of assembly, petition, and expression."

DuBois 4

"Legislation curbing or penalizing *advocacy* even of ideas we despise is, I submit, at war with the First Amendment. Under our Constitution one's belief or ideology is of no concern to government."

DuBois 5

"I see no constitutional method whereby the Government can punish or penalize one for 'being a Communist' or 'promoting Communism.'"

❋   ❋   ❋

"I cannot believe that Dennis has any continuing vitality. It is out of line with Terminiello v. Chicago, 337 US 1, where a fascist was held to be protected by the First Amendment for espousing his creed, which most Americans find as obnoxious as communism."

DuBois 6

"The word 'revolution' has of course acquired a subversive connotation in modern times. But it has roots that are eminently respectable in American history. This country is a product of revolution."

❋   ❋   ❋

"Teaching and espousing revolution—as distinguished from indulging in overt acts—are therefore obviously within the range of the First Amendment."

DuBois   7   **DuBois**   8

"It is evident that Congress has provided a way for appellants to raise their Constitutional claims. But appellants, denying that they are within the coverage of the Act, wish to litigate these claims in an injunctive proceeding in the District Court. The effect would be that important and difficult constitutional issues would be decided devoid of factual context and before it was clear that appellants were covered by the Act."

"Before there may be proceedings to punish appellants for failure to register with the Attorney General, the SACB must first find that the DuBois Clubs is a Communist front organization and issue an order to that effect. The act provides for a full evidentiary hearing which is to be held in public. Appellants may be represented by counsel, offer oral or documentary evidence, submit rebuttal evidence, and conduct cross-examination."

DuBois   9   **DuBois**   10

"If an organization is classified a Communist front, serious consequences follow; employment of its members is restricted, §784; application for or use of passports is made illegal, §785; registration is required, §786; use of the mails and the radio and TV is curtailed, §789; tax exemptions are denied, §790. At least some of these provisions are unconstitutional under our decisions as bills of attainder or as denial of First and Fifth Amendment Rights. Yet vindication would come only after long and protracted hearings and appeals. Meanwhile, there would be a profound 'chilling' effect on the exercise of First Amendment rights within the principle of Dombrowski v. Pfister. . . ."

"If the appellants are aggrieved by the Boards' order, they may obtain review in the United States Court of Appeals for the District of Columbia Circuit which may set aside the order if it is not 'supported by the preponderance of the evidence.'"

UNITED STATES, Petitioner

v.

DAVID PAUL O'BRIEN

———

DAVID PAUL O'BRIEN, Petitioner

v.

UNITED STATES

391 US 672   May 27, 1968

SUMMARY: On March 31, 1966, David O'Brien and three companions burned their Selective Service registration certificates on the steps of the South Boston Courthouse. A crowd, including several FBI agents, witnessed the event. Immediately after the burning, members of the crowd began attacking the foursome. An agent ushered O'Brien to safety and advised him of his right to counsel and to silence. O'Brien produced the charred remains of his draft card, which, with his consent, were photographed.

Justices:	EARL WARREN	JOHN M. HARLAN	BYRON R. WHITE
	HUGO L. BLACK	WILLIAM J. BRENNAN, JR.	ABE FORTAS
	WILLIAM O. DOUGLAS	POTTER STEWART	THURGOOD MARSHALL

O'Brien   1   **O'Brien**   2

"The Court of Appeals, therefore, was of the opinion that conduct punishable under the 1965 Amendment was already punishable under the nonpossession regulation, and consequently that the amendment served no valid purpose; further, that in light of the prior regulation, the amendment must have been 'directed at public as distinguished from private destruction.' On this basis, the Court concluded that the 1965 Amendment ran afoul of the First Amendment by singling out persons engaged in protests for special treatment. The Court ruled, however, that O'Brien's conviction should be affirmed under the statutory provision. . . ."

"O'Brien's argument to the contrary is necessarily premised upon his unrealistic characterization of Selective Service certificates. He essentially adopts the position that such certificates are so many pieces of paper designed to notify registrants of classification, to be retained or tossed in the wastebasket according to the convenience or taste of the registrant."

O'Brien   **3**   **O'Brien**   **4**

"The Court states that the constitutional power of Congress to raise and support armies is 'broad and sweeping' and that Congress' power 'to classify and conscript manpower for military service is "beyond question."' This is undoubtedly true in times when, by declaration of Congress, the Nation is in a state of war. The underlying and basic problem in this case, however, is whether conscription is permissible in the absence of a declaration of war."

"1. The registration certificate serves as proof that the individual described thereon has registered for the draft. . . .
"2. The information supplied on the certificate facilitates communication between registrants and local boards, simplifying the system and benefiting all concerned. . . .
"3. Both certificates carry continued reminders that the registrant must notify his local board of any change of address, and other specified changes in his status. . . .
"4. The regulatory scheme involving Selective Service certificates includes clearly valid prohibitions against the alteration, forgery or similar deceptive misuse of certificates."

—WARREN

O'Brien   **5**   **O'Brien**   **6**

"The underlying and basic problem in this case, however, is whether conscription is permissible in absence of a declaration of war. That question has not been briefed nor was it presented in oral argument; but it is, I submit, a question upon which litigants and the country are entitled to a ruling."

—DOUGLAS

". . . at the time O'Brien burned his certificate an offense was committed by any person, 'who forges, alters, *knowingly destroys, knowingly mutilates*, or in any manner changes any such certificate. . . .' (Italics supplied.)"

O'Brien   7

O'Brien   8

"The rule that this Court will not consider issues not raised by the parties is not inflexible and yields in 'exceptional cases' (Duigan v. United States, 274 US 195, . . .), to the need correctly to decide the case before the court. . . . In such a case it is not unusual to ask for reargument."

"On appeal, the Court of Appeals for the First Circuit held the 1965 Amendment unconstitutional as a law abridging freedom of speech. At the time the Amendment was enacted, a regulation of the Selective Service required registrants to keep their registration certificates in their 'personal possession' at all times."

O'Brien   9

O'Brien   10

"He did not contest the fact that he burned the certificate. He stated in argument to the jury that he burned the certificate publicly to influence others to adopt his antiwar beliefs, as he put it, 'so that other people would reevaluate their positions with Selective Service, with the armed forces, and reevaluate their place in the culture of today, to hopefully consider my position.'"

"We cannot accept the view that an apparently limitless variety of conduct can be labeled 'speech' whenever the person engaging in the conduct intends thereby to express an idea."

SIDNEY STREET, Appellant

v.

STATE OF NEW YORK

394 US 576   April 21, 1969

SUMMARY: On the afternoon of June 6, 1966, Sidney Street, a Negro veteran who had been awarded the Bronze Star, was listening to the radio in his Brooklyn apartment. He heard the news report that James Meredith, when on his march for civil rights in Mississippi, had been shot by a sniper. Upon hearing this, he took from his drawer an American flag and carried it to a street corner where he burned it. He was arrested and convicted under the New York statute which made it a misdemeanor to publicly mutilate, deface, defile, defy, trample upon, or cast contempt upon an American flag by words or act.

Justices:	EARL WARREN	JOHN M. HARLAN	BYRON R. WHITE
	HUGO L. BLACK	WILLIAM J. BRENNAN, JR.	ABE FORTAS
	WILLIAM O. DOUGLAS	POTTER STEWART	THURGOOD MARSHALL

Street   1   **Street**   2

"Except perhaps for appellant's incidental use of the word 'damn,' upon which no emphasis was placed at trial, any shock effect of appellant's speech must be attributed to the content of the ideas expressed. It is firmly settled that under our Constitution the public expression of ideas may not be prohibited merely because the ideas are themselves offensive to some of their hearers."

"I believe that the States and the Federal Government do have the power to protect the flag from acts of desecration and disgrace."

—WARREN

Street 3

"If a state statute provided that it is a misdemeanor to burn one's shirt or trousers or shoes on the public thoroughfare, it could hardly be asserted that the citizen's constitutional right is violated. If the arsonist asserted that he was burning his shirt or trousers or shoes as a protest against the Government's fiscal policies, for example, it is hardly possible that his claim to First Amendment shelter would prevail against the State's claim of a right to avert danger to the public and to avoid obstruction to traffic as a result of a fire."

Street 4

"Appellant's words, taken alone, did not urge anyone to do anything unlawful. They amounted only to somewhat excited public advocacy of the idea that the United States should abandon, at least temporarily, one of its national symbols."

Street 5

"Soon thereafter, a police officer halted his patrol car and found the burning flag. The officer testified that he then crossed the northwest corner of the intersection, where he found appellant "talking out loud" to a small group of persons. The officer estimated that there were some 30 persons on the corner near the flag and 5 to 10 on the corner with appellant. The officer testified that as he approached within 10 or 15 feet of appellant, he heard appellant say, 'We don't need no damn flag,' and that when he asked appellant whether he had burned the flag appellant replied: 'Yes; that is my flag; I burned it. If they let that happen to Meredith we don't need an American flag.'"

Street 6

"Saying to himself, 'They didn't protect him,' appellant, himself a Negro, took from his drawer a neatly folded, 48-star American flag which he formerly had displayed on national holidays. Appellant left his apartment and carried the still-folded flag to the nearby intersection of St. James Place and Lafayette Avenue. Appellant stood on the northeast corner of the intersection, lit the flag with a match, and dropped the flag on the pavement when it began to burn."

Street 7

"Beyond this, however, the flag is a special kind of personality. Its use is traditionally and universally subject to special rules and regulations. A person may "own" a flag, but ownership is subject to special burdens and responsibilities. A flag may be property burdened with peculiar obligations and restrictions. . . .

"One may not justify the burning of a house, even if it is his own, on the ground, however sincere, that he does so as a protest. One may not justify breaking the windows of a government building on that basis. Protest does not exonerate lawlessness. And the prohibition against flag burning on the public thoroughfare being valid, the misdemeanor is not excused merely because it is an act of flamboyant protest."

—Fortas

Street 8

"In these circumstances, we can think of four government interests which might conceivably have been furthered by punishing appellant for his words: (1) an interest in deterring appellant from vocally inciting others to commit unlawful acts; (2) an interest in preventing appellant from uttering words so inflammatory that they would provoke others to retaliate physically against him, thereby causing a breach of the peace; (3) an interest in protecting the sensibilities of passersby who might be shocked by appellant's words about the American flag; and (4) an interest in assuring that appellant, regardless of the impact of his words upon others, showed proper respect for our national emblem."

Street 9

"Q. Did the officer speak to you or did you speak to him? A. He spoke to me.

"Q. What did he say? A. He asked me if I set fire to the flag. I said yes.

"Q. Then what happened? A. I said: 'If they do what they had to Meredith we don't need this flag.'

"Q. While you were burning this flag did anybody say anything to you other than this police officer? A. Nobody.

"Q. Did anybody stop? A. I noticed no unusual crowd."

Street 10

"We are called upon to decide whether the deliberate act of burning an American flag in public as a 'protest' may be punished as a crime."

ROBERT WATTS, Petitioner

v.

UNITED STATES

394 US 705   April 21, 1969

SUMMARY: During a rally on the Washington Monument grounds, Robert Watts, an eighteen-year-old boy, joined in a small gathering scheduled to discuss police brutality. In reply to one member of the group who suggested that the young people present should get more education before expressing their views, Watts, among other things, was reported to have said, "If they make me carry a rifle, the first man I want to get in my sights is L. B. J." On the basis of his statement he was convicted for violating a federal statute making it a felony to knowingly and willfully threaten the President.

Justices: EARL WARREN   JOHN M. HARLAN   BYRON R. WHITE
              HUGO L. BLACK   WILLIAM J. BRENNAN, JR.   ABE FORTAS
              WILLIAM O. DOUGLAS   POTTER STEWART   THURGOOD MARSHALL

Watts   1   **Watts**   2

"The charge in this case is of an ancient vintage.

"The federal statute under which petitioner was convicted traces its ancestry to the Statute of Treasons (25 Edw III) which made it a crime 'to compass and imagine the death of the King.' Note, Threats to Take the Life of the President, 32 Harv L Rev 724, 725 (1919). It is said that one Walter Walker, a 15th-century keeper of an inn known as the 'Crown,' was convicted under the Statute of Treasons for telling his son: 'Tom, if thou behavest thyself well, I will make thee heir to the Crown.' He was found guilty of compassing and imagining the death of the King, hanged, drawn, and quartered. 1 Campbell, Lives of the Chief Justices 151 (1874)."

"18 USC 871 (a) provides:

" 'Whoever knowingly and willfully deposits for conveyance in the mail or for delivery from any post office or by any letter carrier any letter, paper, writing, print, missive, or document containing any threat to take the life of or to inflict bodily harm upon the President of the United States, the President-elect, the Vice President or other officer next in the order of succession to the office of President of the United States, or the Vice President-elect, or knowingly and willfully otherwise makes any such threat against the President, President-elect, Vice President or other officer next in order of succession to the office of President, or Vice President-elect, shall be fined not more than $1,000 or imprisoned not more than five years, or both.' "

Watts 3

"While our Alien and Sedition Laws were in force, John Adams, President of the United States, en route from Philadelphia, Pa., to Quincy, Massachusetts, stopped in Newark, New Jersey, where he was greeted by a crowd and by a committee that saluted him by firing a cannon.

"A bystander said, 'There goes the President and they are firing at his ass.' Luther Baldwin was indicted for replying that he did not care 'if they fired through his ass.' He was convicted in the federal court for speaking 'seditious words tending to defame the President and Government of the United States' and fined, assessed court costs and expenses, and committed to jail until the fine and fees were paid. See Smith, Freedom's Fetters, pp. 270-274 (1956)."

Watts 4

"According to an investigator for the Army Counter Intelligence Corps who was present, petitioner responded: 'They always holler at us to get an education. And now I have already received my draft classification as I-A and I have got to report for my physical this Monday coming. I am not going. If they ever make me carry a rifle the first man I want to get in my sights is L. B. J. They are not going to make me kill my black brothers.'"

Watts 5

"The Alien and Sedition Laws constituted one of our sorriest chapters; and I had thought we had done with them forever.

"Yet the present statute has hardly fared better. 'Like the Statute of Treasons, section 871 was passed in a "relatively calm peacetime spring," but has been construed under circumstances when intolerance for free speech was much greater than it normally might be.' Note, Threatening the President: Protected Dissenter or Assassin, 57 Geo LJ 553, 570 (1969)."

Watts 6

"He [Watts' lawyer] stressed the fact that petitioner's statement was made during a political debate, that it was expressly made conditional upon an event—induction into the Armed Forces—which petitioner vowed would never occur, and that both petitioner and the crowd laughed after the statement was made. He concluded, 'Now actually what happened here in all this was a kind of very crude offensive method of stating a political opposition to the President. What he was saying, he says, I don't want to shoot black people because I don't consider them my enemy, and if they put a rifle in my hand it is the people that put the rifle in my hand, as symbolized by the President, who are my real enemy.'"

"Convictions under 871 have been sustained for displaying posters urging passers-by to 'hang [President] Roosevelt.' United States v. Apel, 44 F Supp 592, 593 (DC ND Ill 1942); for declaring that 'President Wilson ought to be killed. It is a wonder some one has not done it already. If I had an opportunity, I would do it myself.' United States v. Strickrath, 242 F 151, 152 (DC SD Ohio 1917); for declaring that 'Wilson is a wooden-headed son of a bitch. I wish Wilson was in hell, and if I had the power I would put him there,' Clark v. United States, 250 F Supp 449 (CA5th Cir 1918)."

"Certainly the statute under which petitioner was convicted is constitutional on its face. The Nation undoubtedly has a valid, even overwhelming, interest in protecting the safety of its Chief Executive and in allowing him to perform his duties without interference from threats of physical violence. See H. R. Rep No. 652, 64th Cong, 1st Sess (1916). Nevertheless, a statute such as this one, which makes criminal a form of pure speech, must be interpreted with the commands of the First Amendment clearly in mind. What is a threat must be distinguished from what is constitutionally protected speech."

—Per Curiam.

"In the time of Edward IV one Thomas Burdet who predicted that the king would 'soon die with a view to alienate the affections' of the people was indicted for 'compassing and imagining the death of the King,' 79 Eng Rep 705 the crime of constructive treason[1] with which the old reports are filled.

"[1]The prosecution in those cases laid bare to the juries that the treasonous thoughts were the heart of the matters; '. . . the original of his Treasons proceeded from the imagination of his heart; which imagination was in itself High-Treason, albeit the same proceeded not to any overt fact; and the heart being possessed with the abundance of his traitorous imagination, and not being able so to contain itself, burst forth in vile and traitorous Speeches, and from thence to horrible and heinous actions.' Trial of Sir John Perrot, 1 How St Tr 1315, 1318 (1952)."

—Douglas

"But whatever the 'willfulness' requirement implies, the statute initially requires the Government to prove a true 'threat.' We do not believe that the kind of political hyperbole indulged in by petitioner fits within that statutory term. For we must interpret the language Congress chose 'against the background of a profound national commitment to the principle that debate on public issues should be uninhibited, robust, and wide-open, and that it may well include vehement, caustic, and sometimes unpleasantly sharp attacks on government and public officials.' "

DANIEL JAY SCHACHT, Petitioner

v.

UNITED STATES

298 US 58   May 25, 1970

SUMMARY: Daniel Schacht was one of a group of three who took part in a skit in the street as part of a larger peaceful antiwar demonstration at the Houston Armed Forces Induction Center. He was dressed in an army uniform and was indicted in a United States District Court for violating 18 U.S.C. §702 which makes it a crime for any person "without authority [to wear] the uniform or a distinctive part thereof . . . of any of the armed forces of the United States. . . ."

Justices:	WARREN E. BURGER	JOHN M. HARLAN	BYRON R. WHITE
	HUGO L. BLACK	WILLIAM J. BRENNAN, JR.	THURGOOD MARSHALL
	WILLIAM O. DOUGLAS	POTTER STEWART	

Schacht 1

"There is no doubt that Schacht did wear distinctive parts of the uniform of the United States Army and that he was not a member of the Armed Forces. He has defended his conduct since the beginning, however, on the ground that he was authorized to wear the uniform by an Act of Congress, 10 U.S.C. 772 (f), which provides as follows:

"When wearing by persons not on active duty authorized.

.   .   .   .

" '(f) While portraying a member of the Army, Navy, Air Force, or Marine Corps, an actor in a theatrical or motion picture production may wear the uniform of that armed force *if the portrayal does not tend to discredit that armed force.*'" [Emphasis added.]

Schacht 2

"Schacht argued in the trial court and in this Court that he wore the army uniform as an 'actor' in a 'theatrical production' performed several times between 6:30 and 8:30 A.M. on December 4, 1967, in front of the Armed Forces Induction Center at Houston, Texas. The street skit in which Schacht wore the army uniform as a costume was designed, in his view, to expose the evil of the American presence in Vietnam and was part of a larger, peaceful antiwar demonstration at the induction center that morning."

Schacht 3

"This clause on its face simply restricts §772 (f)'s authorization to those dramatic portrayals which do not 'tend to discredit' the military, but, when this restriction is read together with 18 U.S.C. §702, it becomes clear that Congress has in effect made it a crime for an actor wearing a military uniform to say things during his performance critical of the conduct or policies of the Armed Forces. An actor, like everyone else in our country, enjoys a constitutional right to freedom of speech, including the right to criticize the Government during a dramatic performance."

Schacht 4

"In the present case Schacht was free to participate in any skit at the demonstration which praised the Army, but under the final clause of §772 (f) he could be convicted of a federal offense if his portrayal attacked the Army instead of praised it. In light of our earlier finding that the skit in which Schacht participated was a 'theatrical production' within the meaning of 772 (f), it follows that his conviction can be sustained only if he can be punished for speaking out against the role of our Army and our country in Vietnam. Clearly punishment for this reason would be an unconstitutional abridgment of freedom of speech. The final clause of §772 (f), which leaves Americans free to praise the war in Vietnam but can send persons like Schacht to prison for opposing it, cannot survive in a country which has the First Amendment."

—BLACK

Schacht 5

"The Government's brief and argument seriously contend that this Court is without jurisdiction to consider and decide the merits of this case on the ground that the petition for certiorari was not timely filed under Rule 22 (2) of the Rules of this Court. This Rule provides that a petition for certiorari to review a court of appeals' judgment in a criminal case 'shall be deemed in time when . . . filed with the Clerk within thirty days after the entry of such judgment.' We cannot accept the view that this time requirement is jurisdictional and cannot be waived by the Court."

Schacht 6

"The United States has argued that the exception for 'theatrical productions' must be limited to performances in a setting equivalent to a playhouse or theater where observers will necessarily be aware that they are watching a make-believe performance. Under this interpretation, the Government suggests, petitioner must be found as a matter of law not to have been engaged in a 'theatrical production'; hence, his conviction for unauthorized wearing of the uniform is lawful without regard to the validity of the 'tend to discredit' proviso to §772 (f)."

Schacht 7

"The appellants and their colleagues prepared a script to be followed at the induction center and they actually rehearsed their roles at least once prior to the appointed day before a student organization called the Humanists. " 'The skit was composed of three people. There was Schacht who was dressed in a uniform and cap. A second person was wearing "military colored" coveralls. The third person was outfitted in typical Viet Cong apparel. The first two men carried water pistols. One of them would yell, "Be an able America," and then they would shoot the Viet Cong with their pistols. The pistols expelled a red liquid which, when it struck the victim, created the impression that he was bleeding. Once the victim fell down the other two would walk up to him and exclaim. "My God, this is a pregnant woman." Without noticeable variation this skit was reenacted several times during the morning of the demonstration.' "

Schacht 8

"The critical question in deciding what is to count as a 'theatrical production' ought to be whether or not, considering all the circumstances of the performance, an ordinary observer would have thought he was seeing a fictitious portrayal rather than a piece of reality. And, although the judge's instructions here did not precisely reflect this interpretation, this question seems eminently suited to resolution by the jury."

—WHITE

Schacht 9

"Certainly theatrical productions need not always be performed in buildings or even on a defined area such as a conventional stage. Nor need they be performed by professional actors or be heavily financed or elaborately produced. Since time immemorial outdoor theatrical performances, often performed by amateurs, have played an important part in the entertainment and the education of the people of the world. Here, the record shows without dispute the preparation and repeated presentation by amateur actors of a short play designed to create in the audience an understanding of and opposition to our participation in the Vietnam war. *Supra,* at 2-3. It may be that the performances were crude and amateurish and perhaps unappealing, but such can be said about many theatrical performances."

Schacht 10

"Our previous cases would seem to make it clear that 18 U.S.C. §702, making it an offense to wear our military uniforms without authority is, standing alone, a valid statute on its face. See, *e.g., United States v. O'Brien,* 391 U.S. 367. But the general prohibition of 18 U.S.C. §702 cannot always stand alone in view of 10 U.S.C. §772 which authorizes the wearing of military uniforms under certain conditions and circumstances including the circumstances of an actor portraying a member of the armed services in a 'theatrical production.' 10 U.S.C. §772 (f)."

FREDERICK WALZ, Appellant

v.

TAX COMMISSION OF THE CITY OF NEW YORK

397 US 664   May 4, 1970

SUMMARY: New York State, as do all the fifty states, provides for tax exemption of places of worship. Frederick Walz, an owner of real estate, contended that an exemption to church property indirectly requires him to make a contribution to religious bodies and thereby violates provisions prohibiting establishment of religion under the First Amendment.

Justices: WARREN E. BURGER   JOHN M. HARLAN   BYRON R. WHITE
HUGO L. BLACK   WILLIAM J. BRENNAN, JR.   THURGOOD MARSHALL
WILLIAM O. DOUGLAS   POTTER STEWART

Walz   1   **Walz**   2

"It is true that each church contributes to the pluralism of our society through its purely religious activities, but the state encourages these activities not because it champions religion per se but because it values religion among a variety of private, nonprofit enterprises which contribute to the diversity of the Nation. Viewed in this light, there is no nonreligious substitute for religion as an element in our societal mosaic, just as there is no nonliterary substitute for literary groups."

"New York, in common with the other States, has determined that certain entities that exist in a harmonious relationship to the community at large, and that foster its 'moral or mental improvement,' should not be inhibited in their activities by property taxation or the hazard of loss of those properties for nonpayment of taxes. It has not singled out one particular church or religious group or even churches as such; rather, it has granted exemption to all houses of religious worship within a broad class of property owned by nonprofit, quasi-public corporations which include hospitals, libraries, playgrounds, scientific, professional, historical and patriotic groups."

Walz   **3**

"Often a particular church will use the same personnel, facilities and source of funds to carry out both its secular and religious activities. Thus, the same people who gather in church facilities for religious worship and study may return to these facilities to participate in Boy Scout activities, to promote antipoverty causes, to discuss public issues, or to listen to chamber music. Accordingly, the funds used to maintain the facilities as a place for religious worship and study also maintain them as a place for secular activities beneficial to the community as a whole. Even during formal worship services, churches frequently collect the funds used to finance their secular operations and make decisions regarding their nature."

Walz   **4**

"Churches, like newspapers also enjoying First Amendment rights, have no constitutional immunity from all taxes. As we said in Murdock: 'We do not mean to say that religious groups and the press are free from all financial burdens of government. See Grosjean v. American Press Co., 297 US 233, 250, 80 L Ed 660, 668, 56 S Ct 444. We have here something quite different, for example, from a tax on the income of one who engages in religious activities or a tax on property used or employed in connection with those activities. It is one thing to impose a tax on the income or property of a preacher. It is quite another thing to exact a tax from him for the privilege of delivering a sermon.' Ibid."

Walz   **5**

"That is a major difference between churches on the one hand and the rest of the nonprofit organizations on the other. Government could provide or finance operas, hospitals, historical societies, and all the rest because they represent social welfare programs within the reach of the police power. In contrast, government may not provide or finance worship because of the Establishment Clause any more than it may single out 'atheistic' or 'agnostic' centers or groups and create or finance them."

—Douglas

Walz   **6**

"If believers are entitled to public financial support, so are nonbelievers. A believer and nonbeliever under the present law are treated differently because of the articles of their faith. Believers are doubtless comforted that the cause of religion is being fostered by this legislation. Yet one of the mandates of the First Amendment is to promote a viable, pluralistic society and to keep government neutral, not only between sects but between believers and nonbelievers."

"In Torcaso v. Watkins, 367 US 488, 6 L Ed 2d 982, 81 S Ct 1680, we held that a State could not bar an atheist from public office in light of the freedom of belief and religion guaranteed by the First and Fourteenth Amendments. Neither the State nor the Federal Government, we said, 'can constitutionally pass laws or impose requirements which aid all religions as against non-believers, and neither can aid those religions based on a belief in the existence of God as against those religions founded on different beliefs.' Id., at 495, 6 L Ed 2d at 987.

"That principle should govern this case."

"Obviously a direct money subsidy would be a relationship pregnant with involvement and, as with most governmental grant programs, could encompass sustained and detailed administrative relationships for enforcement of statutory or administrative standards, but that is not this case. The hazards of churches supporting government are hardly less in their potential than the hazards of governments supporting churches; each relationship carries some involvement rather than the desired insulation and separation. We cannot ignore the instances in history when church support of government led to the kind of involvement we seek to avoid."

"Nothing in this national attitude toward religious tolerance and two centuries of uninterrupted freedom from taxation has given the remotest sign of leading to an established church or religion and on the contrary it has operated affirmatively to help guarantee the free exercise of all forms of religious beliefs. Thus, it is hardly useful to suggest that tax exemption is but the 'foot in the door' or the 'nose of the camel in the tent' leading to an established church."

—BURGER

"Thomas Jefferson was President when tax exemption was first given Washington churches, and James Madison sat in sessions of the Virginia General Assembly which voted exemption for churches in that Commonwealth. I have found no record of their personal views on the respective acts. The absence of such a record is itself significant. It is unlikely that two men so concerned with the separation of church and state would have remained silent had they thought the exemptions established religion. And if they had not either approved the exemptions, or been mild in their opposition, it is probable that their views would be known to us today." ·

QUESTIONS FOR DISCUSSION

1. Should advocacy of violence and overthrow of the government be permitted in speech or print?

2. Are persons who counsel members of the military to desertion or to disobey orders guilty of a crime?

3. In time of war should what is permissible in speech and press differ from peacetime?

4. What statements in speech and press convey a "clear and present danger"?

5. Do citizens have a right to live in a state or community of their choice in time of war and peace?

6. Should the government control and sometimes prohibit the travel of its citizens?

7. Does the congress have a right to investigate organizations under suspicion of being subversive?

8. Should persons who burn their draft cards be sent to prison?

9. Should speech and acts against the flag be punishable?

Privacy

ROY OLMSTEAD, Jerry L. Finch, Clarence G. Healy,
Cliff Maurice, Tom Nakagawa, Edward Rugdahl,
Myer Berg, John Earl, and Francis Brown, Petitions

v.

UNITED STATES OF AMERICA

277 US 438 June 4, 1928

SUMMARY: Olmstead was convicted by the district court as the leading conspirator and the general manager of a business which violated the National Prohibition Act. The operation involved at least fifty persons who transported liquor from British Columbia into the state of Washington. The information which led to the discovery was largely based upon intercepted telephone messages by Federal prohibition officers. The wiretaps involved no trespass upon the property because they were made in the basement of the large office building and in the streets near the house lines of the petitioners' residences.

Justices:	WILLIAM HOWARD TAFT	JAMES CLARK MCREYNOLDS	PIERCE BUTLER
	OLIVER WENDELL HOLMES	LOUIS DEMBITZ BRANDEIS	EDWARD TERRY SANFORD
	WILLIS VAN DEVANTER	GEORGE SUTHERLAND	HARLAN FISKE STONE

Olmstead   1

"The 4th Amendment provides: 'The right of the people to be secure in their persons, houses, papers, and effects, against unreasonable searches and seizures, shall not be violated, and no warrants shall issue, but upon probable cause, supported by oath or affirmation, and particularly describing the place to be searched, and the persons or things to be seized.' And the 5th: 'No person . . . shall be compelled, in any criminal case, to be a witness against himself.'"

Olmstead   2

"The evidence in the records discloses a conspiracy of amazing magnitude to import, possess and sell liquor unlawfully. [456] It involved the employment of not less than fifty persons, of two seagoing vessels for the transportation of liquor to British Columbia, of small vessels for coastwise transportation to the state of Washington, the purchase and use of a ranch beyond the suburban limits of Seattle, with a large underground cache for storage and a number of smaller caches in that city, the maintenance of a central office manned with operators, the employment of executives, salesmen, deliverymen, dispatchers, scouts, bookkeepers, collectors and an attorney. In a bad month sales amounted to $176,000; the aggregate for a year must have exceeded two millions of dollars."

Olmstead   3

"Olmstead was the leading conspirator and the general manager of the business. He made a contribution of $10,000 to the capital; eleven others contributed $1,000 each. The profits were divided one-half to Olmstead and the remainder to the other eleven. Of the several offices in Seattle the chief one was in a large office building. In this there were three telephones on three different lines. There were telephones in an office of the manager in his own home, at the homes of his associates, and at other places in the city. Communication was had frequently with Vancouver, British Columbia. Times were fixed for the deliveries of the 'stuff,' to places along Puget Sound near Seattle, and from there the liquor was removed and deposited in the caches already referred to. One of the chief men was always on duty at the main office to receive orders by the telephones and to direct their filling by a corps of men stationed in another room—the 'bull pen.'"

Olmstead   4

"Congress may, of course, protect the secrecy of telephone messages by making them, when intercepted, inadmissible as evidence in Federal criminal trials, by direct legislation, [466] and thus depart from the common law of evidence. But the courts may not adopt such a policy by attributing an enlarged and unusual meaning to the 4th Amendment. The reasonable view is that one who installs in his house a telephone instrument with connecting wires intends to project his voice to those quite outside, and that the wires beyond his house and messages while passing over them are not within the protection of the 4th Amendment. Here those who intercepted the projected voices were not in the house of either party to the conversation."

Olmstead   5

"The common-law rule is that the admissibility of evidence is not affected by the illegality of the means by which it was obtained. Professor Greenleaf, in his work on Evidence (vol. 1, 12th ed. by Redfield, sec. 254 (a)) says: 'It may be mentioned in this place, that though papers and other subjects of evidence may have been illegally taken from the possession of the party against whom they are offered, or otherwise unlawfully obtained, this is no valid objection to their admissibility, if they are pertinent to the issue. The court will not take notice how they were obtained, whether lawfully or unlawfully nor will it form an issue, to determine that question.'"

Olmstead   6

"Nor can we, without the sanction of congressional enactment, subscribe to the suggestion that the courts have a discretion to exclude evidence, the admission of which is not unconstitutional because unethically secured. This would be at variance with the common law doctrine generally supported by authority. There is no case that sustains, nor any recognized text book that gives color to such a view. Our general experience shows that much evidence has always been receivable although not obtained by conformity to the highest ethics. The history of criminal trials shows numerous cases of prosecutions of oathbound conspiracies for murder, robbery, and other crimes where officers of the law have disguised themselves and joined the organizations, taken the oaths and given themselves every appearance of active members engaged in the promotion of crime for the purpose of securing evidence. Evidence secured by such means has always been received."

Olmstead   **7**   **Olmstead**   **8**

"A standard which would forbid the reception of evidence if obtained by other than nice ethical conduct by government officials would make society suffer and give criminals greater immunity than has been known heretofore. In the absence of controlling legislation by Congress, those who realize the difficulties in bringing offenders to justice may well deem it wise that the exclusion of evidence should be confined to cases where rights under the Constitution would be violated by admitting it."

—TAFT

"Acting on behalf of the government, and in their official capacity, at least six other prohibition agents listened over the tapped wires and reported the messages taken. Their operations extended over a period of nearly five months. The typewritten record of the notes of conversations overheard occupies 775 typewritten pages. By objections reasonably made and persistently renewed, the defendants objected to the admission of the evidence obtained by wire-tapping on the ground that the government's wire-tapping constituted an unreasonable search and seizure, in violation of the 4th Amendment; and that the use as evidence of the conversations overheard compelled the defendants to be witnesses against themselves, in violation of the 5th Amendment."

Olmstead   **9**   **Olmstead**   **10**

"When the 4th and 5th Amendments were adopted, 'the form that evil had theretofore taken' had been necessarily simple. Force and violence were then the only means known to man by which a government could directly effect self-incrimination. It could compel the individual to testify—a compulsion effected, if need be, by torture. It could secure possession of his papers and other articles incident to his private life—a seizure effected, if need be, by breaking and entry. Protection against such invasion of 'the sanctities of a man's home and the privacies of life' was provided in the 4th and 5th Amendments, by specific language. Boyd v. United States, 116 US 616, 630, 29 L. ed. 746, 751, 6 Sup. Ct. Rep. 524. But 'time works changes, brings into existence new conditions and purposes.' Subtler and more far-reaching means of invading privacy have become available to the government."

—BRANDEIS

"The makers of our Constitution undertook to secure conditions favorable to the pursuit of happiness. They recognized the significance of man's spiritual nature, of his feelings and of his intellect. They knew that only a part of the pain, pleasure and satisfaction of life are to be found in material things. They sought to protect Americans in their beliefs, their thoughts, their emotions and their sensations. They conferred, as against the government, the right to be let alone—the most comprehensive of rights and the right most valued by civilized men. To protect that right, every unjustifiable intrusion by the government upon the privacy of the individual, whatever the means employed, must be deemed a violation of the 4th Amendment. And the use, as evidence [479] in a criminal proceeding, of facts ascertained by such intrusion must be deemed a violation of the 5th."

THELMA MARTIN, Appellant

v.

CITY OF STRUTHERS, OHIO

319 US 141   May 3, 1943

SUMMARY: Thelma Martin was convicted in the Mayor's Court and fined $10.00 on a charge of violating a city ordinance which prohibited distribution of literature at a residence. The appellant was engaged in door-to-door contact in behalf of the Jehovah's Witnesses faith.

Justices:	HARLAN F. STONE	STANLEY REED	FRANK MURPHY
	OWEN J. ROBERTS	FELIX FRANKFURTER	ROBERT H. JACKSON
	HUGO L. BLACK	WILLIAM O. DOUGLAS	WILEY RUTLEDGE

Martin   1   **Martin**   2

"The most, it seems to me, that can be or has been read into the ordinance is a prohibition of free distribution of printed matter by summoning inmates to their doors. There are excellent reasons to support a determination of the city council that such distributors may not disturb householders while permitting salesmen and others to call them to the door. Practical experience may well convince the council that irritations arise frequently from this method of advertising."

"The ordinance does not control anything but the distribution of literature, and in that respect it substitutes the judgment of the community for the judgment of the individual householder."

Martin 3

"The freedom to teach or preach by word or book is unabridged, save only the right to call a householder to the door of his house to receive the summoner's message. I cannot expand this regulation to a violation of the First Amendment."

Martin 4

"If the citizens of Struthers desire to be protected from the annoyance of being called to their doors to receive printed matter, there is to my mind no constitutional provision which forbids their municipal council from modifying the rule that anyone may sound a call for the householder to attend his door. It is the council which is entrusted by the citizens with the power to declare and abate the myriad nuisances which develop in a community."

Martin 5

"While I appreciate the necessity of watchfulness to avoid abridgments of our freedom of expression, it is impossible for me to discover in this trivial town police regulation a violation of the First Amendment. No ideas are being suppressed. No censorship is involved."

Martin 6

"Traditionally the American law punishes persons who enter onto the property of another after having been warned by the owner to keep off. General trespass after warning statutes exist in at least twenty states, while similar statutes of narrower scope are on the books of at least twelve more states. We know of no state which, as does the Struthers ordinance in effect, makes a person a criminal trespasser if he enters the property of another for an innocent purpose without an explicit command from the owners to stay away."

Martin   7   **Martin**   8

"For centuries it has been a common practice in this and other countries for persons not specifically invited to go from home to home and knock on doors or ring doorbells to communicate ideas to the occupants or to invite them to political, religious, or other kinds of public meetings. Whether such visiting shall be permitted has in general been deemed to depend upon the will of the individual master of each household, and not upon the determination of the community. In the instance case, the City of Struthers has attempted to make this decision for all of its inhabitants."

"The First Amendment does not compel a pedestrian to pause on the street to listen to the argument supporting another's views of religion or politics. Once the door is opened, the visitor may not insert a foot and insist on a hearing. He certainly may not enter the home. To knock or ring, however, comes close to such invasions. To prohibit such a call leaves open distribution of the notice on the street or at the home without signal to announce its deposit. Such assurance of privacy falls far short of an abridgment of freedom of the press. The ordinance seems a fair adjustment of the privilege of distributors and the rights of householders."

—Reed

Martin   9   **Martin**   10

"In addition, burglars frequently pose as canvassers, either in order that they may have a pretense to discover whether a house is empty and hence ripe for burglary, or for the purpose of spying out the premises in order that they may return later. Crime prevention may thus be the purpose of regulatory ordinances.
"While door to door distributors may be either a nuisance or a blind for criminal activities, they may also be useful members of society engaged in the dissemination of ideas in accordance with the best tradition of free discussion. The widespread use of this method of communication by many groups espousing various causes attests its major importance."

"Constant callers, whether selling pots or distributing leaflets, may lessen the peaceful enjoyment of a home as much as a neighborhood glue factory or railroad yard which zoning ordinances may prohibit. In the instant case, for example, it is clear from the record that the householder to whom the appellant gave the leaflet which led to her arrest was more irritated than pleased with her visitor. The City, which is an industrial community most of whose residents are engaged in the iron and steel industry, has vigorously argued that its inhabitants frequently work on swing shifts, working nights and sleeping days so that casual bell pushers might seriously interfere with the hours of sleep although they might call at high noon."

—Black

PUBLIC UTILITIES COMMISSION OF THE DISTRICT OF COLUMBIA

Capital Transit Company and Washington Transit Radio, Inc.

v.

FRANKLIN S. POLLAK and Guy Martin

343 US 451   May 26, 1952

SUMMARY: A street railway company in the District of Columbia installed in its streetcars receivers and loudspeakers over which radio programs were broadcast. The transportation company contracted with station WWDC-FM for programming, approximately 90 percent of which was music and 10 percent announcements and commercial advertising. Pollak and Martin brought the case as passengers protesting forced listening. The Public Utilities Commission, after investigation and public hearings, concluded that this practice did not inconvenience comfort and safety, but tended to improve public service.

Justices: FREDRICK M. VINSON   HAROLD H. BURTON   FELIX FRANKFURTER
              TOM C. CLARK   ROBERT H. JACKSON   WILLIAM O. DOUGLAS
              SHERMAN MINTON   STANLEY F. REED   HUGO L. BLACK

Pollak   **1**

"The streetcar audience is a captive audience. It is there as a matter of necessity, not of choice. One who is in a public vehicle may not of course complain of the noise of the crowd and the babble of tongues. One who enters any public place sacrifices some of his privacy. My protest is against the invasion of his privacy over and beyond the risks of travel.

"The government may use the radio (or television) on public vehicles for many purposes. Today it may use it for a cultural end. Tomorrow it may use it for political purposes."

Pollak   **2**

"Transit radio service is a new income producing incident of the operation of railway properties. The profit arises from the rental of facilities for commercial advertising purposes. This aspect of the enterprise bears some relation to the long-established practice of renting space for visual advertising on the inside and outside of streetcars and busses.

"Through these programs Capital Transit seeks to improve its public relations. To minimize objections to the advertising features of the programs, it requires that at least 90% of the radio time be used for purposes other than commercials and announcements. This results in programs generally consisting of 90% music, 5% news, weather reports and matters of civic interest and 5% commercial advertising. The advertising is confined to statements of 15 to 30 seconds each. It occupies a total of about 3 minutes in each hour."

Pollak   **3**

"The principal results obtained through the survey, as presented in this record, were as follows: 'Of those interviewed, 93.4 percent were not opposed; that is, 76.3 were in favor, 13.9 said they didn't care, and 3.2 said they didn't know; 6.6 percent were not in favor, but when asked the question "Well, even though you don't care for such programs personally, would you object if the majority of passengers wanted busses and streetcars equipped with radio receivers," 3.6 said they would not object or oppose the majority will. Thus, a balance of 3 percent of those interviewed were firmly opposed to the use of radios in transit vehicles.' "

Pollak   **4**

"If liberty is to flourish, government should never be allowed to force people to listen to any radio program. The right of privacy should include the right to pick and choose from competing entertainments, competing propaganda, competing political philosophies. If people are let alone in those choices, the right of privacy will pay dividends in character and integrity. The strength of our system is in the dignity, the resourcefulness, and the independence of our people. Our confidence is in their ability as individuals to make the wisest choice. That system cannot flourish if regimentation takes hold. The right of privacy, today violated, is a powerful deterrent to any one who would control men's minds."

—Douglas

Pollak   **5**

"This is a case of first impression. There are no precedents to construe; no principles previously expounded to apply. We write on a clean slate.

"The case comes down to the meaning of 'liberty' as used in the Fifth Amendment. Liberty in the constitutional sense must mean more than freedom from unlawful governmental restraint; it must include privacy as well, if it is to be a repository of freedom. The right to be let alone is indeed the beginning of all freedom. Part of our claim to privacy is in the prohibition of the Fourth Amendment against unreasonable searches and seizures. It gives the guarantee that a man's home is his castle beyond invasion either by inquisitive or by officious people."

Pollak   **6**

"Pollack and Martin contend that the radio programs interfere with their freedom of conversation and that of other passengers by making it necessary for them to compete against the programs in order to be heard. The Commission, however, did not find, and the testimony does not compel a finding, that the programs interfered substantially with the conversation of passengers or with rights of communication constitutionally protected in public places. It is suggested also that the First Amendment guarantees a freedom to listen only to such points of view as the listener wishes to hear. There is no substantial claim that the programs have been used for objectionable propaganda."

—Burton

Pollak 7

"One who tunes in on an offensive program at home can turn it off or tune in another station, as he wishes. One who hears disquieting or unpleasant programs in public places, such as restaurants, can get up and leave. But the man on the streetcar has no choice but to sit and listen, or perhaps to sit and to try *not* to listen.

"When we force people to listen to another's ideas, we give the propagandist a powerful weapon. Today it is a business enterprise working out a radio program under the auspices of government. Tomorrow it may be a dominant political or religious group. Today the purpose is benign; there is no invidious cast to the programs. But the vice is inherent in the system. Once privacy is invaded, privacy is gone. Once a man is forced to submit to one type of radio program, he can be forced to submit to another. It may be but a short step from a cultural program to a political program."

Pollak 8

"The service and equipment of the company are subject to regulation by the Public Utilities Commission of the District of Columbia. The Commission, after an investigation and public hearings disclosing substantial grounds for doing so, has concluded that the radio service is not inconsistent with public convenience, comfort and safety and 'tends to improve the conditions under which the public ride.' The Commission, accordingly, has permitted the radio service to continue despite vigorous protests from some passengers that to do so violates their constitutional rights."

Pollak 9

"Uncontradicted testimony listed approximately the following numbers of vehicles equipped with transit radio in the areas named in October, 1949: St. Louis, Missouri, 1,000; Cincinnati, Ohio, 475; Houston, Texas, 270; Washington, D. C., 220; Worcester, Massachusetts, 220; Tacoma, Washington, 135; Evansville, Indiana, 110; Wilkes-Barre, Pennsylvania, 100; suburban Pittsburgh, Pennsylvania, 75; Allentown, Pennsylvania, 75; Huntington, West Virginia, 55; Des Moines, Iowa, 50; Topeka, Kansas, 50; suburban Washington, D. C., 30. Baltimore, Maryland, was listed but the number of vehicles was not stated."

Pollak 10

"The present case involves a form of coercion to make people listen. The listeners are of course in a public place; they are on streetcars traveling to and from home. In one sense it can be said that those who ride the streetcars do so voluntarily. Yet in a practical sense they are forced to ride, since this mode of transportation is today essential for many thousands. Compulsion which comes from circumstances can be as real as compulsion which comes from a command."

DOLLREE MAPP, etc., Appellant

v.

OHIO

367 US 643   June 19, 1961

SUMMARY: Mrs. Mapp who lived with her fifteen-year-old daughter in a duplex flat in Cleveland was arrested and convicted for possession of "four little pamphlets, a couple of photographs and a little pencil doodle"—all of which were alleged to be pornographic. These materials were obtained during a police search of her home upon a "tip" that a man with information concerning a bombing was hiding in her apartment.

Justices:	EARL WARREN	WILLIAM O. DOUGLAS	WILLIAM J. BRENNAN, JR.
	HUGO L. BLACK	TOM C. CLARK	CHARLES E. WHITTAKER
	FELIX FRANKFURTER	JOHN M. HARLAN	POTTER STEWART

Mapp   1

"At the trial no search warrant was produced by the prosecution, nor was the failure to produce one explained or accounted for. At best 'There is, in the record, considerable doubt as to whether there was ever any warrant for the search of defendant's home.' 170 Ohio St. at 430. . . ."

—CLARK

Mapp   2

"She lived alone with her fifteen-year-old daughter in a second-floor flat of a duplex in Cleveland. At about 1:30 in the afternoon of May 23, 1957, three policemen arrived at this house. They rang the bell, and the appellant, appearing at her window, asked them what they wanted. According to their later testimony, the policemen had come to the house on information from 'a confidential source that there was a person hiding out in the home, who was wanted for questioning in connection with a recent bombing.' To the appellant's question, however, they replied only that they wanted to question her and would not state the subject about which they wanted to talk."

Mapp 3

"A state conviction comes to us as the complete product of a sovereign judicial system. Typically a case will have been tried in a trial court, tested in some final appellate court, and will go no further. In the comparatively rare instance when a conviction is reviewed by us on due process grounds we deal then with a finished product in the creation of which we are allowed no hand, and our task, far from being one of overall supervision, is, speaking generally, restricted to a determination of whether the prosecution was Constitutionally fair. The specifics of trial procedure, which in every mature legal system will vary greatly in detail, are within the sole competence of the States."

Mapp 4

"In the Rochin Case, three police officers, acting with neither a judicial warrant nor probable cause, entered Rochin's home for the purpose of conducting a search and broke down the door to a bedroom occupied by Rochin and his wife. Upon their entry into the room, the officers saw Rochin pick up and swallow two small capsules. They immediately seized him and took him in handcuffs to a hospital where the capsules were recovered by use of a stomach pump. [367 US 644] Investigation showed that the capsules contained morphine and evidence of that fact was made the basis of his conviction of a crime in a state court.

"When the question of the validity of that conviction was brought here, we were presented with an almost perfect example of the interrelationship between the Fourth and Fifth Amendments."

Mapp 5

"At the heart . . . in this case is the following syllogism: (1) the rule excluding in federal criminal trials evidence which is the product of an illegal search and seizure is 'part and parcel' of the Fourth Amendment; (2) Wolf held that the 'privacy' assured against federal action by the Fourth Amendment is also protected against state action by the Fourteenth Amendment; and (3) it is therefore 'logically and constitutionally necessary' that Weeks exclusionary rule should also be enforced against the States."

Mapp 6

"This reasoning ultimately rests on the unsound premise that because Wolf carried into the States, as part of 'the concept of ordered liberty' embodied in the Fourteenth Amendment (338 US, at 27), it must follow that whatever configurations of the Fourth Amendment have been developed in the particularizing federal precedents are likewise to be deemed a part of 'ordered liberty,' and as such are enforceable against the states. For me, this does not follow at all."

—Harlan

"For nearly fifty years, since the decision of this Court in Weeks v. United States, federal courts have refused to permit the introduction into evidence against an accused of his papers and effects obtained by 'unreasonable searches and seizures' in violation of the Fourth Amendment. In Wolf v. Colorado, decided in 1949, however, this Court held that 'in a prosecution in a State court for a State crime the Fourteenth Amendment does not forbid the admission of evidence obtained by an unreasonable search and seizure.' "

"The appellant, who was on the steps going up to her flat, demanded to see the search warrant, but the officer refused to let her see it although he waved a paper in front of her face. She grabbed it and thrust it down the front of her dress. The policeman seized her, took the paper from her, and had her handcuffed to another officer. She was taken upstairs, thus bound, and into the larger of two bedrooms in the apartment; there she was forced to sit on the bed. Meanwhile, the officers entered the house and made a complete search of the four rooms of her flat and of the basement of the house."

"In the final analysis, it seems to me that the Boyd doctrine, though perhaps not required by the express language of the Constitution strictly construed, is amply justified from an historical standpoint, soundly based in reason, [367 US 663] and entirely consistent with what I regard to be the proper approach to interpretation of our Bill of Rights—an approach well set out by Mr. Justice Bradley in the Boyd case:

'[C]onstitutional provisions for the security of person and property should be liberally construed. A close and literal construction deprives them of half their efficacy, and leads to gradual depreciation of the right, as if it consisted more in sound than in substance.' "

"The appellant, who had retained an attorney in connection with a pending civil matter, told the police she would call him to ask if she should let them in. On her attorney's advice, she told them she would let them in only when they produced a valid search warrant. For the next two and one half hours, the police laid siege to the house. At four o'clock, their number was increased to at least seven. Appellant's lawyer appeared on the scene; and one of the policemen told him that now they had a search warrant, but the officer refused to show it. Instead, going to the back door, the officer first tried to kick it in and, when that proved unsuccessful, he broke the glass in the door and opened it from the inside."

ESTELLE T. GRISWOLD et al., Appellant

v.

STATE OF CONNECTICUT

381 US 479   June 7, 1965

SUMMARY: Estelle Griswold, the Executive Director of the Planned Parenthood League of Connecticut, and Dr. Buxton, a licensed physician and a professor at Yale Medical School, were arrested for giving information, instructions, and medical advice to married persons as to the means of contraception in 1961. The Planned Parenthood League operated a center from which they offered both advice and supplies for contraceptive purposes. The statute of Connecticut which was broken read: "Any person who uses any drug, medicinal article or instrument for the purpose of preventing contraception shall be fined not less than fifty dollars or imprisoned not less than sixty days nor more than one year or be both fined and imprisoned."

Justices:	EARL WARREN	TOM C. CLARK	POTTER STEWART
	HUGO L. BLACK	JOHN M. HARLAN	BYRON R. WHITE
	WILLIAM O. DOUGLAS	WILLIAM J. BRENNAN, JR.	ARTHUR J. GOLDBERG

Griswold   1

"But to say that the Ninth Amendment has anything to do with this case is to turn somersaults with history. The Ninth Amendment, like its companion the Tenth, which this court held 'states but a truism that all is retained which has not been surrendered' United States v. Darby, 312 US 100, . . . was formed by James Madison and adopted by the States simply to make clear that the adoption of the Bill of Rights did not alter the plan that the *Federal* Government was to be a government of express and limited powers, and that all rights and powers not delegated to it were retained by the people and the individual States. Until today no member of this Court has ever suggested that the Ninth Amendment meant anything else, and the idea that a federal court could ever use the Ninth Amendment to annul a law passed by the elected representatives of the people of the State of Connecticut would have caused James Madison no little wonder."

Griswold   2

"As to the First, Third, Fourth, and Fifth Amendments, I can find nothing in any of them to invalidate this Connecticut law, even assuming that all of those Amendments are fully applicable against the States. It has not even been argued that this is a law 'respecting an establishment of religion, or prohibiting free exercise thereof.' And surely, unless the solemn process of constitutional adjudication is to descend to the level of a play on words, there is not involved here any abridgment of 'the freedom of speech, or of the press; or of the right of the people to peaceably assemble, and to petition the Government for a redress of grievances.' No soldier has been quartered in any house. There has been no search, and no seizure. Nobody has been compelled to be a witness against himself."

Griswold 3

"Since 1879, Connecticut has had on its books a law which forbids the use of contraceptives by anyone. I think this is an uncommonly silly law. As a practical matter, the law is obviously unenforceable, except in the oblique context of the present case. As a philosophical matter, I believe the use of contraceptives in the relationship of marriage should be left to the personal and private choice, based upon each individual's moral, ethical, and religious beliefs. As a matter of social policy, I think professional counsel about methods of birth control should be available to all, so that each individual's choice can be meaningfully made. But we are not asked in this case to say whether we think this law is unwise, or even asinine. We are asked to hold that it violates the United States Constitution. And that I cannot do."

Griswold 4

"But speech is one thing; conduct and physical activities are quite another. See, e.g., Cox v. Louisiana, 379 US 536, . . . The two defendants here were active participants in an organization which gave physical examinations to women, advised them what kind of contraceptive devices or medicines would most likely be satisfactory for them, and then supplied the devices themselves, all for a graduated scale of fees, based on family income. Thus these defendants admittedly engaged with others in a planned course of conduct to help people violate the Connecticut law. Merely because some speech was used in carrying on that conduct—just as in ordinary life some speech accompanies most kinds of conduct—we are not in my view justified in holding that the First Amendment forbids the State to punish their conduct."

—BLACK

Griswold 5

"For these reasons I get nowhere in this case by talk about a constitutional 'right of privacy' as an emanation from one or more constitutional provisions. I like my privacy as well as the next one, but I am nevertheless compelled to admit that government has a right to invade it unless prohibited by some specific constitutional provision."

Griswold 6

"We do not sit as a super-legislature to determine the wisdom, need, and propriety of laws that touch economic problems, business affairs, or social conditions. This law, however, operates directly on an intimate relationship of husband and wife and their physician's role in one aspect of that relation."

Griswold 7

Griswold 8

"We recently referred in Mapp v. Ohio, 367 US 643, . . . to the Fourth Amendment as creating a 'right to privacy, no less important than any other right carefully and particularly reserved to the people.' "

"The Ninth Amendment to the Constitution may be regarded by some as a recent discovery and may be forgotten by others, but since 1791 it has been a basic part of the Constitution which we are sworn to uphold. To hold that a right so basic and fundamental and so deep-rooted in our society as the right of privacy in marriage may be infringed because that is not guaranteed in so many words by the first eight amendments to the Constitution is to ignore the Ninth Amendment and to give it no effect whatsoever."

* * *

"The Ninth Amendment reads, 'The enumeration in the Constitution, of certain rights, shall not be construed to deny or disparage others retained by the people.' "

Griswold 9

Griswold 10

"Connecticut does not bar the importation or possession of contraceptive devices; they are not considered contraband under state law . . . and their availability in that State is not seriously disputed. The only way Connecticut seeks to limit or control the availability of such devices is through its general aiding and abetting statute whose operation in this context has been obviously ineffective and whose most serious use has been against birth-control clinics rendering advice to married, rather than unmarried persons . . . it would appear that the sale of contraceptives to prevent disease is plainly legal under Connecticut law."

"Would we allow the police to search the sacred precincts of marital bedrooms for telltale signs of the use of contraceptives? The very idea is repulsive to the notions of privacy surrounding the marriage relationship."

"We deal with the right of privacy older than the Bill of Rights—older than our political parties, older than our school system. Marriage is a coming together for better or for worse, hopefully enduring, and intimate to the degree of being sacred. It is an association that promotes a way of life, not causes; a harmony in living, not political faiths; a bilateral loyalty, not commercial or social projects. Yet it is an association for as noble a purpose as any involved in our prior decisions."

—Douglas

BILLIE SOL ESTES, Petitioner

v.

STATE OF TEXAS

381 US 532   June 7, 1965

SUMMARY: Massive pretrial publicity totaling 11 volumes of press clippings indicate the notoriety of the trial of the West Texas financier, Billie Sol Estes, who was convicted of swindling. Initial hearings were carried live by television in which 12 cameramen were engaged in filming the proceedings in the courtroom, but for the actual trial a box concealed the television people and only certain portions of the trial were broadcast.

Justices:	EARL WARREN	TOM C. CLARK	POTTER STEWART
	HUGO L. BLACK	JOHN M. HARLAN	BYRON R. WHITE
	WILLIAM O. DOUGLAS	WILLIAM J. BRENNAN, JR.	ARTHUR J. GOLDBERG

Estes   1   Estes   2

"The suggesting that there are limits upon the public's right to know what goes on in the courts causes me deep concern. The idea of imposing upon any medium of communications the burden of justifying its presence is contrary to where I had always thought the presumption must lie in the area of First Amendment freedoms."

—STEWART

"In Rideau v. Louisiana, 373 US 723, 10 L ed 2d 663, 83 S Ct 1417 (1963), this Court constructed a rule that the televising of a defendant in the act of confessing to a crime was inherently invalid under the Due Process Clause of the Fourteenth Amendment even without a showing of prejudice or a demonstration of the nexus between the televised confession and the trial. Here, although there was nothing so dramatic as a home-viewed confession, there had been a bombardment of the community with the sights and sounds of a two-day hearing during which the original jury panel, the petitioner, the lawyers and the judge were highly publicized. The petitioner was subjected to characterization and minute electronic scrutiny to such an extent that at one point the photographers were found attempting to picture the page of the paper from which he was reading while sitting at the counsel table."

"Because of continual objection, the rules governing live telecasting, as well as radio and still photos, were changed as the exigencies of the situation seemed to require. As a result, live telecasting was prohibited during a great portion of the actual trial. Only the opening and closing arguments of the State, the return of the jury's verdict and its receipt by the trial judge were carried live with sound. Although the order allowed videotapes of the entire proceeding without sound, the cameras operated only intermittently, recording various portions of the trial for broadcast on regularly scheduled newscasts later in the day and evening. At the request of the petitioner, the trial judge prohibited coverage of any kind, still or television, of the defense counsel during their summations to the jury."

"Moreover, should television become an accepted part of the courtroom, greater sacrifices would be made for the benefit of broadcasters. In the present case construction of a television booth in the courtroom made it necessary to alter the physical layout of the courtroom and to move from their accustomed position two benches reserved for spectators. If this can be done in order to better accommodate the television industry, I see no reason why another court might not move a trial to a theater, if such a move would provide improved television coverage. Our memories are short indeed if we have already forgotten the wave of horror that swept over this country when Premier Fidel Castro conducted his prosecutions before 18,000 people in Havana Stadium."

"I believe that it violates the Sixth Amendment for federal courts and the Fourteenth Amendment for state courts to allow criminal trials to be televised to the public at large. I base this conclusion on three grounds: (1) that the television of trials diverts the trial from its proper purpose in that it has an inevitable impact on all the trial participants; (2) that it gives the public the wrong impression about the purpose of trials, thereby detracting from the dignity of court proceedings and lessening the reliability of trials; and (3) that it singles out certain defendants and subjects them to trials under prejudicial conditions not experienced by others."

"Telecasting is particularly bad where the judge is elected, as is the case in all save a half dozen of our States. The telecasting of a trial becomes a political weapon, which, along with other distractions inherent in broadcasting, diverts his attention from the task at hand—the fair trial of the accused. But this is not all. There is the initial decision that must be made as to whether the use of television will be permitted. This is perhaps an even more crucial consideration. Our judges are high-minded men and women. But it is difficult to remain oblivious to the pressures that the news media can bring to bear on them both directly and through the shaping of public opinion. Moreover, where one judge in a district or even in a State permits telecasting, the requirement that the others do the same is almost mandatory."

"Moreover, while it is practically impossible to assess the effect of television on jury attentiveness, those of us who know juries realize the problem of jury 'distraction.' The State argues this is de minimis since the physical disturbances have been eliminated. But we know that distractions are not caused solely by the physical presence of the camera and its telltale red lights. It is the awareness of the fact of telecasting that is felt by the juror throughout the trial. We are all self-conscious and uneasy when being televised. Human nature being what it is, not only will a juror's eyes be fixed on the camera, but also his mind will be preoccupied with the telecasting rather than with the testimony."

—Clark

"The State contends that the televising of portions of a criminal trial does not constitute a denial of due process. Its position is that because no prejudice has been shown by the petitioner as resulting from the televising, it is permissible that claims of 'distractions' during the trial due to the physical presence of television are wholly unfounded; and that psychological considerations are for psychologists, not courts, because they are purely hypothetical. It argues further that the public has a right to know what goes on in the courts; that the court has no power to 'suppress, edit, or censor events which transpire in proceedings before it,' citing Craig v. Harney, 331 US 367, 374, 91 L ed 1546, 1551 67 S Ct 1249 (1947); and that the televising of criminal trials would be enlightening to the public and would promote greater respect for the courts."

"It is said, however, that the freedoms granted in the First Amendment extend a right to the news media to televise from the courtroom, and that to refuse to honor this privilege is to discriminate between the newspapers and television. This is a misconception of the rights of the press.

"The free press has been a mighty catalyst in awakening public interest in governmental affairs, exposing corruption among public officers and employees and generally informing the citizenry of public events and occurrences, including court proceedings. While maximum freedom must be allowed the press in carrying on this important function in a democratic society its exercise must necessarily be subject to the maintenance of absolute fairness in the judicial process."

"The purpose of the requirement of a public trial was to guarantee that the accused would be fairly dealt with and not unjustly condemned. History had proven that secret tribunals were effective instruments of oppression. As our Brother Black so well said in In re Oliver, 333 US 257, 92 L ed 682, 68 S Ct 499 (1948): 'The traditional Anglo-American distrust for secret trials has been variously ascribed to the notorious use of this practice by the Spanish Inquisition, to the excesses of the English Court of Star Chamber, and to the French monarchy's abuse of the lettre de cachet. . . . Whatever other benefits the guarantee to an accused that his trial be conducted in public may confer upon our society, the guarantee has always been recognized as a safeguard against any attempt to employ our courts as instruments of persecution.'"

SAMUEL H. SHEPPARD, Petitioner

v.

E. L. MAXWELL, Warden
384 US 333   June 6, 1966

SUMMARY: Dr. Samuel Sheppard was convicted for murdering his wife, Marilyn, on July 4, 1954. Previous to and during the nine-week trial, representatives of the news media provided massive coverage, handled and photographed trial exhibits, broadcast in a room adjacent to where the jury recessed, published the names of the jury, interviewed witnesses, and published articles by Sheppard, himself.

Justices:	EARL WARREN	TOM C. CLARK	POTTER STEWART
	HUGO L. BLACK	JOHN M. HARLAN	BYRON R. WHITE
	WILLIAM O. DOUGLAS	WILLIAM J. BRENNAN, JR.	ABE FORTAS

Sheppard   1

"The principle that justice cannot survive behind walls of silence has long been reflected in the 'Anglo-American distrust for secret trials.'"

—CLARK

Sheppard   2

"Twenty-five days before the case was set, 75 veniremen were called as prospective jurors. All three Cleveland newspapers published the names and addresses of the veniremen. As a consequence, anonymous letters and telephone calls, as well as calls from friends, regarding the impending prosecution were received by all of the prospective jurors."

Sheppard   **3**   **Sheppard**   **4**

"The following day, July 21, another one page editorial was headed: 'Why No Inquest? Do It Now, Dr. Gerber.' The Coroner called an inquest the same day and subpoenaed Sheppard. It was staged in the gymnasium. . . . In the front of the room was a long table occupied by reporters, television and radio personnel, and broadcasting equipment. The hearing was broadcast with live microphones placed at the Coroner's seat and the witness stand. A swarm of reporters and photographers attended. Sheppard was brought into the room by police who searched him in full view of several hundred spectators. Sheppard's counsel were present during the three-day inquest but were not permitted to participate."

"During the Coroner's inquest Sheppard was questioned five and one-half hours about his actions on the night of the murder, his married life, and a love affair, with Susan Hayes. . . . Throughout this period the newspapers emphasized evidence that tended to incriminate Sheppard and pointed out discrepancies in his statements to authorities. At the same time, Sheppard made many public statements to the press and wrote feature articles asserting his innocence."

Sheppard   **5**   **Sheppard**   **6**

"Marilyn Sheppard, petitioner's pregnant wife, was bludgeoned to death in the upstairs bedroom of their lakeshore home in Bay Village, Ohio, a suburb of Cleveland. On the day of the tragedy, July 4, 1954, Sheppard pieced together for several local officials the following story: He and his wife had entertained neighborhood friends, the Aherns, on the previous evening at their home. After dinner they watched television in the livingroom. Sheppard became drowsy and dozed off to sleep on the couch. Later, Marilyn partially awoke him saying that she was going to bed. The next thing he remembered was hearing his wife cry out in the early morning hours. He hurried upstairs and in the dim light from the hall saw a 'form' standing next to his wife's bed. As he struggled with the 'form' he was struck on the back of the neck and rendered unconscious."

"This federal habeas corpus application involves the question whether Sheppard was deprived of a fair trial in his state conviction for the second-degree murder of his wife because of the trial judge's failure to protect Sheppard sufficiently from the massive, pervasive and prejudicial publicity that attended his prosecution."

Sheppard 7

"From the cases coming here we note that unfair prejudicial news comment on pending trials has become increasingly prevalent. Due process requires that the accused receive a trial by an impartial jury free from outside influences. Given the pervasiveness of modern communications and the difficulty of effacing prejudicial publicity from the minds of the jurors, the trial courts must take strong measure to insure that the balance is never weighed against the accused."

—Clark

Sheppard 8

"The press does not simply publish information about trials but guards against the miscarriage of justice by subjecting the police, prosecutors, and judicial processes to extensive public scrutiny and criticism. This Court has, therefore, been unwilling to place any direct limitations on the freedom traditionally exercised by the news media for '[w]hat transpires in the court room is public property.' Craig v. Harney, 331 US 367. . . ."

Sheppard 9

"As has been mentioned, the jury viewed the scene of the murder on the first day of the trial. Hundreds of reporters, cameramen and onlookers were there, and one representative of the news media was permitted to accompany the jury while it inspected the Sheppard home. The time of the jury's visit was revealed so far in advance that one of the newspapers was able to rent a helicopter and fly over the house taking pictures of the jurors on their tour."

"When the trial was in its seventh week, Walter Winchell broadcast over WXEL television and WJW radio that Carole Beasley, who was under arrest in New York City for robbery, had stated that, as Sheppard's mistress, she had borne him a child. The defense asked the jury to be queried on the broadcast. Two jurors admitted in open court that each had heard it. The judge . . . merely asked the jury to 'pay no attention whatever to that type of scavenging.'"

Sheppard 10

"Unlike Estes, Sheppard was not granted a change of venue to a locale away from where the publicity originated, nor was his jury sequestered. The Estes jury saw none of the television broadcasts from the courtroom. On the contrary, the Sheppard jurors were subjected to newspaper, radio, and television coverage of the trial while not taking part in the proceedings."

CLYDE FRANKLIN LEE et al., Petitioners

v.

STATE OF FLORIDA

392 US 378   June 17, 1968

SUMMARY: The police for more than a week used recording equipment to monitor telephone calls to and from Lee and two other petitioners from private and public phones. The three petitioners were convicted in a Florida trial court for violating the state lottery laws.

Justices:	EARL WARREN	JOHN M. HARLAN	BYRON R. WHITE
	HUGO L. BLACK	WILLIAM J. BRENNAN, JR.	ABE FORTAS
	WILLIAM O. DOUGLAS	POTTER STEWART	THURGOOD MARSHALL

Lee   **1**   **Lee**   **2**

"In the summer of 1963 petitioner Lee ordered the installation of a private telephone in the house where he lived near Orlando, Florida. The local telephone company informed him that no private lines were available, and he was given a telephone on a four-party line instead. A week later, at the direction of the Orlando police department, the company connected a telephone in a neighboring house to the same party line. The police attached to this telephone an automatic activator, a tape recorder and a set of ear phones."

—STEWART

"There clearly is a federal statute, applicable in Florida and every other State, that made illegal the conduct of the Orlando authorities in this case."

Lee 3

"[T]he plain words of §605 forbid anyone, unless authorized by the sender, to intercept a telephone message, and direct in equally clear language that *'no person'* shall divulge or publish the message or its substance to *'any person.'*"

Lee 4

"More than 15 years ago, in Schwartz v. Texas, 344 US 199, . . . this Court decided that §605 did not render state convictions based on such interceptions invalid."

Lee 5

"Congress has ample power to proscribe any particular use of intercepted telephone conversations. The question here is simply whether §605 of the Communications Act proscribes basing state criminal convictions on such interceptions. This statutory question does not involve any constitutional exclusionary rule, cf. Mapp v. Ohio, 367 US 643 . . . , or the supervisory power of this Court over the lower federal courts, of Weeks v. United States 232 US 383. . . ."

Lee 6

"It is not at all obvious that a statute which by its terms prohibits only interception and divulgence of conversations, meant also to prohibit state-court reliance on the perfectly probative evidence gained thereby."

Lee   7   **Lee**   8

"I cannot agree that there is the slightest justification for overruling Schwartz and would
affirm these Florida gambling convictions."

"Waiting for Congress to rewrite its law, however, is too slow for the Court in this day of
rapid creation of new judicial rules, many of
which inevitably tend to make convictions of
criminals more difficult."

—BLACK

Lee   9   **Lee**   10

". . . the police cannot be deemed to have
'intercepted' the telephone conversations, because people who use party lines should realize that their conversations might be overheard."

"In the Mapp case, the Court in overruling
Wolf imposed a judicially exclusionary rule in
order to insure that a State could not adopt
rules of evidence calculated to permit the invasion of rights protected by federal organic
law. In the present case the federal law itself
explicitly protects intercepted communications
from divulgence, in a court or any other place."

DICK GREGORY et al., Petitioners

v.

CITY OF CHICAGO

394 US 111   March 10, 1969

SUMMARY: A band of Negroes demonstrating against Dr. Benjamin Willis, Superintendent of Chicago public school system, marched to the city hall and then to Mayor Daley's home. Fearful that a threatening crowd of on-lookers could no longer be contained, the police asked Dick Gregory, Negro leader of the march, to leave the area. When Gregory and his marchers refused, they were arrested and charged with disorderly conduct.

Justices:	EARL WARREN	JOHN M. HARLAN	BYRON R. WHITE
	HUGO L. BLACK	WILLIAM J. BRENNAN, JR.	ABE FORTAS
	WILLIAM O. DOUGLAS	POTTER STEWART	THURGOOD MARSHALL

Gregory   **1**

"Sergeant Golden testified that between 8:00 o'clock and 9:00 o'clock the crowd increased steadily to a few hundred, but that from 9:00 o'clock until about 9:20 o'clock the people just seemed to come from everywhere until it reached between 1,000 and 1,200. During this time the crowd became unruly. There was shouting and threats. 'God damned nigger, get the hell out of here'; 'Get out of here niggers —go back where you belong or we will get you out of here' and 'Get the hell out of here or we will break your blankety-blank head open.' Cars were stopped in the streets with their horns blowing. There were Ku Klux Klan signs and there was singing of the Alabama Trooper song. Children in the crowd were playing various musical instruments such as a cymbal, trumpet and drum."

Gregory   **2**

"When they refused, they were arrested and charged with violation of Chicago's disorderly conduct ordinance, which provides as follows: 'All persons who shall make, aid, countenance, or assist in making any improper noise, riot, disturbance, breach of the peace, within the limits of the city; all persons who shall collect in bodies or crowds for unlawful purposes, or for any purpose, to the annoyance or disturbance of other persons; . . . shall be deemed guilty of disorderly conduct, and upon conviction thereof, shall be severely fined not less than one dollar nor more than two hundred dollars for each offense.' "

Gregory   3

"Men and women who hold public office would be compelled, simply because they did not hold public office, to lose the comforts and privacy of an unpicketed home. We believe that our Constitution, written for the ages, to endure except as changed in the manner it provides, did not create a government with such monumental weaknesses. Speech and press are, of course, to be free, so that public matters can be discussed with impunity. But picketing and demonstrating can be regulated like other conduct of men. We believe that the homes of men, sometimes the last citadel of the tired, the weary and the sick, can be protected by government from noisy, marching, tramping, threatening picketers and demonstrators bent on filling the minds of men, women, and children with fears of the unknown."

Gregory   4

"This is a simple case. Petitioners, accompanied by Chicago police and an assistant city attorney, marched in a peaceful and orderly procession from city hall to the mayor's residence to press their claims for desegregation of the public schools. Having promised to cease singing at 8:30 P.M., the marchers did so. Although petitioners and the other demonstrators continued to march in a completely lawful fashion, the onlookers became unruly as the number of bystanders increased. Chicago police, to prevent what they regarded as an impending civil disorder, demanded that the demonstrators, upon pain of arrest, disperse. When this command was not obeyed, petitioners were arrested for disorderly conduct."

—WARREN

Gregory   5

"Petitioner Gregory and his group had become dissatisfied because Benjamin Willis, Superintendent of Chicago's public school system, was not moving speedily enough to desegregate the public schools. While Mayor Daley did not appear to have legal authority to remove Dr. Willis, the group evidently believed the Mayor could cause him to be removed if he wanted to do so, and their prodding was therefore directed at the Mayor as well as against Willis. The group march began near the Chicago Loop District at 4:30 P.M. and ended five miles away in the neighborhood of Daley's home. A lieutenant of police, four police sergeants and about forty policemen met Gregory at the gathering place in Grant Park."

Gregory   6

"There Gregory addressed the marchers saying: 'First we will go over to the snake pit [city hall]. When we leave there, we will go out to the snake's house [the mayor's home]. Then, we will continue to go out to Mayor Daley's home until he fires Ben Willis [Superintendent of Schools].' The demonstrators marched to the city hall, and then they marched to the Mayor's home about five miles away, arriving at about 8 P.M. The demonstrators were accompanied by the police and by the Assistant City Attorney from the park to the Mayor's home. When they reached this neighborhood, the demonstrators began marching around and around near the Mayor's home."

"Meanwhile the crowd of spectators from the neighborhood kept increasing, and its language and conduct became rougher and tougher. The events leading up to the arrest of the demonstrators are set out in detail in the opinion of the Illinois Supreme Court, and we agree fully with that court's description of these events, which we have reprinted as an appendix to this opinion. This episode finally came to a conclusion at about 9:30 P.M. Fearful that the threatening crowd of onlookers could no longer be contained, the police asked Gregory and his marchers to leave the area."

"These facts disclosed by the record point unerringly to one conclusion, namely, that when groups with diametrically opposed, deep-seated views are permitted to air their emotional grievances, side by side, on city streets, tranquility and order cannot be maintained even by the joint efforts of the finest and best officers and of those who desire to be the most law-abiding protestors of their grievances."

—BLACK

"Indeed, in the face of jeers, insults and assaults with rocks and eggs, Gregory and his group maintained a decorum that speaks well for their determination simply to tell their side of their grievances and complaints. Even the 'snake' and 'snake pit' invectives used by Gregory and his demonstrators, unlike some used by their hecklers, remained within the general give and take of heated political argument. Thus both police and demonstrators made their best efforts faithfully to discharge their responsibilities as officers and citizens, but they were nevertheless unable to restrain these hostile hecklers within decent and orderly bounds."

"The disorderly conduct ordinance under which these petitioners were charged and convicted is not, however, a narrowly drawn law, particularly designed to regulate certain kinds of conduct such as marching or picketing or demonstrating along the streets or highways. Nor does it regulate the times or places or manner of carrying on such activities. To the contrary, it might better be described as a meat ax ordinance, gathering in one comprehensive definition of an offense a number of words which have a multiplicity of meanings, some of which would cover activity specifically protected by the First Amendment."

ROBERT ELI STANLEY, Appellant

v.

STATE OF GEORGIA

394 US 557   April 7, 1969

SUMMARY: Under authority of a warrant to search for bookmaking activities, federal and state agents entered Stanley's two-story residence in Atlanta. Very little evidence of bookmaking was found, but while looking through a desk drawer in an upstairs bedroom, three reels of film were discovered. Using a projector and screen, the agents viewed the films for fifty minutes, concluded they were obscene, and arrested Stanley for "knowingly hav[ing] possession of obscene matter" in violation of Georgia law.

Justices:	WARREN E. BURGER	JOHN M. HARLAN	BYRON R. WHITE
	HUGO L. BLACK	WILLIAM J. BRENNAN, JR.	THURGOOD MARSHALL
	WILLIAM O. DOUGLAS	POTTER STEWART	

Stanley   **1**

"It is true that Roth does declare, seemingly without qualification, that obscenity is not protected by the First Amendment. That statement has been repeated in various forms in subsequent cases. See, e.g., Smith v. California, 361 US 147, 152, 4 L Ed 2d 205, 210, 80 S Ct 215 (1959); Jacobellis v. Ohio, 378 US 184, 186-187, 12 L Ed 2d 793, 796, 797, 84 S Ct 1676 (1964) (opinion of Brennan, J.); Ginsberg v. New York, supra, 390 US, at 635, 20 L Ed 2d at 201. However, neither Roth nor any subsequent decision of this Court dealt with the precise problem involved in the present case."

—MARSHALL

Stanley   **2**

"Neither Roth nor any other decision of this Court reaches that far. As the Court said in Roth itself, '[c]easeless vigilance is the watchword to prevent . . . erosion [of First Amendment rights] by Congress or by the States. The door barring federal and state intrusion into this area cannot be left ajar; it must be kept tightly closed and opened only the slightest crack necessary to prevent encroachment upon more important interests.' 354 US, at 488, 1 L Ed 2d at 1509."

Stanley 3

"It is now well established that the Constitution protects the right to receive information and ideas. 'This freedom [of speech and press] . . .' necessarily protects the right to receive. . . .' Martin v. City of Struthers, 319 US 141, 143, 87 L Ed 1313, 1316, 63 S Ct 862 (1943); see Griswold v. Connecticut, 381 US 479, 482, 14 L Ed 2d 510, 513, 85 S Ct 1678 (1965); Lamont v. Postmaster General, 381 US 301, 307-308, 14 L Ed 2d 398, 402, 403, 85 S Ct 1493 (1965) (Brennan, J., concurring); cf. Pierce v. Society of Sisters, 268 US 510, 69 L Ed 1070, 45 S Ct 571, 39 ALR 468 (1925). This right to receive information and ideas, regardless of their social worth, see Winters v. New York, 333 US 507, 510, 92 L Ed 840, 847, 68 S Ct 665 (1948), is fundamental to our free society."

Stanley 4

"These are the rights that appellant is asserting in the case before us. He is asserting the right to read or observe what he pleases—the right to satisfy his intellectual and emotional needs in the privacy of his own home. He is asserting the right to be free from state inquiry into the contents of his library. Georgia contends that appellant does not have these rights, that there are certain types of materials that the individual may not read or even possess. Georgia justifies this assertion by arguing that the films in the present case are obscene."

Stanley 5

"If the First Amendment means anything, it means that a State has no business telling a man, sitting alone in his own house, what books he may read or what films he may watch. Our whole constitutional heritage rebels at the thought of giving government the power to control men's minds."

Stanley 6

"Communities believe, and act on the belief, that obscenity is immoral, is wrong for the individual, and has no place in a decent society. They believe, too, that adults as well as children are corruptible in morals and character, and that obscenity is a source of corruption that should be eliminated. Obscenity is not suppressed primarily for the protection of others. Much of it is suppressed for the purity of the community and for the salvation and welfare of the 'consumer.' Obscenity, at bottom, is not crime. Obscenity is sin." Henkin, Morals and the Constitution: The Sin of Obscenity, 63 Col L Rev 391, 395 (1963).

"Perhaps recognizing this, Georgia asserts that exposure to obscenity may lead to deviant sexual behavior or crimes of sexual violence. There appears to be little empirical basis for that assertion. But more importantly, if the State is only concerned about literature inducing antisocial conduct, we believe that in the context of private consumption of ideas and information we should adhere to the view that '[a]mong free men, the deterrents ordinarily to be applied to prevent crime are education and punishment for violations of the law. . . .' Whitney v. California, 274 US 357, 378, 71 L Ed 1095, 1107, 47 S Ct 641 (1927) (Brandeis, J., concurring)."

"The Fourth Amendment provides that 'no warrants shall issue, but upon probable cause, supported by Oath or affirmation, and particulary describing the place to be searched, and the persons or things to be seized.' The purpose of these clear and precise words was to guarantee to the people of this Nation that they should forever be secure from the general searches and unrestrained seizures that had been a hated hallmark of colonial rule under the notorious writs of assistance of the British Crown."

"There can be no doubt, therefore, that the agents were lawfully present in the appellant's house, lawfully authorized to search for any and all of the items specified in the warrant, and lawfully empowered to seize any such items they might find. It follows, therefore, that the agents were acting within the authority of the warrant when they proceeded to the appellant's upstairs bedroom and pulled open the drawers of his desk. But when they found in one of those drawers not gambling material but moving picture films, the warrant gave them no authority to seize the films."

"For the record makes clear that the contents of the films could not be determined by mere inspection. And this is not a case that presents any questions as to the permissible scope of a search made incident to a lawful arrest. For the appellant had not been arrested when the agents found the films. After finding them, the agents spent some 50 minutes exhibiting them by means of the appellant's projector in another upstairs room. Only then did the agents return downstairs and arrest the appellant."

—STEWART

DANIEL ROWAN, dba American Book Service et al., Appellants

v.

UNITED STATES POST OFFICE DEPARTMENT et al.

397 US 728   May 4, 1970

SUMMARY: Publishers, distributors, owners, and operators of mail-order houses and mailing-list brokers here sought a declaratory judgment that Title III of the Postal Revenue and Federal Salary Act of 1967 was unconstitutional. They argued that the act infringed upon the rights to freedom of the press when it permitted a household to stop mailings from certain firms coming to his door.

Justices:	WARREN E. BURGER	JOHN M. HARLAN	BYRON R. WHITE
	HUGO L. BLACK	WILLIAM J. BRENNAN, JR.	THURGOOD MARSHALL
	WILLIAM O. DOUGLAS	POTTER STEWART	

Rowan   1

"A brief description of the statutory framework will facilitate our analysis of the questions raised in this appeal. Title III of the Act is entitled 'Prohibition of pandering advertisements in the mails.' It provides a procedure whereby any householder may insulate himself from advertisements that offer for sale 'matter which the addressee in his sole discretion believes to be erotically arousing or sexually provocative.'"

Rowan   2

"Section 4009 was a response to public and congressional concern with use of mail facilities to distribute unsolicited advertisements that recipients found to be offensive because of their lewd and salacious character. Such mail was found to be pressed upon minors as well as adults who did not seek and did not want it. Use of mailing lists of youth organizations was part of the mode of doing business. At the congressional hearings it developed that complaints to the Postmaster General increased from 50,000 to 250,000 annually."

Rowan   **3**   Rowan   **4**

"The legislative history, including testimony of child psychology specialists and psychiatrists, reflected concern over the impact of the materials before the Committee on the development of children. A declared objective of Congress was to protect minors and the privacy of homes from such material and to place the judgment of what constitutes an offensive invasion of those interests in the hands of the addressee."

—Burger

"Senator Monroney, a major proponent of the legislation in the Senate, described the bill as follows:

" 'With respect to the test contained in the bill, if the addressee declared it to be erotically arousing or sexually provocative the Postmaster General would have to notify the sender to send no more mail to that address. . . .' 113 Cong Rec 34231 (1967)."

Rowan   **5**   Rowan   **6**

"The essence of appellants' argument is that the statute violates their constitutional right to communicate. One sentence in appellants' brief perhaps characterizes their entire position:

" 'The freedom to communicate orally and by the written word and, indeed, in every manner whatsoever is imperative to a free and sane society.' Brief for Appellants at 15."

"In today's complex society we are inescapably captive audiences for many purposes, but a sufficient measure of individual autonomy must survive to permit every householder to exercise control over unwanted mail. To make the householder the exclusive and final judge of what will cross his threshold undoubtedly has the effect of impeding the flow of ideas, information and arguments which, ideally, he should receive and consider."

"Today's merchandising methods, the plethora of mass mailings subsidized by low postal rates, and the growth of the sale of large mailing lists as an industry in itself have changed the mailman from a carrier of primarily private communications, as he was in a more leisurely day, and has made him an adjunct of the mass mailer who sends unsolicited and often unwanted mail into every home. It places no strain on the doctrine of judicial notice to observe that whether measured by pieces or pounds, Everyman's mail today is made up overwhelmingly of material he did not seek from persons he does not know. And all too often it is matter he finds offensive."

"In this case the mailer's right to communicate is circumscribed only by an affirmative act of the addressee giving notice that he wishes no further mailings from that mailer.

"To hold less would tend to license a form of trespass and would make hardly more sense than to say that a radio or television viewer may not twist the dial to cut off an offensive or boring communication and thus bar its entering his home. Nothing in the Constitution compels us to listen to or view any unwanted communication, whatever its merit; we see no basis for according the printed word or pictures a different or more preferred status because they are sent by mail."

"The ancient concept that 'a man's home is his castle' into which 'not even the king may enter' has lost none of its vitality, and none of the recognized exceptions includes any right to communicate offensively with another. See Camara v. Municipal Court, 387 US 523, 18 L Ed 2d 930, 87 S Ct 1727 (1967).

"Both the absoluteness of the citizen's right under §4009 and its finality are essential; what may not be provocative to one person may well be to another. In operative effect the power of the householder under the statute is unlimited; he or she may prohibit the mailing of a dry goods catalog because he objects to the contents—or indeed the text of the language touting the merchandise."

"I agree that 39 USC §4009 is constitutional insofar as it permits an *addressee* to require a mailer to remove *his* name from its mailing lists and to stop all future mailings to the addressee. As the Court notes, however, subsection (g) of §4009 also allows an addressee to request the Postmaster General to include in any prohibitory order 'the names of any of his minor children who have not attained their nineteenth birthday, and who reside with the addressee.' "

—BRENNAN

QUESTIONS FOR DISCUSSION

1. What is the Constitutional basis for the right to privacy?

2. Under what circumstances would you defend the electronic surveillance and/or bugging of a residence, business, or office?

3. Would you object to a public transportation company's broadcasting music and news within its vehicles?

4. What, if any, limitations should be placed on television and press coverage of trials?

5. Do you support residential picketing?

6. Should the state protect the public from mailings of obscene materials?

7. Do you agree with the Court's finding concerning obscene materials within the home?

8. In order to maintain your privacy would you support an ordinance which prohibits solicitors, salesmen, evangelists, politicians, and tax collectors from coming to your door? Why? Why not?

Provocation and Demonstration

FRANK HAGUE, Individually and as Mayor of Jersey City, et al., etc., Petitioners

v.

COMMITTEE FOR INDUSTRIAL ORGANIZATION et al.
307 US 496   June 5, 1939

SUMMARY: In Jersey City the Director of Public Safety was authorized to grant permits for parades and public assembly. The union charged that it was repeatedly refused permits for its organizers to arrange meetings to speak in behalf of the union movement, and consequently won an injunction from a federal court against enforcement of the city's parade and assembly ordinance. The Mayor Frank "I am the Law" Hague argued that since the famous 1897 Davis v. Massachusetts case a city had the right to control the use of his private property.

Justices:	CHARLES E. HUGHES	PIERCE BUTLER	JAMES C. McREYNOLDS
	STANLEY F. REED	OWEN J. ROBERTS	FELIX FRANKFURTER
	HUGO L. BLACK	HARLAN F. STONE	WILLIAM O. DOUGLAS

Hague   1   **Hague**   2

"The Board of Commissioners of Jersey City do ordain: '1. From and after the passage of this ordinance, no public parades or public assembly in or upon the public streets, highways, public parks or public buildings of Jersey City shall take place or be conducted until a permit shall be obtained from the Director of Public Safety. 2. The Director of Public Safety is hereby authorized and empowered to grant permits for parades and public assembly, upon application made to him at least three days prior to the proposed parade or public assembly.' "

"The District Court should have refused to interfere by injunction with the essential rights of the municipality to control its own parks and streets. Wise management of such intimate local affairs, generally at least, is beyond the competency of federal courts, and essays in that direction should be avoided."

—McREYNOLDS

Hague   **3**   **Hague**   **4**

"There was ample opportunity for respondents to assert their claims through an orderly proceeding in courts of the state empowered authoritatively to interpret her laws with final review here in respect of federal questions."

". . . the petitioners rely upon Davis v. Massachusetts, 167 US 43, 42 L Ed 71, 17 S. Ct. 731. There it appeared that, pursuant to enabling legislation, the city of Boston adopted an ordinance prohibiting anyone from speaking, discharging fire arms, selling goods, or maintaining any booth for public amusement on any of the public grounds of the city except under a permit from the Mayor. Davis spoke on Boston Common without a permit and without applying to the Mayor for one. He was charged with a violation of the ordinance and moved to quash the complaint, inter alia, on the ground that the ordinance abridged his privileges and immunities as a citizen of the United States and denied him due process of law because it was arbitrary and unreasonable. His contentions were overruled and he was convicted."

Hague   **5**   **Hague**   **6**

"In the Slaughter-House Cases it was said, 16 Wall. 79, 21 L Ed 490: 'The right to peaceably assemble and petition for redress of grievances, the privilege of the writ of habeas corpus, are rights of the citizen guaranteed by the Federal Constitution.' "

"Although it has been held that the Fourteenth Amendment created no rights in citizens of the United States, but merely secured existing rights against state abridgment, it is clear that the right peaceably to assemble and to discuss these topics, and to communicate respecting them, whether orally or in writing, is a privilege inherent in citizenship of the United States which the Amendment protects."

Hague   7   **Hague**   8

"In the United States v. Cruikshank, 92 US 542, 552, 553, 23 L Ed 588, 591, 592, the court said: 'The right of the people peaceably to assemble for the purpose of petitioning Congress for a redress of grievances, or for anything else connected with the powers or the duties of the national government, is an attribute of national citizenship, and, as such, under the protection of, and guaranteed by, the United States. The very idea of a government, republican in form, implies a right on the part of its citizens to meet peaceably for consultation in respect to public affairs and to petition for a redress of grievances. If it had been alleged in these counts that the object of the defendants was to prevent a meeting for such a purpose, the case would have been within the statute, and within the scope of the sovereignty of the United States.'"

"Wherever the title of streets and parks may rest, they have immemorially been held in trust for the use of the public and, time out of mind, have been used for purposes of assembly, communicating thoughts between citizens, and discussing public questions. Such use of the streets and public places has, from ancient times, been a part of the privileges, immunities, rights and liberties of citizens. The privilege of a citizen of the United States to use the streets and parks for communication of views on national questions may be regulated in the interest of all; it is not absolute, but relative, and must be exercised in subordination to the general comfort and convenience, and in consonance with peace and good order; but it must not, in the guise of regulation, be abridged or denied."

—ROBERTS

Hague   9   **Hague**   10

". . . the challenged ordinance is not void on its face; that in principle it does not differ from the Boston ordinance, as applied and upheld by this Court, speaking through Mr. Justice White, in Davis v. Massachusetts, 167 US 43, 42. . . ."

"Prior to the Civil War there was confusion and debate as to the relation between United States citizenship and state citizenship. Beyond dispute, citizenship of the United States, as such, existed. The Constitution, in various clauses, recognized it but nowhere defined it. Many thought state citizenship, and that only created United States citizenship.

"After the adoption of the Thirteenth Amendment a bill, which became the first Civil Rights Act, was introduced in the 39th Congress, the major purpose of which was to secure the recently freed Negroes all the civil rights secured to white men."

WALTER CHAPLINSKY, Appellant

v.

STATE OF NEW HAMPSHIRE

315 US 568   March 9, 1942

SUMMARY: Chaplinsky, a Jehovah's Witness, was convicted for violation of a N. H. law which stated: "No person shall address any offensive, derisive or annoying word to any other person who is lawfully in any street or other public place, nor call him by any offensive or derisive name, nor make any noise or exclamation in his presence and hearing with intent to deride, offend or annoy him, or to prevent him from pursuing his lawful business or occupation." On a Saturday afternoon, Chaplinsky spoke to a crowd which appeared to a traffic officer to become restless; when he did not stop upon an officer's request and a disturbance at the busy intersection occurred, the officer took Chaplinsky to the station. To this point Chaplinsky had only distributed his literature and denounced religion as a racket. Enroute to the station he called the city marshall, ". . . a God-damned racketeer" and "A damned Fascist and the whole government of Rochester are Fascists or agents of Fascists."

Justices:	HARLAN F. STONE	STANLEY F. REED	FRANK MURPHY
	OWEN J. ROBERTS	FELIX FRANKFURTER	JAMES F. BYRNES
	HUGO L. BLACK	WILLIAM O. DOUGLAS	ROBERT H. JACKSON

Chaplinsky   1   **Chaplinsky**   2

"Chaplinsky's version was slightly different. He testified that when he met Bowering, he asked him to arrest the ones responsible for the disturbance. In reply Bowering cursed him and told him to come along. Appellant admitted that he said the words charged in the complaint with the exception of the name of the Deity."

"Over appellant's objection the trial court excluded as immaterial testimony relating to appellant's mission to 'preach the true facts of the Bible,' his treatment at the hands of the crowd, and the alleged neglect of duty on the part of the police."

—MURPHY

Chaplinsky 3

"And we cannot conceive that cursing a public officer is the exercise of religion in any sense of the term."

Chaplinsky 4

"Appellant assails the statute as a violation of all three freedoms, speech, press and worship, but only an attack on the basis of free speech is warranted. The spoken and not the written word is involved."

Chaplinsky 5

"The statute's purpose was to preserve the public peace, no words being 'forbidden except such as have a tendency to cause acts of violence by the persons to whom, individually, the remark is addressed.' . . . 'The word "offensive" is not to be defined in terms of what a particular addressee thinks. . . . The test is what men of common intelligence would understand would be words likely to cause an average addressee to fight. . . .'"

Chaplinsky 6

"Resort to epithets or personal abuse is not in any proper sense communication of information or opinion safeguarded by the constitution, and its punishment as a criminal act could raise no question under that instrument."

Chaplinsky   7   **Chaplinsky**   8

"These include the lewd and obscene, the profane, the libelous, and the insulting or "fighting" words—those which by their very utterance inflict injury or tend to incite an immediate breach of the peace. It has been well observed that such utterances are no essential part of any exposition of ideas, and are of such slight social value as a step to truth that any benefit that may be derived from them is clearly outweighed by the social interest in order and morality."

                                        —MURPHY

"Argument is unnecessary to demonstrate that Chaplinsky's words 'damned racketeer' and 'damned Fascist' are epithets likely to provoke the average person to retaliation, and therefore cause a breach of the peace."

Chaplinsky   9   **Chaplinsky**   10

"Allowing the broadest scope to the language and purpose of the Fourteenth Amendment, it is well understood that the right of free speech is not absolute at all times and under all circumstances."

"The refusal of the state court to admit evidence of provocation and evidence bearing on the truth or falsity of the utterances is open to no Constitutional objection."

CHARLES KOVACS, Appellant

v.

ALBERT COOPER, JR., Judge of the First District Police Court of Trenton

336 US 77   January 31, 1949

SUMMARY: Kovacs was found guilty of violating a city ordinance which forbade loudspeaking instruments which emit "loud and raucous noises." Kovacs was arrested for operating a sound truck near a municipal building at the time of a labor dispute.

Justices: FRED M. VINSON   FELIX FRANKFURTER   ROBERT H. JACKSON
               HUGO L. BLACK   WILLIAM O. DOUGLAS   WILEY RUTLEDGE
               STANLEY F. REED   FRANK MURPHY   HAROLD H. BURTON

Kovacs 1

"Opportunity to gain the public ears by objectionably amplified sound on the streets is no more assured by the right of free speech than is the unlimited opportunity to address gatherings on the streets."

Kovacs 2

"Of course, even the fundamental rights of the Bill of Rights are not absolute. The said case recognized that in this field by stating 'The hours and place of public discussion can by controlled.' . . . Hecklers may be expelled from assemblies and religious worship may not be disturbed by those anxious to preach a doctrine of atheism. The right to speak one's mind would often be an empty privilege in a place and at a time beyond the protecting hand of the guardians of public order."

Kovacs 3

"There are many people who have ideas that they wish to disseminate but who do not have enough money to own or control publishing plants, newspapers, radio, moving picture studios, or chains of show places. Yet everybody knows the vast reaches of these powerful channels of communication which from the very nature of our economic system must be under the control and guidance of comparatively few people. On the other hand, public speaking is done by many men of divergent minds with no centralized control over the ideas they entertain so as to limit the causes they espouse. . . . And it is an obvious fact that public speaking today without the sound amplifier is a wholly inadequate way to reach the people on a large scale."

—BLACK

Kovacs 4

"I am aware that the 'blare' of this new method of carrying ideas is susceptible of abuse and may under circumstances constitute an intolerable nuisance. But ordinances can be drawn which adequately protect a community from unreasonable use of public speaking devices without absolutely denying to the community's citizens all information that may be disseminated or received through this new avenue for trade in ideas. I would agree without reservation to the sentiment that (unrestrained use throughout a municipality of all sound amplifying devices would be intolerable). And of course cities may restrict or absolutely ban the use of amplifiers on busy streets in the business area. A city ordinance that reasonably restricts the volume of sound, or the hours during which an amplifier may be used, does not, in my mind, infringe the constitutionally protected area of speech."

Kovacs 5

"In Saia v. New York . . . we held that the ordinance was applied to keep a minister from using an amplifier while preaching in a public park. We held that the ordinance, aimed at the use of an amplifying device, invaded an area of free speech guaranteed to the people by the First and Fourteenth Amendments. The ordinance, so we decided, amounted to censorship in its baldest form."

Kovacs 6

"The question in this case is not whether appellant may Constitutionally be convicted of operating a sound truck that emits 'loud and raucous noises.' The appellant was neither charged with nor convicted of operating a sound truck that emitted 'loud and raucous noises.' The charge against him in the police court was that he violated the city ordinance 'in that he did, on South Stockton Street, in said City, play, use and operate a device known as a sound truck.' The record reflects not even a shadow of evidence to prove that the noise was either 'loud or raucous,' unless these words of the ordinance refer to any noise coming from an amplifier, whatever its volume or tone."

Kovacs   7   **Kovacs**   8

"The use of sound trucks and other peripatetic or stationary broadcasting devices for advertising, for religious exercises and for discussion of issues or controversies has brought forth numerous municipal ordinances. The avowed and obvious purpose of these ordinances is to prohibit or minimize such sounds on or near the streets since some citizens find these noises objectionable and to some degree an interference with the business or social activities in which they are engaged or the quiet that they would like to enjoy."

—REED

"The Court said in the Saia Case at 560, 561: 'The right to be heard is placed in the uncontrolled discretion of the Chief of Police. He stands athwart the channels of communication as an obstruction which can be removed only after criminal trial and conviction and lengthy appeal. A more effective previous restraint is difficult to imagine.' "This ordinance is not of that character."

Kovacs   9   **Kovacs**   10

"This objection centers around the use of the words 'loud and raucous.' While these are abstract words, they have through daily use acquired a content that conveys to any interested person a sufficiently accurate concept of what is forbidden."

"But that the First Amendment limited its protections of speech to the natural range of the human voice as it existed in 1790 would be for me like saying that the commerce power remains limited to navigation by sail and travel by the use of horses and oxen in accordance with the principal modes of carrying on commerce in 1789. The Constitution was not drawn with any such limited vision of time, space and mechanics."

IRVING FEINER, Petitioner

v.

PEOPLE OF THE STATE OF NEW YORK

340 US 315   January 15, 1951

SUMMARY: Irving Feiner, a young college student, made an inflammatory speech, using a loud-speaker, to a crowd of seventy-five to eighty Negroes and white people gathered on a Syracuse sidewalk. Feiner was protesting the cancellation of a permit granted by public officials for a speech in a public school on the subject of racial discrimination and civil liberties. The speech which was to be presented by a former Assistant Attorney General had been transferred to Hotel Syracuse, and Feiner was trying to publicize its new location. He made derogatory remarks about the American Legion, local political officials, called President Truman a "bum," and urged that Negroes rise up in arms and fight for equal rights. As the crowd became restless, a police officer thrice requested Feiner to stop speaking, and when he continued, he was arrested. Subsequently, he was convicted of disorderly conduct and sentenced to thirty days in jail.

Justices:	FRED M. VINSON	FELIX FRANKFURTER	HAROLD H. BURTON
	HUGO L. BLACK	WILLIAM O. DOUGLAS	TOM C. CLARK
	STANLEY F. REED	ROBERT H. JACKSON	SHERMON MINTON

Feiner   1   **Feiner**   2

"On the evening of March 8, 1949, petitioner Irving Feiner was addressing an open air meeting at the corner of South McBride and Harrison Streets in the City of Syracuse. At approximately 6:30 P.M., the police received a telephone complaint concerning the meeting, and two officers were detailed to investigate. . . . They found a crowd of about seventy-five to eighty people, both Negro and white, filling the sidewalk and spreading out into the street."

"The police officers made no effort to interfere with the petitioner's speech, but were first concerned with the effect of the crowd on both pedestrian and vehicular traffic. They observed the situation from the opposite side of the street, noting that some pedestrians were forced to walk in the street to avoid the crowd. Since traffic was passing at the same time, the officers attempted to get the people listening to the petitioner back on the sidewalk."

Feiner 3

Penal Code of New York, Section 722
"Any person who with intent to provoke a breach of the peace, or whereby a breach of the peace may be occasioned, commits any of the following acts shall be deemed to have committed the offense of disorderly conduct:

1. Uses offensive, disorderly, threatening, abusive or insulting language, conduct or behavior.
2. . . .
3. Congregates with others on a public street and refuses to move on when ordered by the police. . . ."

Feiner 4

"But after Feiner had been speaking 20 minutes, a man said to the police officers; 'If you don't get that son-of-a-bitch off, I will go over and get him off there myself.' It was then that the police ordered Feiner to stop speaking, when he refused, they arrested him."

Feiner 5

"No one would have the hardihood to suggest that the principle of freedom of speech sanctions incitement to riot or that religious liberty connotes the privilege to exhort others to physical attack upon those belonging to another sect."

—Vinson

Feiner 6

"The record before us convinces me that the petitioner, a college student, has been sentenced to the penitentiary for the unpopular views he expressed on matters of public interest while lawfully making a street-corner speech in Syracuse, New York."

Feiner 7

Feiner 8

". . . if, in the name of preserving order, they (the police) ever can interfere with a lawful public speaker they first must make all reasonable efforts to protect him."

"There was some pushing and shoving in the crowd and some angry muttering. That is the testimony of the police. But there were no fights and no 'disorder' even by the standards of the police. There was not even any heckling of the speaker."

—Douglas

Feiner 9

Feiner 10

"Public assemblies and public speech occupy an important role in American life. One high function of the police is to protect these lawful gatherings so that the speakers may exercise their constitutional rights."

"The petitioner was speaking in a 'loud, high pitched voice.' He gave the impression that he was endeavoring to arouse the Negro people against the whites, urging that they arise up in arms and fight for equal rights."

B. ELTON COX, Appellant

v.

STATE OF LOUISIANA

379 US 536   January 18, 1965

SUMMARY: A demonstration of 2,000 Negro college students was held at the state capitol building and on a sidewalk 101 feet from the Baton Rouge Courthouse where 23 fellow students were jailed by previous arrests for picketing segregated lunch counters. The Reverend Mr. B. Elton Cox, a Field Secretary of CORE, was arrested at the demonstration because the demonstrators failed to disperse after a police order was given indicating that they had exceeded their time for demonstrating.

Justices:	EARL WARREN	TOM C. CLARK	POTTER STEWART
	HUGO L. BLACK	JOHN M. HARLAN	BYRON R. WHITE
	WILLIAM O. DOUGLAS	WILLIAM J. BRENNAN, JR.	ARTHUR J. GOLDBERG

Cox 1

"There was ample evidence for the jury to have found the following to be the facts: On December 14, 1961, 23 persons were arrested and put in jail on a charge of illegal picketing. That night appellant Cox and others made plans to carry on a 'demonstration,' that is a parade and march, through parts of Baton Rouge, ending at the courthouse. Their purpose was to 'protest' against what they called the 'illegal arrest' of the 23 picketers. They neither sought nor obtained any permit for such use of the streets. The next morning the plan was carried out."

Cox 2

"Some 2,000 protestors marched to a point 101 feet across from the courthouse which also contained the jail. State and County police officers, for reasons as to which there was a conflict in the evidence from which different inferences could be drawn, agreed that the picketers might stay there for a few minutes. The group sang songs along with the prisoners in the jail and did other things set out in the Court's opinion. Later state and county officials told Cox, the group's leader, that the crowd had to 'move on.' Cox told his followers to stay where they were and they did. Officers then used tear gas and the picketers ran away. Cox was later arrested."

Cox   **3**

"Cox testified that they gave him permission to conduct the demonstration on the far side of the street. This testimony is not only uncontradicted but is corroborated by the State's witnesses who were present."

Cox   **4**

"One would not be justified in ignoring the familiar red light because this was thought to be a means of social protest. Nor could one, contrary to traffic regulations, insist upon a street meeting in the middle of Times Square at the rush hour as a form of freedom of speech or assembly. Government authorities have the duty and responsibility to keep their streets open and available for movement. A group of demonstrators could not insist upon the right to cordon off a street, or entrance to a public or private building, and allow no one to pass who did not agree to listen to their exhortations."

Cox   **5**

"It is clear from the record, however, that Cox and the demonstrators did not then and there break up the demonstration. Two of the Sheriff's deputies immediately started across the street and told the group, 'You have heard what the Sheriff said, now, do what he said.' A state witness testified that they put their hands on the shoulders of some of the students 'as though to shove them away.'

"Almost immediately thereafter—within a time estimated variously from two to five minutes —one of the policemen exploded a tear gas shell at the crowd. This was followed by several other shells. The demonstrators quickly dispersed, running back towards the State Capitol and the downtown area; Cox tried to calm them as they ran and was himself one of the last to leave."

—GOLDBERG

Cox   **6**

"The First and Fourteenth Amendments, I think, take away from government, state and federal power to restrict freedom of speech, press, and assembly *where people have a right to be for such purposes.* This does not mean, however, that these amendments also grant a constitutional right to engage in the conduct of picketing or patrolling, whether on publicly owned streets or on privately owned property."

—BLACK

Cox   **7**   **Cox**   **8**

"The students were then directed by Cox to the west sidewalk, across the street from the courthouse, 101 feet from its steps. They were lined on this sidewalk about five deep and spread almost the entire block. The group did not obstruct the street. It was close to noon and, being lunch time, a small crowd of 100 to 300 curious white people, mostly courthouse personnel, gathered on the east sidewalk and courthouse steps, about 100 feet from the demonstrators. Seventy-five to eighty policemen and members of the Sheriff's staff, as well as members of the fire department and fire truck, were stationed in the street between the two groups. Rain fell throughout the demonstration."

"On the other hand, I have no doubt that the State has power to protect judges, jurors, witnesses, and court officers from intimidation by crowds which seek to influence them by picketing, patrolling, or parading in or near the courthouses in which they do their business or the homes in which they live, and I therefore believe that the Louisiana statute which protects the administration of justice forbidding such interference is constitutional, both as written and as applied. Since I believe that the evidence showed practically without dispute that appellant violated this statute I think this conviction should be affirmed."

Cox   **9**   **Cox**   **10**

"Several of the students took from beneath their coats picket signs similar to those which had been used the day before. These signs bore legends such as 'Don't buy discrimination for Christmas,' 'Sacrifice for Christ, don't buy,' and named stores which were proclaimed 'unfair.' They sang 'God Bless America,' pledged allegiance to the flag, prayed briefly, and sang one or two hymns, including 'We shall Overcome.' The 23 students, who were locked in jail cells in the courthouse building out of sight of the demonstrators, responded by themselves singing; this in turn was greeted by cheers and applause by the demonstrators."

"Cox then said: 'All right. It's lunch time. Let's go eat. There are twelve stores we are protesting. A number of these stores have twenty counters; they accept your money from nineteen. They won't accept it from the twentieth counter. This is an act of discrimination. These stores are open to the public. You are members of the public. We pay taxes to the State.'

"In apparent reaction to these last remarks, there was what state witnesses described as 'muttering' and grumbling by the white onlookers.

"The Sheriff, deeming, as he testified, Cox's appeal to the students to sit in at the lunch counters to be 'inflammatory,' then took a power microphone and said, 'Now you have been allowed to demonstrate. Up until now your demonstration has been more or less peaceful, but what you are doing now is a direct violation of the peace, and it has got to be broken up immediately.'"

HARRIET LOUISE ADDERLEY et al., Petitioners

v.

STATE OF FLORIDA

385 US 39   November 14, 1966

SUMMARY: Thirty-two Negro students from Florida A&M University in Talahassee were convicted for trespassing with a malicious and mischievous intent upon the premises of the county jail. The defendants, along with many other students, were demonstrating at the jail to protest previous arrests of other students trying to integrate a public theater. The students sang "freedom" songs outside the jail but were not accused of disorderly conduct other than refusing to disperse from jail premises upon the repeated requests of the sheriff.

Justices:	EARL WARREN	TOM C. CLARK	POTTER STEWART
	HUGO L. BLACK	JOHN M. HARLAN	BYRON R. WHITE
	WILLIAM O. DOUGLAS	WILLIAM J. BRENNAN, JR.	ABE FORTAS

Adderley   **1**

"Today a trespassing law is used to penalize people for exercising a constitutional right. Tomorrow a disorderly conduct statute, a breech-of-peace statute, a vagrancy statute will be put to the same end. It is said that the sheriff did not make the arrests because of the views which petitioners espoused. That excuse is usually given, as we know from many cases involving arrests of minority groups, for breeches of the peace, unlawful assemblies, and parading without a permit. . . . by allowing these orderly and civilized protests against injustice to be suppressed, we only increase the forces of frustration which the conditions of second-class citizenship are generating amongst us."

—DOUGLAS

Adderley   **2**

"There was no violence; no threat of violence; no attempted jail break; no storming of a prison; no plan or plot to do anything but protest. . . . Indeed they moved back from the entrance when instructed. There was no shoving or pushing, no disorder or threat of riot. It is said that some of the group blocked part of the driveway leading to the jail entrance. . . . Further it is undisputed that the entrance to the jail was not blocked. And whenever the students were requested to move they did so. If there was congestion, the solution was a further request to move to lawns or parking areas, not complete ejection and arrest."

Adderley 3

"The constitutional guarantee of liberty implies the existence of an organized society maintaining public order, without which liberty itself would be lost in excuses of anarchy. . . . A group of demonstrators could not insist upon the right to cordon off a street or entrance to a public or private building and allow no one to pass who did not agree to listen to their exhortations."

Adderley 4

"The U. S. Constitution does not forbid a State to control the use of its own property for its own lawful nondiscriminatory purpose."

Adderley 5

"The State, no less than a private owner of property, has power to preserve the property under its control for the use to which it is lawfully dedicated."

Adderley 6

"The record reveals that he objected only to their presence on that part of the jail grounds preserved for jail uses. . . . Nothing in the Constitution of the U.S. prevents Florida from even-handed enforcement of its general trespass statute against those refusing to obey the sheriff's order to remove themselves from what amounted to the curtilage of the jail-house."

—BLACK

Adderley 7

"The fact that no one gave a formal speech, that no elaborate handbills were distributed, and that the group was not laden with signs would seem immaterial. Such methods are not for the sine qua non of petitioning for the redress of grievances. The group did sing 'freedom' songs. And history shows that a song can be a powerful tool of protest."

Adderley 8

"The rights of free speech and assembly, while fundamental in our democratic society, still do not mean that everyone with opinions or beliefs may address a group at any public place and at any time."

Adderley 9

"We do violence to the First Amendment when we permit this 'petition for redress of grievances' to be turned into a trespass action. It does not help to analogize this problem to the problem of picketing. Picketing is a form of protest usually directed against private interests."

Adderley 10

"The jailhouse, like an executive mansion, a legislative chamber, a courthouse, or the statehouse itself (Edwards v. S. Carolina, Supra) is one of the seats of government whether it be the Tower of London, the Bastille, or a small county jail. And when it houses political prisoners or those whom many think are unjustly held, it is an obvious center for protest."

WYATT TEE WALKER et al., Petitioners

v.

CITY OF BIRMINGHAM

388 US 307   January 27, 1967

SUMMARY: During the spring of 1963, sit-ins, kneel-ins and parades were conducted by the Negro community to protest discrimination. City officials secured affidavits stating that the demonstrators had trespassed upon private property, unlawfully picketed private places of business, congregated in mobs, and that this had caused undue burden and strain upon the manpower of the Police Department. The Circuit Court of Jefferson County, Alabama, granted a temporary injunction enjoining the leaders of the civil rights demonstrations from encouraging mass street parades without a permit as required by law in a city ordinance. The rights' leaders had been denied permits, and after the injunction was issued on Wednesday, April 10, 1963, Easter Week, no further move was made to request that the injunction be dissolved, but rather, marches were held on Good Friday and Easter. In the days which followed, tension and hostility focused the attention of the nation upon the climate of Birmingham.

Justices:	EARL WARREN	TOM C. CLARK	POTTER STEWART
	HUGO L. BLACK	JOHN M. HARLAN	BYRON R. WHITE
	WILLIAM O. DOUGLAS	WILLIAM J. BRENNAN, JR.	ABE FORTAS

Walker   **1**

"... Kasper arrived from somewhere in the East and organized a campaign to 'run the Negroes out of the school.' The federal court issued an ex parte restraining order enjoining Kasper from interfering with desegregation. Relying on the First Amendment, Kasper harangued the crowd 'to the effect that although he had been served with the restraining order, it did not mean anything. ...' His conviction for criminal contempt was affirmed by the Court of Appeals for the Sixth Circuit. That court concluded that 'an injunction order issued by a court must be obeyed' whatever its seeming invalidity. ..."

Walker   **2**

"Picketing and parading are methods of expression protected by the First Amendment against both state and federal abridgment. Edwards v. South Carolina, Cox v. Louisiana. Since they involve more than speech itself and implicate street traffic, the accommodations of the public and the like, they may be regulated as to the times and places of the demonstrations. ... But a state cannot deny the right to use streets and parks or other public grounds for the purpose of petitioning for the redress of grievances."

Walker   **3**   **Walker**   **4**

"An ordinance—unconstitutional on its face or patently unconstitutional as applied—is not made sacred by an unconstitutional injunction that enforces it. It can and should be flouted in the manner of the ordinance itself."

"The evidence shows that a permit was applied for . . . Commissioner Conner replied, 'No, you will not get a permit in Birmingham, Alabama, to picket. I will picket you over to City Jail.'"

Walker   **5**   **Walker**   **6**

" 'It is for the court . . . to determine the question of the validity of the law, and until its decision is reversed for error by orderly review, either by itself or by a higher court, its orders based upon its decisions are to be respected, and disobedience of them is contempt of its lawful authority, to be punished.'"

—STEWART

". . . where a permit has been arbitrarily denied, one need not pursue the long and expensive route to this court to obtain a remedy.

". . . For if a person must pursue his judicial remedy before he may speak, parade or assemble, the occasion when protest is desired or needed will have become history and later speech, parade or assembly will be futile or pointless."

Walker 7

". . . in the fair administration of justice no man can be judge in his own case, however exalted his station, however righteous his motives, and irrespective of his race, color, politics, or religion."

Walker 8

"The ex parte temporary injunction has a long and odious history in this country, and its susceptibility to misuse is all too apparent from the facts of the case. As a weapon against strikes, it proved so effective in the hands of judges friendly to employers that congress was forced to take the drastic step of removing from federal district courts the jurisdiction to issue injunctions in labor disputes."

—WARREN

Walker 9

"The breadth and vagueness of the injunction itself would also be subject to substantial constitutional question. But the way to raise that question was to apply to the Alabama Courts to have the injunction modified or dissolved. The injunction in all events clearly prohibited mass parading without a permit, and the evidence shows that the petitioners fully understood that prohibition when they violated it."

Walker 10

"We have consistently recognized the strong interest of state and local governments in regulating the use of their streets and other public places."

JOHN EARL CAMERON et al., Appellants

v.

PAUL JOHNSON, etc., et al.
390 US 611   April 22, 1968

SUMMARY: A large rally to increase voter registration of Negroes was held at the courthouse on January 22, 1964. Thereafter, from January 23 until May 18, 1964, Negroes maintained a picket line every day except Sundays outside the County Courthouse at Hattiesburg, Mississippi. On April 8, the Governor signed an Anti-Picketing Law. Ignoring warnings to disperse and arrests of pickets, the picketing continued until May 18 when nine more Negroes were arrested. The Appellants sought a permanent injunction against the enforcement of the Anti-Picketing statute.

Justices:	EARL WARREN	JOHN M. HARLAN	BYRON R. WHITE
	HUGO L. BLACK	POTTER STEWART	ABE FORTAS
	WILLIAM O. DOUGLAS	WILLIAM J. BRENNAN, JR.	THURGOOD MARSHALL

Cameron   1   **Cameron**   2

"The statute is therefore 'a valid law dealing with conduct subject to regulation so as to vindicate important interests of society and . . . the fact that free speech is intermingled with such conduct does not bring it within constitutional protection.' Cox v. Louisiana. . . ."

"But 'picketing and parading [are] subject to regulation even though intertwined with expression and association. Cox v. Louisiana . . . and this statute does not prohibit picketing so intertwined unless engaged in a manner which obstructs or unreasonably interferes with ingress or egress to or from the courthouse. Prohibition of conduct which has this effect does not abridge constitutional liberty' since such activity bears no necessary relationship to the freedom to . . . distribute information or opinion."

Cameron   **3**   **Cameron**   **4**

"Shortly after the first day of picketing, the sheriff marked out a 'march route.' The pickets thereafter confined themselves to this route. They were allowed to continue picketing unmolested. The march route never took the pickets directly in front of any entrance to the courthouse. The picketing, by all accounts, was peaceful without incident. The pickets at first sang, chanted, preached, and prayed, but within a few days and beginning well before the arrests, they confined themselves to a slow, quiet walk. This continued throughout the relevant dates.

"The evidence in this record that the picketing interfered with or even inconvenienced pedestrians is negligible."

"The arrests and their sequence demonstrate that the State was not here engaged in policing access to the courthouse or even freedom of the sidewalks, but in a deliberate plan to put an end to the voting-rights demonstration."

Cameron   **5**   **Cameron**   **6**

"I agree that the statute in question is not 'unconstitutional on its face.' But that conclusion is not the end of the matter. Dombrowski stands for the proposition that 'the abstention doctrine . . . is inappropriate for cases . . . where . . . statutes are justifiably attacked on their face as abridging free expression, *or as applied for the purpose of discouraging protected activities.'*"

—FORTAS

"Appellants were arrested and prosecuted 'without any hope of ultimate success.' There is no evidence that their activities 'obstructed . . . or unreasonably interfered with ingress or egress to and from any . . . courthouse. . . .'"

Cameron 7

Cameron 8

"Federal courts are available to enjoin the invocation of state criminal process when that process is abusively invoked 'without any hope of ultimate success, but only to discourage' the assertion of constitutionally protected rights."

"The second prong of appellants' argument is that the statute, even assuming that it is 'lacking neither clarity nor precision, is void for overbreadth,' that is, that it offends the constitutional principle that 'a governmental purpose to control or prevent activities constitutionally subject to state regulation may not be achieved by means which sweep unnecessarily broadly and thereby invade the area of protected freedoms'. . . ."

Cameron 9

Cameron 10

"It is a 'precise and narrowly drawn regulatory statute evincing a legislative judgment that certain specific conduct be . . . prescribed.' Edwards v. South Carolina."

"The terms 'obstruct' and 'unreasonably to interfere' plainly require no 'guess[ing] at [their] meaning.' Appellants focus on the word 'unreasonably.' It is a widely used and well understood word and clearly so when juxtaposed with 'obstruct' and 'interfere.'"

—Brennan

AMALGAMATED FOOD EMPLOYEES UNION LOCAL 590 et al., Petitioners

v.

LOGAN VALLEY PLAZA, Inc., et al.

391 US 308   May 20, 1968

SUMMARY: Union members of a competitor of a supermarket in Logan Valley Plaza picketed the Logan Valley nonunion supermarket. The pickets varied between four and thirteen and were peaceful. The picketing was conducted in the parcel pickup area and the adjacent shopping center parking lot. A court of Common Pleas of Blair County, Pennsylvania, ordered an injunction restricting the union to picketing along berms beside the public roads outside the shopping center.

Justices:	EARL WARREN	JOHN M. HARLAN	BYRON R. WHITE
	HUGO L. BLACK	WILLIAM J. BRENNAN, JR.	ABE FORTAS
	WILLIAM O. DOUGLAS	POTTER STEWART	THURGOOD MARSHALL

Logan Valley   1

"It is said that the picketers may be banished to the publicly owned berms, several hundred feet from the target of their criticism. But that is to make "private property" a sanctuary from which some members of the public may be excluded merely because of the ideas they espouse."

Logan Valley   2

"Logan Valley Plaza is not a town but only a collection of stores. In no sense are any parts of the shopping center dedicated to the public for general purposes or the occupants of the Plaza exercising official powers."

"The state may not delegate the power, through the use of its trespass laws, wholly to exclude those members of the public wishing to exercise their First Amendment rights on the premises in a manner and for a purpose generally consonant with the use to which the property is actually put."

—MARSHALL

"Streets, sidewalks, parks and other similar public places are so historically associated with the exercise of First Amendment rights that access to them for the purpose of exercising such rights cannot constitutionally be denied broadly and absolutely."

"I would go further, however, and hold that the entire injunction is valid. With the exception of the Weis property mentioned above, the land on which this shopping center (composed of only two stores at the time of trial and approximately 17 now) is located is owned by respondent Logan Valley Plaza, Inc. Logan has improved its property by putting shops and parking spaces thereon for the use of business customers. Now petitioners contend that they can come onto Logan property for the purpose of picketing and refuse to leave when asked, and that Logan cannot use trespass laws to keep them out."

"The mere fact that speech is accompanied by conduct does not mean that the speech can be suppressed under the guise of prohibiting the conduct."

"Petitioners cannot under the guise of exercising First Amendment rights, trespass on respondent Weis' private property for the purpose of picketing. It would be just as sensible for this court to allow the pickets to stand on the check-out counters, thus interfering with customers who wish to pay for their goods, as to approve of picketing in the pick-up zone which interferes with customers' loading of their cars."

—BLACK

"Picketing is free speech plus, the plus being physical activity that may implicate traffic and related matters. Hence the latter aspects of picketing may be regulated."

"The First Amendment provides that no person shall be deprived of life, liberty or property, without due process of law; nor shall private property be taken for public use without just compensation. This means to me that there is no right to picket on the private premises of another to try to convert the owner or others to the views of the pickets."

"It has been estimated that by the end of 1966 there were between 10,000 and 11,000 shopping centers in the U.S. and Canada, accounting for approximately 37% of the total retail sales in those two countries. These figures illustrate the substantial consequences for workers seeking to challenge substandard working conditions, consumers protesting shoddy or overpriced merchandise, and minority groups seeking nondiscriminatory hiring policies that a contrary decision here would have."

JOSEPH CARROLL et al., Petitioner

v.

PRESIDENT AND COMMISSIONERS OF PRINCESS ANNE et al.

393 US 175   November 19, 1968

SUMMARY: The National States Rights Party, a "white supremacist" organization, on July 6, 1966, held a rally near the Courthouse of Princess Anne, Maryland. The speeches attacked and insulted Negroes and Jews and were amplified so that they could be heard for several blocks. About sixty state policemen were brought in because of the tenseness of the crowd which grew to number about 125, one-fourth of which were Negroes. The Princess Anne Commissioners obtained a ten-day restraining order to prevent another rally announced for the following night. The proceedings were ex parte, no notice being given to the States Rights Party to appear. The August 7 rally was not held, and the injunction was extended for ten months. At the injunctive proceedings, witnesses testified as to the tense atmosphere, and a tape recording of the August 6 rally was played.

Justices:	EARL WARREN	JOHN M. HARLAN	BYRON R. WHITE
	HUGO L. BLACK	WILLIAM J. BRENNAN, JR.	ABE FORTAS
	WILLIAM O. DOUGLAS	POTTER STEWART	THURGOOD MARSHALL

Carroll   1

"An order issued in the area of First Amendment rights must be couched in the narrowest terms that will accomplish the pinpointed objective permitted by Constitutional mandate and the essential need of the public order."

Carroll   2

"As Mr. Justice Harlan, dissenting in A Quantity of Books v. Kansas, pointed out, speaking of political and social expression: 'It is vital to the operation of democratic government that the citizens have facts and ideas on important issues before them. A delay of even a day or two may be of crucial importance in some instances. On the other hand, the subject of sex is of constant but rarely particular topical interest. 378 US, at 224, 12 L Ed 2d at 821.'"

—FORTAS

Carroll   3

"This conclusion—that the question is not moot and ought to be adjudicated by this Court—is particularly appropriate in view of this Court's decision in Walker v. Birmingham, 388 US 307. . . . In that case, the Court held that demonstrators who had proceeded with their protest march in face of the prohibition of an injunctive order against such a march, could not defend contempt charges by asserting the unconstitutionality of the injunction. The proper procedure, it was held, was to seek judicial review of the injunction and not to disobey it, no matter how well-founded their doubts might be as to its validity. Petitioners have here pursued the course indicated by Walker, and in view of the continuing vitality of petitioner's grievance we cannot say their case is moot."

Carroll   4

"The issuance of an injunction which aborts a scheduled rally or public meeting, even if the restraint is of short duration, is a matter of importance and consequence in view of the First Amendment's imperative."

Carroll   5

"We need not decide the thorny problem of whether, on the facts of this case, an injunction against the announced rally could be justified. The 10-day order here must be set aside because of a basic infirmity in the procedure by which it was obtained. It was issued ex parte, without any effort, however informal, to invite or permit their participation in the proceedings."

—Fortas

Carroll   6

"Petitioners recite that they were denied the right to hold a rally in Princess Anne on July 17, 1967, and that the letter of rejection relied upon the Court of Appeals decision. They acknowledge that on July 25 they were authorized to hold rallies in Princess Anne on July 28, 29, and 30, 1967; but they appear to complain that the permit stipulated that the sound should not be amplified for more than 250 feet, and that 'you will not be permitted to use racial epithets or to make slanderous remarks about the members of any race or ethnic group.'"

Carroll 7

Carroll 8

"Finally, respondents urge that the failure to give notice and an opportunity for hearing should not be considered to invalidate the order because, under Maryland procedure, petitioners might have obtained a hearing on not more than two days' notice."

"Petitioner Norton said, 'I want you to . . . be back here at the same place tomorrow night, bring every friend you have. . . . We're going to take it easy tonight . . .' and 'You white folks bring your friends, come back tomorrow night. . . . Come on back tomorrow night, let's raise a little bit of hell for the white race.' "

Carroll 9

Carroll 10

"In Cantwell v. Connecticut, 310 US 296, . . . this Court said that 'No one would have the hardihood to suggest that the principle of freedom of speech sanctions incitement to riot.' "

"The Court has emphasized that '[a] system of prior restraints comes to this Court bearing a heavy presumption against its constitutional validity.' Bantam Books v. Sullivan, 372 US 58, . . . (1963); Freedman v. Maryland, 380 US 51, . . . 1965."

CLARENCE BRANDENBURG, Appellant

v.

STATE OF OHIO

395 US 444   June 9, 1969

SUMMARY: Brandenburg, a leader of the Ku Klux Klan, spoke at a rally at which a wooden cross was burned, and some of the persons present carried firearms. His speech included such statements as "Bury the niggers," and "send the Jews back to Israel." Brandenburg was convicted under the Ohio Criminal Syndicalism statute for "advocating . . . the duty, necessity, or propriety of crime, sabotage, violence, or unlawful methods of terrorism as a means of accomplishing industrial or political reform," and for assembling a group to advocate such doctrines.

Justices:	EARL WARREN	JOHN M. HARLAN	BYRON R. WHITE
	HUGO L. BLACK	WILLIAM J. BRENNAN, JR.	THURGOOD MARSHALL
	WILLIAM O. DOUGLAS	POTTER STEWART	

Brandenburg 1

"The lines drawn by the Court between the criminal act of being an 'active' Communist and the innocent act of being a nominal or inactive Communist mark the difference only between deep and abiding belief and casual or uncertain belief. But I think that all matters of belief are beyond the reach of subpoenas or the probings of investigators. That is why the invasions of privacy made by investigating committees were notoriously unconstitutional. That is the deep-seated fault in the infamous loyalty-security hearings which, since 1947 when President Truman launched them, have processed 20,000,000 men and women. Those hearings were primarily concerned with one's thoughts, ideas, beliefs, and convictions. They were the most blatant violations of the First Amendment we have ever known."

—DOUGLAS

Brandenburg 2

"The line between what is permissible and not subject to control and what may be made impermissible and subject to regulation is the line between ideas and overt acts.

"The example usually given by those who would punish speech is the case of one who falsely shouts fire in a crowded theatre.

"This is, however, a classic case where speech is brigaded with action. See Speiser v. Randall, 357 US 513, 536-537, 2 L Ed 2d 1460, 1478, 1479, 78 S Ct 1332 (Douglas, J., concurring). They are indeed inseparable and a prosecution can be launched for the overt acts actually caused."

Brandenburg 3

"The case was Schenck v. United States, 249 US 47, 52, 63 L Ed 470, 473, 39 S Ct 247, where the defendant was charged with attempts to cause insubordination in the military and obstruction of enlistment. The pamphlets that were distributed urged resistance to the draft, denounced conscription, and impugned the motives of those backing the war effort. The First Amendment was tendered as a defense. Mr. Justice Holmes in rejecting that defense said:

" 'The question in every case is whether the words used are used in such circumstances and are of such a nature as to create a clear and present danger that they will bring about the substantive evils that Congress has a right to prevent. It is a question of proximity and degree.' "

Brandenburg 4

"Mr. Justice Holmes, though never formally abandoning the 'clear and present danger' test, moved closer to the First Amendment ideal when he said in dissent in Gitlow v. New York, 268 US 652, 673, 69 L Ed 1138, 1148, 45 S Ct 625:

" 'Every idea is an incitement. It offers itself for belief and if believed it is acted on unless some other belief outweighs it or some failure of energy stifles the movement at its birth. The only difference between the expression of an opinion and an incitement in the narrower sense is the speaker's enthusiasm for the result.' "

Brandenburg 5

"As we said in Noto v. United States, 367 US 290, 297-298, 6 L Ed 2d 836, 841, 81 S Ct 1517 (1961), 'the mere abstract teaching . . . of the moral propriety or even moral necessity for a resort to force and violence, is not the same as preparing a group for violent action and steeling it to such action.' "

Brandenburg 6

"The prosecution's case rested on the films and on testimony identifying the appellant as the person who communicated with the reporter and who spoke at the rally. The State also introduced into evidence several articles appearing in the film, including a pistol, a rifle, a shotgun, ammunition, a Bible, and a red hood worn by the speaker in the films. One film showed 12 hooded figures, some of whom carried firearms. They were gathered around a large wooden cross, which they burned."

Brandenburg 7

"Measured by this test, Ohio's Criminal Syndicalism Act cannot be sustained. The Act punishes persons who 'advocate or teach the duty, necessity, or propriety' of violence 'as a means of accomplishing industrial or political reform'; or who publish or circulate or display any book or paper containing such advocacy; or who 'justify' the commission of violent acts 'with intent to exemplify, spread or advocate the propriety of the doctrines of criminal syndicalism'; or who 'voluntarily assemble' with a group formed 'to teach or advocate the doctrines of criminal syndicalism.'"

Brandenburg 8

"Another scene on the same film showed the appellant, in Klan regalia, making a speech. The speech, in full, was as follows: 'This is an organizers' meeting. We have had quite a few members here today which are——we have hundreds, hundreds of members throughout the State of Ohio. I can quote from a newspaper clipping from the Columbus, Ohio, Dispatch, five weeks ago Sunday morning. The Klan has more members in the State of Ohio than does any other organization. We're not a revengent organization, but if our President, our Congress, our Supreme Court, continues to suppress the white, Caucasian race, it's possible that there might have to be some revenge taken.

"'We are marching on Congress July the Fourth, four hundred thousand strong. From there we are dividing into two groups, one group to march on St. Augustine, Florida, the other group to march into Mississippi. Thank you.'"

Brandenburg 9

"The Ohio Criminal Syndicalism Statute was enacted in 1919. From 1917 to 1920, identical or quite similar laws were adopted by 20 States and two territories. E. Dowell, A History of Criminal Syndicalism Legislation in the United States 21 (1939). In 1927, this Court sustained the constitutionality of California's Criminal Syndicalism Act, Cal Penal Code sec. 11400-11402, the text of which is quite similar to that of the laws of Ohio. Whitney v. California, 274 US 357, 71 L Ed 1095, 47 S Ct 641 (1927). The Court upheld the statute on the ground that, without more, 'advocating' violent means to effect political and economic change involves such danger to the security of the State that the State may outlaw it. Cf. Fiske v. Kansas, 274 US 380, 71 L Ed 1108, 47 S Ct 655 (1927). But Whitney has been thoroughly discredited by later decisions."

—Per Curiam

Brandenburg 10

"The significant portions that could be understood were:
'How far is the nigger going to—yeah.'
'This is what we are going to do to the niggers.'
'A dirty nigger.'
'Send the Jews back to Israel.'
'Let's give them back to the dark garden.'
'Save America.'
'Let's go back to constitutional betterment.'
'Bury the niggers.'
'We intend to do our part.'
'Give us our state rights.'
'Freedom for the whites.'
'Nigger will have to fight for every inch he gets from now on.'"

STATE OF ILLINOIS, Petitioner

v.

WILLIAM ALLEN

397 US 337   March 31, 1970

SUMMARY: During a hearing and jury trial in 1950 for robbery, the trial judge, after repeated outbursts by William Allen who was on trial, removed him from the courtroom. Allen had insisted upon being his own attorney, to which the judge consented, but he asked a court-appointed attorney to "sit in and protect the record." At one point Allen shouted to the judge: "When I go out for lunchtime, you're going to be a corpse here," and he tore the file which his attorney had and threw the paper on the floor. Allen was removed from the courtroom and convicted of robbery.

Justices:	WARREN E. BURGER	JOHN M. HARLAN	BYRON R. WHITE
	HUGO L. BLACK	WILLIAM J. BRENNAN, JR.	THURGOOD MARSHALL
	WILLIAM O. DOUGLAS	POTTER STEWART	

Allen   1

"After his indictment and during the pretrial stage, the petitioner [Allen] refused court-appointed counsel and indicated to the trial court on several occasions that he wished to conduct his own defense. After considerable argument by the petitioner, the trial judge told him, 'I'll let you be your own lawyer, but I'll ask Mr. Kelly [court-appointed counsel] [to] sit in and protect the record for you, insofar as possible.' "

Allen   2

"The Court of Appeals felt that the defendant's Sixth Amendment right to be present at his own trial was so 'absolute' that, no matter how unruly or disruptive the defendant's conduct might be, he could never be held to have lost that right so long as he continued to insist upon it, as Allen clearly did. Therefore the Court of Appeals concluded that a trial judge could never expel a defendant from his own trial and that the judge's ultimate remedy when faced with an obstreperous defendant like Allen who determines to make his trial impossible is to bind and gag him."

Allen   3

"Another aspect of the contempt remedy is the judge's power, when exercised consistently with state and federal law, to imprison an unruly defendant such as Allen for civil contempt and discontinue the trial until such time as the defendant promises to behave himself. This procedure is consistent with the defendant's right to be present at trial, and yet it avoids the serious shortcomings of the use of shackles and gags. It must be recognized, however, that a defendant might conceivably, as a matter of calculated strategy, elect to spend a prolonged period in confinement for contempt in the hope that adverse witnesses might be unavailable after a lapse of time. A court must guard against allowing a defendant to profit from his own wrong in this way."

Allen   4

"There is more than an intimation in the present record that the defendant was a mental case. The passage of time since 1957, the date of the trial, makes it, however, impossible to determine what the mental condition of the defendant was at that time. The fact that a defendant has been found to understand 'the nature and object of the proceedings against him' and thus competent to stand trial does not answer the difficult questions as to what a trial judge should do with an otherwise mentally ill defendant who creates a courtroom disturbance. What a judge should do with a defendant whose courtroom antics may not be volitional is a perplexing problem which we should not reach except on a clear record."

Allen   5

"Radicals on the left historically have used those tactics to incite the extreme right with the calculated design of fostering a regime of repression from which the radicals on the left hope to emerge as the ultimate victor. The left in that role is the provocateur. The Constitution was not designed as an instrument for that form of rough-and-tumble contest. The social compact has room for tolerance, patience, and restraint, but not for sabotage and violence. Trials involving that spectacle strike at the very heart of constitutional government."

Allen   6

"The panel of judges who tried William Penn were sincere, law-and-order men of their day. Though Penn was acquitted by the jury, he was jailed by the court for his contemptuous conduct. Would we tolerate removal of a defendant from the courtroom during a trial because he was insisting on his constitutional rights, albeit vociferously, no matter how obnoxious his philosophy might have been to the bench that tried him? Would we uphold contempt in that situation?

"Problems of political indictments and of political judges raise profound questions going to the heart of the social compact. For that compact is two-sided: majorities undertake to press their grievances within limits of the Constitution and in accord with its procedures minorities agree to abide by constitutional procedures in resisting those claims."

"This defendant had no lawyer and refused one, though the trial judge properly insisted that a member of the bar be present to represent him. He tried to be his own lawyer and what transpired was pathetic, as well as disgusting and disgraceful.

"We should not reach the merits but should reverse the case for staleness of the record and affirm the denial of relief by the District Court. After all, behind the issuance of a writ of habeas corpus is the exercise of an informed discretion. The question, how to proceed in a criminal case against a defendant who is a mental case, should be resolved only on a full and adequate record."

—DOUGLAS

"It is not pleasant to hold that the respondent Allen was properly banished from the court for a part of his own trial. But our courts, palladiums of liberty as they are, cannot be treated disrespectfully with impunity. Nor can the accused be permitted by his disruptive conduct indefinitely to avoid being tried on the charges brought against him. It would degrade our country and our judicial system to permit our courts to be bullied, insulted, and humiliated and their orderly progress thwarted and obstructed by defendants brought before them charged with crimes."

"Trying a defendant for a crime while he sits bound and gagged before the judge and jury would to an extent comply with that part of the Sixth Amendment's purposes that accords the defendant an opportunity to confront the witnesses at the trial. But even to contemplate such a technique, much less see it, arouses a feeling that no person should be tried while shackled and gagged except as a last resort. Not only is it possible that the sight of shackles and gags might have a significant effect on the jury's feelings about the defendant, but the use of this technique is itself something of an affront to the very dignity and decorum of judicial proceedings that the judge is seeking to uphold."

"One of the most basic of the rights guaranteed by the Confrontation Clause is the accused's right to be present in the courtroom at every stage of his trial. Lewis v. United States, 146 US 370, 36 L Ed 1011, 13 S Ct 136 (1892). The question presented in this case is whether an accused can claim the benefit of this constitutional right to remain in the courtroom while at the same time he engages in speech and conduct which is so noisy, disorderly, and disruptive that it is exceedingly difficult or wholly impossible to carry on the trial."

QUESTIONS FOR DISCUSSION

1. Should a person have to get a permit to make a speech or a group to assemble in a public place?

2. What words, if any, should cause a man to be guilty of provoking another to fight?

3. Does a community have the right to prohibit sound trucks in certain neighborhoods?

4. Should the speaker and/or the crowd be arrested if an audience becomes hostile?

5. May a crowd assemble on courthouse or jail grounds to protest arrests of their number?

6. Do city and state officials have the right to stop a parade by an injunction?

7. What are the tolerable limits to picketing?

Conclusion

The Lessons from the Court
for the Classroom

Scott Chisholm, an instructor of English at Indiana State University, and a Canadian citizen residing permanently in the United States, on April 14, 1967, during a unit on symbolic language in an English composition class, burned a small American flag in response to a challenge by a student. In so doing he stated that "This is not to be misconstrued as an unpatriotic act, because I am not herein involved with abstract questions about the values of my government . . . . I am not attacking the principles for which it stands, nor am I making a political comment about democracy. I am burning a concrete object—a stick and a piece of cloth—not my country or its principles." Mr. Chisholm was immediately suspended and after hearings, his contract for the following year was rescinded. The American Association of University Professors placed Indiana State on the list of censured institutions in the Spring of 1970.

"Academic Freedom and Tenure Indiana State University," Report of Committee A, *AAUP Bulletin*, LVI (March 1970), pp. 52-61.

Every tribe and nation is indebted to its sages who have brought the cherished wisdom of the past to bear upon uncertainties and conflicts of the present. This is the mantle we have placed upon nine men who serve as the most distinguished court of our land. Before studying this text we may have been their critics without ever having examined one of their carefully prepared decisions. We may have doubted their wisdom after having hurriedly read a cursory editorial in the local newspaper. After participating in the simulation, we cannot treat their deliberation so lightly.

We have listened thoughtfully to their words as primitive children have sat at the feet of the wise men of their village. They have spoken to us about freedom to assemble, freedom of press, and freedom of speech. On that they have spoken often. They have deliberated at length on church and state, on race, on loyalty, on demonstration and discipline. On these they have debated at length and with passion. But what do the wise men have to say to the classroom, to the place where the youth lives most of the hours of his day for fifteen of his first twenty years?

The High Court has spoken often and eloquently about the classroom, that "cradle of democracy," and its policy-making interpretations are particularly important lessons for these troubled times. The hope of this text is that students might continue to study, converse, and debate the decisions of the High Court, particularly those which affect students. The purpose of this concluding section is to alert the student to those many Court decisions which speak to the schoolroom and to his freedoms of speech and press. In addition to those *Nine Men Plus* cases which especially speak to the classroom, a number of other opinions will be discussed. For example, a section has been included on those famous decisions which have affected the integration of schools, though not specifically in the free speech-free press area. It is not the intention of the writer to summarize all that has been said in the opinions included, but rather to focus our thinking upon the relationship of the Court's words to the territory of the classroom.

Consider for a moment, for instance, a Court decision which affects every child when he is admitted to his first year of school. At that time, if not before, he is persuaded or coerced to be vaccinated. The Court's opinion on vaccination traces the story of immunization from England in the early years of the nineteenth century to the many state statutes which made vaccination a condition for the right to enter or remain in public schools (*Jacobson* v. *Massachusetts* (1905)). The classroom which examines this case is not only introduced to an unusual story of medical history but to the social contract which was clearly a part of the 1780 Massachusetts Constitution—that government is instituted "for the common good, for the protection, safety, prosperity, and happiness of the people, and not for the profit, honor or private interest of any one man, family, or class of men."

The message of the classroom is more than achievement in the new math, science, or literature. The message is larger than course content. How a school functions, who gives orders and makes policies, may be the loudest message learned. There is a message in the process. It is a feeling for a way of life. Hopefully, it may be a feeling for the efficacy of the democratic process. It was Justice Frankfurter who said, "The history of American freedom is, in no small measure, the history of procedure." Thus we should be pleased, rather than alarmed, over the present concern for due process and students' rights. It is this tangible struggle to realize Constitutional freedoms in the school environment which may cultivate feelings about citizenship that are more than sentimental. Attention of young citizens to make democratic ideals realized in and about the classroom may do much to foster that "hard kind of patriotism" of which Adlai Stevenson spoke. What then are these high opinions which ought to be very much a part of the curriculum of the classroom? I have grouped the lessons taught by the Court under the five headings: religion, race, censorship, loyalty, demonstration and discipline.

Religion

Does a student have a right to silence? In 1925 the Court reasoned that parents who object to the teachings of the public school could send their children to a religious school (*Pierce* v. *Society of Sisters*), and in 1934 it held that a student at the University of California could not be excused for religious objections to courses in military training (*Hamilton* v. *University of California*). In the early forties the issue was God and the flag salute. Twelve-year-old Lillian Gobitis, and her ten-year-old brother William, were affiliated with the Jehovah's Witnesses sect. They had been reared to conscientiously believe that the gesture of saluting the flag was forbidden by the scripture, as was bowing before a graven image. But the school authorities ruled the children must pledge allegiance. Justice Frankfurter, in delivering the majority opinion of the Court (*Minersville School District* v. *Walter Gobitis* (1940)), recognized that mankind lives by symbols. He further reasoned that the morale and cohesive sentiment are intimately entwined with the patriotic gesture of the flag symbol. He spoke for the majority of the Court when he ruled in favor of "training children in the patriotic impulse." The world was at war and the social order depended upon it. Of course the totalitarian nations reasoned likewise.

Approximately three years after Gobitis, in an almost identical circumstance arising from the teaching of another Jehovah's Witnesses household, the compulsory flag salute of West Virginia was declared unconstitutional (*West Virginia* v. *Barnette* (1943)). The failure to salute, it was at this time argued, did not create a "clear and present danger." The right at least to silent conscientious objection in the classroom was then affirmed.

The flag and how it is handled, once again, is a live issue. A rash of state and national flag desecration statutes have come into being to punish those who would burn or spit upon the work of Betsy Ross. We are a very touchy people about our symbols, and we react with passion when anyone mistreats them.

In Cleveland, at Adelbert College of Western Reserve University, not long ago, Chris Wood was a starter on the basketball team. At one game in which he did not start he was seated on the bench and did not stand to face the flag during the singing of the national anthem. He argued he was consistent in that when he was standing, as he had been in previous games during the warm-up sessions, he remained standing when the national anthem was played, but that when he was seated upon such an occasion, he remained seated. "A flag is just a piece of cloth," he declared in a telephone conversation with this writer, and of late he didn't feel he could stand in honor of his country. Within minutes of his inaction, he was "kicked off" the team. Moreover, the college administration later supported the coach, and this occurred in the 1968-69 season. The right to conscientious silence has not yet been won in the school.

Should children be granted release time for religious instruction? Religious instruction in the public schools came before the Supreme Court in 1947 (*Illinois* v. *Board of Education*). Vashti McCollum, a parent of a child in the Champaign public schools, charged that the religious instruction in the classroom violated the First and Fourteenth Amendments. The practice she was opposed to was an arrangement by which Jewish, Protestant, and Catholic clergy were permitted to conduct weekly 30- to 45-minute doctrinal classes. Children who did not wish to participate were permitted to leave their classroom to go to another location for study during that period. In the majority opinion siding against "released time," the Court persuasively referred to Jefferson's intention to erect a "wall of separation between church and State" and to President Grant's pledge to "Encourage free schools and resolve that not one dollar appropriated for their support shall be appropriated to the support of sectarian school." In discussing early attempts of religious groups, which near the turn of the century tried to conduct after-school religious sessions and met with unpopular response, one justice wrote: "But children continue to be children; they wanted to play when school was out, particularly when other children were free to do so."

Are daily Bible readings in public schools unconstitutional? The decision against use of the public school period for religious instruction, however, apparently did not apply to religious exercises conducted by the teacher or student. The right to silence did not mollify the objection of two Unitarian families to daily religious exercises (*Abington Township* v. *Schempp* and *Murray* v. *Curlett* (1963)). The Schempps and Murrays, in separate actions, objected upon the basis of the Established Clause in the First Amendment. Mere excusal from the room, they reasoned, not only was psychologically and socially injurious to their children but also failed to void a statute which in effect established, by daily classroom, indoctrination in the Jewish-Christian religion. Incidentally, those who study the Schempp-Murray opinion will read about the history of disestablishmentarianism from the beginning in Virginia as compared to the "established church" in Massachusetts which continued well into the nineteenth century. Children or their parents who study the written opinions of the Court will be able to answer the $64,000 question: What is antidisestablishmentarianism?

Few other Supreme Court cases have involved religion and the schools. Each time prayer or Bible reading in the classroom has again come before the High Court, virtually the same decision has resulted. Many schools simply ignore the mandate of the Court. This kind of defiance of the judicial process in the classroom, strange as it may seem, may be observed to occur most often in the communities where Law and Order sloganizing is most common.

Should the state-operated buses and state-purchased textbooks be provided children who attend parochial schools? Of late there is reason to argue that the court has backslid from the Establishment Clause in its recent interpretations which have sided with the use of state-operated school buses and state-purchased school texts for students who attend parochial schools. For example, the New York book-lending program was held to be a benefit to all children and, therefore, did not violate the Establishment Clause (*Board of Education of Central School District No. 1* v. *Allen* (1968)).

Dare a teacher teach theories and information contrary to religious doctrines? The Epperson decision of 1968 was one of the few cases to directly deal with the subject matter in the school curriculum. By ruling that the state may not make illegal the teaching of evolution, the Court was saying that theories and facts contrary to religious doctrines may be taught. Justice Fortas sets forth the argument with candor,

> In the present case, there can be no doubt that Arkansas has sought to prevent its teachers from discussing the theory of evolution because it is contrary to the belief of some that the Book of Genesis must be the exclusive source of the doctrine as to the origin of man.

Studying the Epperson case brings to life once again the famous courtroom debates between William Jennings Bryan and Clarence Darrow and might prove particularly stimulating for students of biology as well as religion, law, and political history. The fact that Mrs. Epperson won the right to teach about evolution in her biology class in Little Rock, Arkansas, in 1968, forty-three years after John

Scopes in 1925 was convicted and lost his job for doing so, is dramatic evidence to the student that normal channels for change do not always work. Should teachers of biology in such states as Tennessee and Arkansas have withheld from their students knowledge of Darwinian theory for all these years or should they, like Thoreau, deplore those who "will wait, well disposed, for others to remedy the evil that they will no longer have to regret it"?

Race

How can separate and equal education for the races be unequal? As early as 1908 the Supreme Court heard a case considering a state's right to make integrated schooling unlawful. The Court ruled the State had such a privilege (*Berea College* v. *Commonwealth of Kentucky*). Little else needs to be said in this area than to point to the now famous 1954 *Brown* v. *Board of Education of Topeka* which overturned the separate but equal doctrine enunciated in *Plessy* v. *Ferguson* of 1896.

The individual who examines this famous opinion must then examine values which may be supported by the outdated assumption that physical things alone are what make people equal or unequal. The Court's opinion again and again affirms its belief in the primary role of the school in the life of our Nation:

> Today, education is perhaps the most important function of state and local governments. Compulsory school attendance laws and the great expenditures for education both demonstrate our recognition of the importance of education to our democratic society. It is required in the performance of our most basic public responsibilities, even service in the armed forces. It is the very foundation of good citizenship. Today it is a principal instrument in awakening the child to cultural values, in preparing him for later professional training, and in helping him to adjust normally to his environment. In these days, it is doubtful that any child may reasonably be expected to succeed in life if he is denied the opportunity of an education. Such an opportunity, where the state has undertaken to provide it, is a right which must be made available to all on equal terms.

The implementation of this ruling through the lower courts is no small lesson in government. And, today, in light of the despair of the Negro for equality and the rush to black separation, members of the Court such as Justice Black have expressed concern that "all due speed" has not been fast enough.

Censorship

Should we not protect our youth from immoral teachings? Court influence upon censorship in the classroom has been indirect. That is to say that most cases of censorship in the school have been decided before they have reached the High Court. The Koch case, for example, is one in which a professor lost in the lower courts and did not appeal beyond the state court. Leo Koch, an assistant professor of biology at the University of Illinois, a specialist in lichens, in 1960 was dismissed because of a letter printed in the student newspaper in which he expressed his liberal opinion concerning premarital sexual relations. Many such incidents involving teachers have provoked community uproar. A San Diego high school teacher, Geri Turner Davis, for instance, in 1965 was investigated by the State Board of Education after the community little theater production of the play she wrote, entitled "A Cat Called Jesus." The investigation resulting from this outside-of-school activity found Mrs. Davis to teach "no evil"; however, the controversy was long and personally difficult. A teacher of theater does not have to direct *Peter Pan* in the nude or do the *Beard* to bring the censor to the school!

Does a student have a right to read? Of course the court decisions concerning obscenity have indirectly governed what the student may see and read. Perhaps the most pervasive statute to be overturned was the Michigan law which made it a crime to disseminate any communication "tending to incite minors to violent or depraved or immoral acts" (*Butler* v. *Michigan* (1957)).

Two recent cases more specifically have spelled out limitations for minors. The Court upheld the conviction of Sam Ginsberg, proprietor of Sam's Stationery and Luncheonette on Long Island, for selling "girlie" magazines to a sixteen-year-old boy (*Ginsberg* v. *New York* (1968)). Could the school librarian or English teacher be arrested for permitting a student to read certain magazines?

School authorities usually are very cautious. *Playboy* magazine, in spite of its contributions by noted authors, for example, is not yet even available in most college libraries, nor is it listed in the standard guide to periodical literature. The Sam Ginsberg decision may be interpreted to prevent school libraries from housing certain periodicals, thus abridging the right to read.

In a companion case, the Court sided against the Dallas City Ordinance which attempted to classify films according to the age of those who may view them (*Interstate Circuit Inc.* v. *Dallas* (1968)). The ordinance was declared overbroad, but the majority opinion implied that a more narrowly written statute could stand. Each of these cases, thus, defines more narrowly than Roth the difficult-to-define term of obscenity ("whether to the average person, applying contemporary community standards, the dominant theme of the material taken as a whole appeals to prurient interest"). Therefore, the Court seems to be saying that teachers ought to avoid any work which might be labeled prurient in part, even though the dominant theme may be "pure."

Sex education presently is the target of those who would censor the curriculum. This battle, which the High Court likely will carefully avoid, undoubtedly will continue to cause teachers and school administrators to design cautious, noncontroversial curricula.

May a teacher criticize his school? Another form of censorship recently was attacked in two cases concerning teacher criticism of the school administration. Marvin Pickering, a high school teacher in Illinois, was dismissed because of a letter he wrote to a local newspaper (*Pickering* v. *Board of Education of Township High School* (1968)). The letter primarily criticized the use of school funds. It also objected to a policy which stipulated that any letter written by teachers had to be approved by the superintendent before it could be sent to the newspaper. The court record shows that some of the figures of expenditures and their allocation mentioned in Pickering's allegations against the school board were erroneous. Justice Thurgood Marshall, however, stated in his writing of the majority opinion:

> The public interest in having free and unhindered debate on matters of public importance—the core value of the Free Speech Clause of the First Amendment is so great that it has been held that a State cannot authorize the recovery of damages by a public official for defamatory statements directed at him except when statements are shown to have been either with knowledge of their falsity or with reckless disregard for their truth or falsity.

Justice Marshall's reference to the important *New York Times* v. *Sullivan* principle provides yet other vital questions of a rhetorical nature for the classroom, such as—What kinds of communication produce beneficial response? And how do we insult and offend others? Is a teacher subject to suit for libel or obscenity if he does not stop certain publications or speech of students which might be so labeled?

In a similar case of criticism of a school administration, two teachers in Alaska prompted their state to rewrite a statute defining "immorality" (*Watts* v. *Seward School Board* (1968)). The Supreme Court of Alaska had upheld the conviction of the two teachers who allegedly were reported to have said in a conversation, "We have been unable to get rid of the [school] superintendent, so we are going to get rid of the Board." The United States Supreme Court remanded the case because law had subsequently been rewritten to permit such criticism and "immorality" had been rightfully more narrowly defined as the "Commission of an act which involves moral turpitude."

Loyalty

Should teachers be required to sign an oath of loyalty to the State? The New York State Feinberg law, passed in 1949, specifically demanded the "elimination of subversive persons from the public school systems." The Court in upholding this law reasoned that mere association was prima facie evidence of disqualification (*Adler* v. *Board of Education* (1952)). Justice Minton, echoing the McCarthy hysteria of the times, stated:

> One's associates, past and present, as well as one's conduct, may properly be considered in determining fitness and loyalty. From time immemorial, one's reputation has been determined in part by the company he keeps. In the employment of officials and teachers of the school system, the state may very properly inquire into the company they keep, and we know of no

rule, constitutional or otherwise, that prevents the state, when determining the fitness and loyalty of such persons, from considering the organizations and persons with whom they associate.

Not until 1957 was there a case which rebuffed the Adler position. Paul Sweezy, who referred to himself as a "classical Marxist" and "socialist," was a visiting lecturer at the University of New Hampshire. That state's attorney general summoned Sweezy for testimony, and upon Sweezy's refusal to answer questions, the state court found him in contempt. The Supreme Court, however, sided with Sweezy (*Sweezy* v. *New Hampshire*).

Just two years later, in a swing back toward Adler, the Court supported the conviction of Lloyd Barenblatt, a psychology professor at Vassar, who refused to answer questions put to him by the House Un-American Activities Committee (*Barenblatt* v. *United States* (1959)).

Some of the southern states have had their own peculiar brand of loyalty statutes. Arkansas, for one, compelled every teacher, as a condition of employment to state-supported schools, to file annually a listing of every organization to which he had belonged or contributed within the preceding five years. In 1960, in a five to four decision, the Court ruled in favor of three Arkansas teachers who refused to comply with the statute (*Shelton* v. *Tucker*).

The Court found it particularly unconstitutional that a teacher's employment could be terminated "without bringing charges, without notice, without affording an opportunity to explain" and that there was no provision that the information "be kept confidential." The heart of the issue obviously was not Communist membership because Shelden, a Negro, and the other teachers involved declared they were not Communist and had never been Communists, but it was "public pressures upon school boards to discharge teachers who belong to unpopular or minority organizations," more specifically such organizations as the National Association for the Advancement of Colored People.

In the mid-sixties the loyalty oath required of professors employed by the University of Washington was held to be unconstitutional (*Baggett* v. *Bullitt* (1964)), and more recently the New York statute which called for an "annual review of every teacher to determine whether any utterance or act of his, inside the classroom or out, came within the sanctions of law" was overturned (*Keyishian* v. *Board of Regents of University of New York* (1967)) Justice Douglas, in this case, declared,

> Our Nation is deeply committed to safeguarding academic freedom, which is of transcendent value to all of us and not merely to the teachers concerned. That freedom is therefore a special concern of the First Amendment which does not tolerate laws that cast a pall of orthodoxy over the classroom.

Are speaker bans constitutional? A number of state legislatures have passed laws which banned certain persons from speaking in their schools and universities. In 1963, North Carolina enacted a statute which restricted guest speakers who were known members of the Communist Party, had pleaded the Fifth Amendment, or were known to advocate the overthrow of the Constitution. In 1968, a United States District Court declared this North Carolina law unconstitutional. The District Court's decision relied on such cases as Keyishian and Baggett, referred to earlier. The open speaking policy, however, is not a settled issue and likely will continue to be abridged from time to time on campuses and public schools upon the pretext of preventing incitement to riot.

What kinds of dissent must be tolerated in the public schools? The most recent and probably the most important case to date concerning student loyalty is *Tinker* v. *Des Moines Independent Community School District* (1969). Three teen-age students were suspended in 1965 for wearing black armbands as a protest against the war in Vietnam. Justice Fortas said the issue was not a frivolous one, such as skirt length or hair style, but one of political expression, and therefore suspension violated the right to free speech.

Previous to the Tinker decision, two lower courts had made, on the same day, opposite rulings concerning the wearing of "freedom buttons," and at this writing, the suspension of students for wearing buttons protesting the war is before the courts in Cleveland.

It is interesting to note that the principals of the Des Moines schools came to their decision to suspend students who would wear armbands in order "to avoid controversy." The meeting in which this decision was reached, Justice Fortas points out, was called "in response to a student's statement to the journalism teacher in one of the schools that he wanted to write an article on Vietnam and have it published in the school paper. (The student was dissuaded.)"

The Tinker decision is also significant in its statement that students' rights to express controversial opinions "do not embrace merely the classroom house," but also the cafeteria and playing field. The line seems to be drawn where conduct "materially disrupts classroom work or involves substantial disorder." In a dissenting opinion, Justice Black argues that the armband did exactly that, "that is, it took the students' minds off their classroom work and diverted them to thoughts about the highly emotional subject of the Vietnam War." Black vehemently continues:

> And I repeat that if the time has come when pupils of state-supported schools, kindergartens, grammar schools, or high schools, can defy and flout orders of the school officials to keep their minds on their school work, it is the beginning of a new revolutionary era of permissiveness in this country fostered by the judiciary.

This *reductio ad absurdum* argument of our senior justice spells out an apparent backlash to student activism. It reaffirms the all-too-common point of view that students are less than citizens and that constitutional freedoms do not really apply to the school. The "clear and present danger" test of student speech and conduct is then not so much the rule as is the does-the-student-disobey-the-teacher test. Black asserts that teachers are hired to teach that which the state so designates as part of the curriculum and that children have "not yet reached the point of experience and wisdom which enable[d] them to teach all of their elders."

Black also exposes the depth of his dismay over current dissent by his retreat to the ancient precedent set by the Supreme Court in which it ruled that the state of Mississippi had the right to bar student membership in Greek fraternities (*Waugh* v. *Mississippi University* (1915)). The argument, which Black himself had printed in italics for emphasis, reads:

> . . . *membership in the prohibited societies divided the attention of the students and distracted from that singleness of purpose which the State desired to exist in its public educational institutions.*

This precedent justifies, Black argues, "Curtailment of the First Amendment right of peaceable assembly" and administrative control over students.

Demonstration and Discipline

Has the State the same right to control its property as a private landowner? The recent dramatic, and sometimes destructive, expression of students has brought to the classroom the court's deliberations across the years on assembly, demonstrations, and due process. Southern Negro college students were the first to become aware that parades and use of public places for rallies required permits and that these permits were to be granted without discrimination. In earlier decisions, the High Court tended to side with Negro student demonstrators against discrimination even when held on a courthouse lawn or street nearby. Students convicted in lower courts for a courthouse rally in South Carolina, for example, won their case (*Edwards* v. *South Carolina* (1963)). A majority of the Court similarly sided with a Regional Field Secretary of the Congress of Racial Equality who had led the band of 2,000 students from Louisiana Southern University to sing and pray 101 feet across the street from the building where some of their fellow students were jailed because of civil rights activities the previous day (*Cox* v. *Louisiana* (1965)). Justice Black, however, explicitly stated that parading and picketing do not qualify for the same constitutional protections as "pure speech."

The landmark decision for would-be demonstrators is *Adderley* v. *Florida* (1966). The pattern was similar to previous demonstrations by Negro students but the decision went against the thirty-two students who had congregated with many others from Florida A & M University on the premises of the jail grounds in Tallahassee. They also sang freedom songs while others of their school-mates were locked within. There was no violence or destruction, but the assembled students were arrested for failing to disperse from the jail's driveway and grounds upon the request of the Sheriff. The regulatory powers of the state were therefore asserted over the behavior of demonstrators: where they assemble, when they assemble, and what they do on the public streets and properties. Consequently, today's student who would parade or assemble in public streets and on state- or federally-owned property, if he wishes to avoid arrest, must obtain a permit, must abide by certain regulations concerning numbers and spacing in order to interfere minimally in case of sidewalk or street traffic, and he must not use amplification instruments without permission. If dramatic, or destructive, protest is rather the tactic, students must weigh the consequences of arrest, often prolonged judicial involvement, and public antagonism against the possible acceptance of their message or "demands."

Does the school have a right to discipline? No Supreme Court opinion has given the last word concerning a school administrator's right to discipline. But the Court's refusal to grant certiorari to several lower court rulings tends to uphold the administrator's right to insure the orderly conduct of school business. The basic relationship is a contractual one between the student and the school. The courts have generally refused to interfere in the domestic affairs of the educational institution unless there is evidence that uncalled-for punishment has been administered and/or a spirit of fair play is lacking.

In a case as early as 1901, an Ohio Circuit Court attempted to answer the question concerning discipline meted out by Western Reserve University:

> What are the terms of such a contract? He [the student] upon making that contract agrees to submit himself to the *reasonable discipline* of the school. He agrees that his conduct and character shall be such as to in no manner be detrimental to the school. . . . He agrees that he will conform to the customs of the school; if it is the custom of the school that the professors shall discipline the scholars, reprimand and inflict such punishment as is proper under the circumstances, then he has agreed that he will conform to that custom.

On the other hand,

> The University agrees with him that it will impart to him instructions; that it will aid him in the ordinary ways in his studies; that it will treat him fairly, that it will give him every opportunity to improve himself, and that it will not impose upon him penalties which he in no wise merits, and that will deal with him impartially. (*Koblitz* v. *Western Reserve University*)

The contractual relationship has not substantially changed in these sixty-eight years since the *Western Reserve* case. The process, however, has changed. The rights to fair hearing for both teacher and student have been carefully spelled out by such organizations as the American Association of University Professors, the National Student Association, and the American Civil Liberties Union. Due process guidelines in the schools increasingly have been based upon Supreme Court rulings handed down concerning the legal handling of juveniles (See *Re Gault* (1967)). These guidelines include written notice of the specific charge or allegations sufficiently in advance of a hearing, a right to counsel, a right to face one's accusers and to cross-examine witnesses, and the constitutional privilege against self-incrimination.

It is safe to conclude that the day has arrived when no school, whether it be private or public, elementary or university, has a legal right to expel a student without a hearing should the student ask for one.

George Wald, the Nobel Prize-winning Harvard biologist, recently proclaimed that young people have good reason to feel that "something has gone sour in teaching and in learning." The school must somehow help these students to *feel* that there are wise men in our society who are giving the best years of their lives to make democracy work and that the struggle for freedom in the classroom is part of the larger struggle against repression elsewhere.

Decisions

Decision Index

SCHOOL DISTRICT OF ABINGTON TOWNSHIP PENNSYLVANIA
et al., Appellants

v.

EDWARD LEWIS SCHEMPP et al.

___

WILLIAM J. MURRAY III, etc., Petitioners

v.

JOHN N. CURLETT et al.
374 US 203   June 17, 1963

The Court ruled in favor of Schempp and Murray, holding that the exercise of religious rituals within the public school violated the Establishment Clause of the First Amendment as applied to the states through the 14th Amendment.

Majority			*Dissenting*
GOLDBERG*	BRENNAN	HARLAN	STEWART
WARREN	DOUGLAS	WHITE	
BLACK	CLARK		

*The justice whose name appears first under the majority wrote that opinion.

___

HARRIET LOUISE ADDERLEY et al., Petitioners

v.

STATE OF FLORIDA
385 US 39   November 14, 1966

The Court held that the state's conviction of students for trespassing on jail grounds by demonstrating there and failing to leave upon the sheriff's request did not violate freedom of speech and assembly. The Court sided with Florida.

Majority		*Dissenting*	
BLACK	STEWART	DOUGLAS	BRENNAN
CLARK	WHITE	WARREN	FORTAS
HARLAN			

___

AMALGAMATED FOOD EMPLOYEES UNION LOCAL 590 et al., Petitioners

v.

LOGAN VALLEY PLAZA, Inc., et al.
391 US 308   May 20, 1968

The Court held that since the shopping center served as a community business block and was freely accessible and open to the people in the area and to those passing through, the state could not delegate the power, through the use of its trespass laws, wholly to exclude those members of the public wishing to exercise their First Amendment rights on the premises. The state's generally valid rules against trespass to private property therefore could not be applied to bar the union from the premises of the shopping center and supermarket. The Court sided with the union.

Majority			*Dissenting*	
WARREN	BRENNAN	MARSHALL	BLACK	WHITE
DOUGLAS	STEWART	FORTAS	HARLAN	

JOSEPH BEAUHARNAIS, Petitioner

v.

PEOPLE OF THE STATE OF ILLINOIS

343 US 250   April 28, 1952

The Court sided with the State holding that the rules against libel to the individual are particularly applicable to attacks upon minority groups. Beauharnais, therefore, was convicted for "group libel."

Majority		Dissenting	
FRANKFURTER	CLARK	BLACK	DOUGLAS
VINSON	MINTON	REED	JACKSON
BURTON			

A BOOK NAMED "JOHN CLELAND'S MEMOIRS
OF A WOMAN OF PLEASURE" et al., Appellant

v.

ATTORNEY GENERAL OF THE
COMMONWEALTH OF MASSACHUSETTS

383 US 413   March 21, 1966

The majority ruled that Massachusett's courts had erred in ruling *Memoirs* to be obscene. The six justices' opinions, however, stated different reasons. Some stated that a book to be ruled obscene must be unqualifiably worthless, others that no court can constitutionally censor, and another that the book was not "hard-core pornography."

Majority		Dissenting
BRENNAN	BLACK	CLARK
WARREN	DOUGLAS	HARLAN
FORTAS	STEWART	WHITE

CLARENCE BRANDENBURG, Appellant

v.

STATE OF OHIO

395 US 444   June 9, 1969

The Court overturned Brandenburg's conviction and thus overruled the 1927 Whitney v. California decision. It was held the constitutional guarantees of free speech and press do not permit a state to proscribe advocacy of the use of force or of law violation, except where it is directed to producing imminent lawless action and was likely to produce such action. The Ohio statute was unconstitutional because it punished mere advocacy.

Decision Unanimous	
WARREN	BRENNAN
BLACK	STEWART
DOUGLAS	WHITE
HARLAN	MARSHALL

JOSEPH BURSTYN, Inc., Appellant,

v.

LEWIS A. WILSON, Commissioner of Education
of the State of New York et al.

343 US 495   May 26, 1952

The Court held that the basic principles of freedom of speech and press applied to motion pictures, even though their exhibition was a large-scale business conducted for profit. The Court recognized that precise rules may differ from media to media, and decided that banning a film on the censor's conclusion that it was "sacrilegious" was unconstitutionally vague. The court sided with Burstyn.

Decision Unanimous

VINSON	FRANKFURTER	BURTON
BLACK	DOUGLAS	CLARK
REED	JACKSON	MINTON

JOHN EARL CAMERON et al., Appellants

v.

PAUL JOHNSON, etc., et al.

390 US 611   April 22, 1968

The Court upheld the earlier proceedings, and it held that (1) the Anti-Picketing statute was not unconstitutional on its face either for vagueness or for overbreadth, and (2) since the record did not establish the plaintiffs' charges of bad faith or selective enforcement designed to harass them with no expectation of obtaining convictions, the District Court did not err in denying injunctive relief. The court sided with Johnson.

Majority		*Dissenting*
BRENNAN	STEWART	FORTAS
WARREN	WHITE	DOUGLAS
BLACK	MARSHALL	
HARLAN		

JOSEPH CARROLL et al., Petitioner

v.

PRESIDENT AND COMMISSIONERS OF PRINCESS ANNE et al.

393 US 175   November 19, 1968

The Court sided with the National States Rights Party, holding that the Princess Anne Commissioners had violated due process in obtaining an ex parte injunction without having issued a notice to the petitioners. Justice Douglas concurred, insisting that a temporary injunction under which a decree can issue an ex parte before a hearing is held gives a state the paralyzing power of a censor.

Decision Unanimous

WARREN	HARLAN	WHITE
BLACK	BRENNAN	FORTAS
DOUGLAS	STEWART	MARSHALL

CHAPLINSKY

v.

NEW HAMPSHIRE

315 US 588   March 9, 1942

Chaplinsky was convicted of "fighting words" and thereby a breach of the peace.

Decision Unanimous

MURPHY	BLACK	DOUGLAS
STONE	REED	BYRNES
ROBERTS	FRANKFURTER	JACKSON

B. ELTON COX, Appellant

v.

STATE OF LOUISIANA

379 US 536   January 18, 1965

The majority sided with Cox, holding that (1) the breach of the peace conviction infringed on his rights to free speech and assembly, (2) the demonstration did not obstruct public passages, and (3) the city officials had in effect told the demonstrators they could meet where they did. The 5 to 4 decision pertains specifically to courthouse picketing. The Court split 7 to 2 on the obstruction charge with White and Harlan dissenting in favor of upholding the convictions.

Majority		*Dissenting*	
GOLDBERG	BRENNAN	BLACK	HARLAN
WARREN	STEWART	CLARK	WHITE
DOUGLAS			

CURTIS PUBLISHING COMPANY	ASSOCIATED PRESS
v.	v.
WALLACE BUTTS	EDWIN A. WALKER
388 US 130	388 US 889

June 12, 1967

The Court upheld the verdict against Curtis Publishing Company holding that the *Saturday Evening Post* had been guilty of libel. The preparation of the article was judged to have "cast serious doubt on the adequacy of the investigation underlying the article," that the truth of the reporting was not clearly proven, and that the periodical's recent pledge to do "sophisticated muckraking" combined with statements in the article supported "actual malice." On the other hand, the Associated Press was not found to be guilty on these counts, and thus General Walker's award of $500,000 for compensatory damages and $300,000 punitive damages was reversed.

CURTIS   WALKER

Majority			*Dissenting*		*Unanimous*
HARLAN	STEWART	WARREN	BRENNAN	BLACK	
CLARK	FORTAS		WHITE	DOUGLAS	

W. E. B. DuBOIS CLUBS OF AMERICA et al., Appellants

v.

RAMSEY CLARK, ATTORNEY GENERAL OF THE UNITED STATES
389 US 309 December 11, 1967

The Court sided against the DuBois Clubs, stating that the organization had not exhausted other channels for exempting themselves from the order to register as a front organization. Thus the Subversive Activities Control Board became free to call hearings to "investigate" the DuBois Club.

Per Curiam (Concurring-Majority)		*Dissenting*
WARREN	WHITE	BLACK
HARLAN	FORTAS	DOUGLAS
BRENNAN	MARSHALL	
STEWART		

BILLIE SOL ESTES, Petitioner

v.

STATE OF TEXAS
381 US 532 June 7, 1965

The majority of the Court held that the notoriety of the trial combined with televising the proceedings denied due process. A strong dissenting foursome voiced the opinion that televising the trial did not violate Estes' constitutional rights.

Majority	*Dissenting*
CLARK	STEWART
WARREN	BLACK
DOUGLAS	BRENNAN
GOLDBERG	WHITE
HARLAN	

IRVING FEINER, Petitioner

v.

PEOPLE OF THE STATE OF NEW YORK
340 US 315 January 15, 1951

The Court upheld the conviction of disorderly conduct against Feiner. Douglas and Minton dissented on the ground that there was no danger of riot. Black dissented stating that Feiner had been sentenced for the unpopular views he expressed.

Majority	*Dissenting*
VINSON	BLACK
REED	DOUGLAS
FRANKFURTER	MINTON
JACKSON	
BURTON	
CLARK	

RONALD L. FREEDMAN, Appellant

v.

STATE OF MARYLAND

380 US 51   March 1, 1965

The court sided with Freedman, holding that the Maryland statute was overly broad. The majority opinion stipulated that the burden of proving a film obscene was on the censor, and that submission for review would be permissible if the action were reasonably speedy. Douglas and Black insisted that no censorship should be permitted, in keeping with a literal interpretation of the First Amendment.

Decision Unanimous

BRENNAN	DOUGLAS	STEWART
WARREN	CLARK	WHITE
BLACK	HARLAN	GOLDBERG

JIM GARRISON, Appellant

v.

STATE OF LOUISIANA

379 US 64   November 23, 1964

The Court reversed the Louisiana Supreme Court conviction of Garrison, holding that accusations of public officials did not become private defamation because they might also reflect on the officials' private character. Truth was held to be the best defense for accusations of libel. To protect public officials from verbal abuse would create a chilling effect upon debate of public issues.

Decision Unanimous

BRENNAN	DOUGLAS	STEWART
WARREN	CLARK	WHITE
BLACK	HARLAN	GOLDBERG

THEODORE R. GIBSON, Petitioner

v.

FLORIDA LEGISLATIVE INVESTIGATING COMMITTEE

372 US 539   March 25, 1963

The Court in a 5-4 decision sided with Gibson. The Florida contempt conviction was held to violate the First and Fourteenth Amendment rights of free speech and free association since the record was insufficient to demonstrate a substantial connection between the NAACP and Communist activities.

Majority		*Dissenting*	
GOLDBERG	DOUGLAS	HARLAN	STEWART
WARREN	BRENNAN	CLARK	WHITE
BLACK			

SAM GINSBERG, Appellant

v.

STATE OF NEW YORK

390 US 629   April 22, 1968

The Court affirmed the conviction of the lower courts—thus supporting anti-pornography statutes when applied to children.

Majority		*Dissenting*
BRENNAN	STEWART	DOUGLAS
WARREN	WHITE	BLACK
HARLAN	MARSHALL	FORTAS

RALPH GINZBURG et al., Petitioners

v.

UNITED STATES

383 US 436   March 21, 1966

The Court ruled that Ginzburg was guilty of pandering, that is, the business of openly advertising to appeal to the erotic of customers. His five-year sentence was confirmed. The same day the Court likewise upheld Mishkin's sentence of three years and fines totaling $12,000 for publishing and distributing "hard core" pornography.

Majority	*Dissenting*
BRENNAN	BLACK
WARREN	DOUGLAS
CLARK	HARLAN
WHITE	STEWART
FORTAS	

GITLOW

v.

PEOPLE OF NEW YORK

268 US 652   June 8, 1925

The Court sided with the State of New York. For the first time the Court agreed that the due process clause of the Fourteenth Amendment made the First Amendment protections applicable to the states, but they held that free speech and press were limited and that criminal anarchy was such a limitation.

Majority		*Dissenting*
SANFORD	SUTHERLAND	HOLMES
TAFT	BUTLER	BRANDEIS
VAN DEVANTER	STONE	
McREYNOLDS		

GREENBELT COOPERATIVE PUBLISHING
ASSOCIATION, Inc., et al., Petitioners

v.

CHARLES S. BRESLER
398 US 6   May 18, 1970

The Court reversed the libel award to Bresler. The *Greenbelt News Record*'s articles in question were considered to perform a legitimate function in reporting fully the public debates. Bresler was admittedly a "public figure" and therefore was not privileged to an award for defamation unless it could be proved that the defamatory publication was not only false but uttered with "actual malice." The word "blackmail" when referring to negotiations and land dealings was not considered to fall into the criminal definition of blackmail.

Decision Unanimous

STEWART	BLACK	BRENNAN	WHITE
BURGER	DOUGLAS	HARLAN	MARSHALL

DICK GREGORY et al., Petitioners

v.

CITY OF CHICAGO
394 US 111   March 10, 1969

The Court reversed the conviction holding that the demonstration had been peaceful and orderly and that their conduct was protected by the First Amendment. The Chicago disorderly conduct ordinance was considered too sweeping and vague.

Decision Unanimous

WARREN	HARLAN	WHITE
BLACK	BRENNAN	FORTAS
DOUGLAS	STEWART	MARSHALL

ESTELLE T. GRISWOLD et al., Appellant

v.

STATE OF CONNECTICUT
381 US 479   June 7, 1965

The Court held the Connecticut law concerning the aiding and abetting the sale or use of contraceptives was an unconstitutional invasion of the right to privacy of married persons.

Majority		*Dissenting*
DOUGLAS	BRENNAN	BLACK
WARREN	WHITE	STEWART
CLARK	GOLDBERG	
HARLAN		

FRANK HAGUE, Individually and as Mayor of
Jersey City, et al., etc., Petitioners

v.

COMMITTEE FOR INDUSTRIAL ORGANIZATION et al.
307 US 496   June 5, 1939

The Court sided with the union, holding that the ordinance which enabled the mayor to consent to or withhold assembly in public places permitted arbitrary and discriminate application and that the right to peaceably assemble was abridged.

Majority		*Dissenting*	*Took No Part*
ROBERTS	BLACK	McREYNOLDS	FRANKFURTER
HUGHES	REED	BUTLER	DOUGLAS
STONE			

STATE OF ILLINOIS, Petitioner

v.

WILLIAM ALLEN
397 US 337   March 31, 1970

The Court held that the accused lost his constitutional right to be present throughout his trial and that it was not unconstitutional to remove him because of his disruptive behavior. Justice Douglas agreed that the court could not tolerate disruptive behavior, however in his dissent he warned that (1) the power of the judge had historically been misused in political trials and (2) that because Allen likely was mentally ill and (3) the record was so stale that it was much too late to discover what were the true facts concerning his mental condition.

Majority			*Dissenting*
BLACK	HARLAN	STEWART	DOUGLAS
BURGER	BRENNAN	WHITE	

INTERSTATE CIRCUIT, Inc., Appellant

v.

CITY OF DALLAS
390 US 676   April 22, 1968

The Court held that the ordinance was unconstitutionally vague. For example, the lack of definition for such terms as "sexual promiscuity" was considered an inadequate basis for a "not suitable" classification. Only Harlan dissented on the ground that it was unfair to demand a greater precision of language in the ordinance than the Court itself can give.

Majority			*Dissenting*
MARSHALL	DOUGLAS	WHITE	HARLAN
WARREN	BRENNAN	FORTAS	
BLACK	STEWART		

NICO JACOBELLIS, Appellant

v.

OHIO

378 US 184   June 22, 1964

The Court sided with Jacobellis but was anything but unified in its opinion. Brennan, who wrote the majority opinion, stated that community standards should be interpreted as national standards. The Chief Justice, however, in his dissent argued that community standards are local.

Majority		*Dissenting*
BRENNAN	DOUGLAS	WARREN
GOLDBERG	STEWART	CLARK
BLACK	WHITE	HARLAN

HARRY KEYISHIAN et al., Appellants

v.

BOARD OF REGENTS OF THE UNIVERSITY OF
THE STATE OF NEW YORK et al.

385 US 589   January 23, 1967

The High Court reversed the lower court's decision, siding for the Keyishian and thus ruled the "loyalty" plan unconstitutional. Mere "knowing membership" without any specific showing of intent to further the unlawful aims of the Communist Party were considered invalid criteria for the New York statute.

Majority	*Dissenting*
BRENNAN	CLARK
WARREN	HARLAN
BLACK	STEWART
DOUGLAS	WHITE
FORTAS	

FRED TOYOSABUBO KOREMATSU, Petitioner

v.

UNITED STATES OF AMERICA

323 US 214   December 18, 1944

The Court upheld the conviction of Fred Korematsu. The act which permitted the internment was considered necessary under the war power of Congress and the Executive.

Majority		*Dissenting*
BLACK	FRANKFURTER	ROBERTS
STONE	DOUGLAS	MURPHY
REED	RUTLEDGE	JACKSON

CHARLES KOVACS, Appellant

v.

ALBERT COOPER, JR., Judge of the
First District Police Court of Trenton
336 US 77 January 31, 1949

Eight members of the Court agreed that sound amplification in streets is subject to reasonable regulation. Kovacs stood convicted by the High Court. But those dissenting contended that the charge was not proved.

Majority	Dissenting
REED	MURPHY
VINSON	BLACK
FRANKFURTER	DOUGLAS
JACKSON	RUTLEDGE
BURTON	

CLYDE FRANKLIN LEE et al., Petitioner

v.

STATE OF FLORIDA
392 US 378 June 17, 1968

Wiretapping by the police of Lee's phone and the use of that information was held by the Court to be unlawful interception and divulgence of information.

Majority		Dissenting
STEWART	BRENNAN	BLACK
WARREN	FORTAS	HARLAN
DOUGLAS	MARSHALL	WHITE

WILLIAM C. LINN, Petitioner

v.

UNITED PLANT GUARD WORKERS OF AMERICA, Local 114, et al.
383 US 53 February 21, 1966

The Court held that where either party to a labor dispute circulates false and defamatory statements during a unionizing campaign, the National Labor Relations Act does not bar a civil action for libel, providing that the statements were proved to be made with malice and resulted in injury. The dissenting justices expressed the opinion that in siding for Linn opened a breach in the wall which had previously insulated labor disputes from the vagaries of lawsuits.

Majority	Dissenting
CLARK	BLACK
HARLAN	FORTAS
BRENNAN	WARREN
STEWART	DOUGLAS
WHITE	

MANUAL ENTERPRISES, Inc., et al., Petitioners

v.

J. EDWARD DAY, Postmaster General of the United States
370 US 478   June 25, 1962

The Court could not agree upon an opinion but did agree to reverse the Postmaster's ruling. Some of the reasons given for this decision were (1) The magazines were not patently offensive, (2) the law does not authorize the Postmaster to exclude matter from the mails on his own determination that it is obscene.

Majority		*Dissenting*	*Took No Part*
HARLAN	DOUGLAS	CLARK	FRANKFURTER
WARREN	BRENNAN		WHITE
BLACK	STEWART		

DOLLREE MAPP, etc., Appellant

v.

OHIO
367 US 643   June 19, 1961

The Court sided with Mapp holding that evidence obtained by search and seizure in violation of the Fourth Amendment is inadmissible in a state court as it is in a federal court. The Court also remanded the clause in the state law which made possession of obscene material criminal.

Majority	*Dissenting*	
CLARK	HARLAN	Agreeing with reversal but dis-
WARREN	FRANKFURTER	senting in part: STEWART
BLACK	WHITTAKER	
DOUGLAS		
BRENNAN		

THELMA MARTIN, Appellant

v.

CITY OF STRUTHERS, OHIO
319 US 141   May 3, 1943

The Court sided with Thelma Martin, holding the Struthers' ordinance which prohibited the right to door-to-door distribution of literature abridged the right to freedom of speech and press for the individual householder.

Majority	*Dissenting*
BLACK	FRANKFURTER
STONE	REED
DOUGLAS	ROBERTS
MURPHY	JACKSON
RUTLEDGE	

MUTUAL FILM CORPORATION

v.

INDUSTRIAL COMMISSION OF OHIO

236 US 230   February 23, 1915

The Court held that motion picture films are "capable of evil, having power for it, the greater because of their attractiveness," and therefore are in need of a censor. The opinion expressed seriously questioned their inclusion in the category of speech and press, particularly because of their commercial nature and their more tangible media.

Decision Unanimous

McKenna	Pitney	Hughes
White	Van Devanter	Holmes
McReynolds	Lamar	Day

J. M. NEAR, Appellant

v.

STATE OF MINNESOTA, EX. REL. FLOYD OLSON

283 US 697   June 1, 1931

The Court ruled in favor of Near, holding that previous restraint upon publication abridged freedom of the press.

Majority		*Dissenting*	
Hughes	Stone	Butler	McReynolds
Holmes	Roberts	Van Devanter	Sutherland
Brandeis			

NEW YORK TIMES COMPANY, Petitioner

v.

L. B. SULLIVAN

RALPH D. ABERNATHY et al., Petitioner

v.

L. B. SULLIVAN

376 US 254   March 9, 1964

The Court reversed the lower court's libel judgment and remanded the case to the Alabama Courts, holding that state libel laws which permit no latitude for error in publishing critical views of public officials and affairs threaten the existence of a free press.

Decision Unanimous

Brennan	Douglas	Stewart
Warren	Clark	White
Black	Harlan	Goldberg

UNITED STATES, Petitioner

v.

DAVID PAUL O'BRIEN

———

DAVID PAUL O'BRIEN, Petitioner

v.

UNITED STATES

391 US 672   May 27, 1968

The Court vacated the judgment of the Court of Appeals and reinstated the judgment and sentence of the District Court. Burning registration certificates could not be protected by the First Amendment. Justice Douglas dissented, expressing the opinion that the case should be reargued on the question of a peacetime draft.

Majority			*Dissenting*	*Did Not Participate*
WARREN	STEWART	WHITE	DOUGLAS	MARSHALL
BLACK	BRENNAN	FORTAS		
HARLAN				

———

ROY OLMSTEAD, Jerry L. Finch, Clarence G. Healy, Cliff Maurice,
Tom Nakagawa, Edward Rugdahl, Myer Berg, John Earl,
and Francis Brown, Petitioners

v.

UNITED STATES OF AMERICA (No. 493)

277 US 438   June 4, 1928

The Court held that wiretapping did not constitute search and seizure and that illegally obtained information could not be excluded from evidence in the trial. Brandeis and the other dissenting justices maintained that wiretapping was an invasion of privacy.

Majority			*Dissenting*	
TAFT	DEVANTER	SUTHERFORD	BRANDEIS	STONE
HOLMES	McREYNOLDS	SANFORD	BUTLER	

———

MARVIN L. PICKERING, Appellant

v.

BOARD OF EDUCATION OF TOWNSHIP HIGH SCHOOL

District 205, Will County, Illinois

391 US 563   June 3, 1968

The Court ruled in favor of Pickering. It was held that there was an absence of proof of false statements knowingly or recklessly made by the teacher. His right to speak on issues of public importance was supported and his dismissal violated his constitutional right to free speech.

Majority			*Dissenting*
MARSHALL	BRENNAN	STEWART	White concurring in
WARREN	BLACK	WHITE	part and dissenting
HARLAN	DOUGLAS	FORTAS	in part.

PUBLIC UTILITIES COMMISSION OF THE DISTRICT OF COLUMBIA, CAPITAL TRANSIT COMPANY AND WASHINGTON TRANSIT RADIO, INC.

v.

FRANKLIN S. POLLAK AND GUY MARTIN
343 US 451   May 26, 1952

Six members of the Court sided with the Commission et al., holding neither the operation of the service nor the action of the Commission was precluded by the constitutional guarantees of free speech and due process. Justice Black concurred but made it clear that if the passengers were subjected to news, public speeches or propaganda of any kind that this would violate the First Amendment.

Majority			Dissenting	Did Not Participate
BURTON	MINTON	REED	DOUGLAS	FRANKFURTER
VINSON	JACKSON	BLACK		
CLARK				

RED LION BROADCASTING COMPANY, Inc., et al.

v.

FEDERAL COMMUNICATIONS COMMISSION
395 US 367   June 9, 1969

The Court affirmed the Federal Communications declaratory order to the effect that the station had failed to meet its obligation under the fairness doctrine. The equal time rules were held not to abridge freedoms of speech and press.

Decision Unanimous			Took No Part
WHITE	BRENNAN	STEWART	DOUGLAS
WARREN	HARLAN	MARSHALL	
BLACK			

SAMUEL ROTH

v.

UNITED STATES

DAVID S. ALBERTS

v.

STATE OF CALIFORNIA
354 US 476   June 24, 1957

Both Roth and Alberts were convicted for mailing obscene matter. The Court set forth this test for obscenity: whether to the average person, applying contemporary community standards, the dominant theme of the material taken as a whole appeals to prurient interest.

Majority		Dissenting	
BRENNAN	BURTON	DOUGLAS	Harlan concurred in Alberts
WARREN	CLARK	BLACK	and dissented in Roth on the
FRANKFURTER	WHITTAKER		basis of state's jurisdiction.

DANIEL ROWAN, dba American Book Service, et al., Appellants

v.

UNITED STATES POST OFFICE DEPARTMENT et al.

397 US 728   May 4, 1970

The Court upheld Title III of the Postal Act (39 USC 4009) maintaining that a statute giving the addressee unfettered discretion in deciding whether to receive future materials from a particular sender neither violated the free speech guarantee of the First Amendment nor the due process guarantee of the Fourteenth Amendment.

Decision Unanimous

BURGER	DOUGLAS	BRENNAN	WHITE
BLACK	HARLAN	STEWART	MARSHALL

JANIUS IRVING SCALES, Petitioner

v.

UNITED STATES

367 US 203   June 5, 1961

The Court confirmed the six-year sentence of Scales for "active knowing membership" in the Communist Party and that evidence was presented of advocacy of revolutionary action rather than abstract revolutionary doctrine. In the companion case, also decided on June 5, 1961, John Francis Noto's conviction was reversed upon the ground that the evidence presented at the trial was insufficient to show his membership in the Communist Party was more than abstract doctrine of forcible overthrow. In yet another case handed down that same day, Communist Party v. Subversive Activities Control Board, the Court sustained a government order under the 1950 McCarran Act requiring the Communist Party to register as a subversive organization.

Majority			*Dissenting*	
HARLAN	CLARK	STEWART	BLACK	BRENNAN
FRANKFURTER	WHITTAKER		DOUGLAS	WARREN

DANIEL JAY SCHACHT, Petitioner

v.

UNITED STATES

298 US 58   May 25, 1970

The Court held that the section of 10 U.S.C. §772 (f) which stipulated that dramatic portrayal is only lawful if it "does not tend to discredit that armed force" was ruled an unconstitutional abridgment of freedom of speech. Three members of the Court in a separate concurring opinion argued that "theatrical production" in which a military uniform is permitted must be limited to a setting where observers will realize that they are "watching a make-believe performance." Under this definition Schacht must be found not to have been engaged in a "theatrical production" and therefore could be found guilty.

Decision Unanimous

BLACK	DOUGLAS	BRENNAN	WHITE
BURGER	HARLAN	STEWART	MARSHALL

CHARLES I. SCHENCK, Plff. in Err.,

v.

UNITED STATES

———

ELIZABETH BAER, Plff. in Err.,

v.

UNITED STATES

249 US 47   March 3, 1919

The Court found Schenck guilty as charged with violating the Espionage Act of June 15, 1917, by sending leaflets to prospective military draftees urging them to resist the Conscription Act. Justice Holmes enunciated the famous clear and present danger doctrine as applied to press and speech in time of war.

Decision Unanimous

HOLMES	DAY	McREYNOLDS
WHITE	DEVANTER	BRANDEIS
McKENNA	PITNEY	CLARK

———

SAMUEL SHEPPARD, Petitioner

v.

E. L. MAXWELL, Warden

384 US 333   June 6, 1966

The Court held that the trial judge failed to protect Sheppard from massive prejudicial publicity and thus deprived him of a fair trial.

Majority		*Dissenting* *Without Opinion*
CLARK	BRENNAN	BLACK
WARREN	STEWART	
DOUGLAS	WHITE	
HARLAN	FORTAS	

———

ROBERT ELI STANLEY, Appellant

v.

STATE OF GEORGIA

394 US 557   April 7, 1969

The Court unanimously reversed Stanley's conviction holding that the Georgia statute, insofar as it made mere private possession of obscene matter a crime, was unconstitutional. Stewart stressed that the conviction be reversed because unlawfully seized materials were inadmissible as evidence.

Decision Unanimous

MARSHALL	DOUGLAS	STEWART
BURGER	HARLAN	WHITE
BLACK	BRENNAN	

SIDNEY STREET, Appellant

v.

STATE OF NEW YORK

394 US 576   April 21, 1969

In remanding the case, the Court ruled that the accused had a constitutional right to express publicly his opinion about the flag, even if his opinion was contemptuous, and in effect ruled the New York statute overbroad. The Court avoided judgment whether the deed of desecration was symbolic speech deserving First Amendment protection.

Majority		*Dissenting*	
HARLAN	STEWART	WARREN	FORTAS
DOUGLAS	MARSHALL	BLACK	WHITE
BRENNAN			

MANUEL D. TALLEY, Petitioner

v.

CALIFORNIA

362 US 60   March 7, 1960

The majority held the ordinance void, but refused to pass upon the possible validity of an ordinance limited to prevent fraud, false advertising, and libel which might be anonymous. Three members of the court dissented, expressing the view that an ordinance which demanded identity of the sponsor of a handbill did not interfere with First Amendment protections.

Majority		*Dissenting*
BLACK	HARLAN	CLARK
WARREN	BRENNAN	FRANKFURTER
DOUGLAS	STEWART	WHITTAKER

TIMES FILM CORPORATION, Petitioner

v.

CHICAGO et al.

365 US 43   January 23, 1961

The Court sided with the city's right to review films and to restrict exhibition. The four dissenting justices expressed the view that the constitutional guarantee of freedom of speech prohibited unlimited censorship of motion pictures before exhibition through a system of administrative licensing.

Majority		*Dissenting*	
CLARK	WHITTAKER	WARREN	DOUGLAS
FRANKFURTER	STEWART	BLACK	BRENNAN
HARLAN			

JOHN F. TINKER and Mary Beth Tinker, Minors, etc., et al., Petitioners

v.

DES MOINES INDEPENDENT COMMUNITY SCHOOL DISTRICT et al.

393 US 503   February 24, 1969

The large majority of the Court was of the opinion that wearing armbands in the circumstances of the case was not disruptive conduct and was symbolic expression akin to "pure speech" which is entitled to First Amendment guarantees. The school armband regulation, therefore, violated the students' right of free speech. Black, in dissenting, stressed that such a decision subjects all public schools to the caprices of their "loudest-mouthed" students and that First Amendment protections have limits, particularly for children.

Majority				*Dissenting*
FORTAS	DOUGLAS	STEWART	MARSHALL	BLACK
WARREN	BRENNAN	WHITE		HARLAN

WYATT TEE WALKER et al., Petitioners

v.

CITY OF BIRMINGHAM

388 US 307   June 12, 1967

The Court affirmed the conviction of contempt against Walker for disobeying the injunction even though the parade ordinance was subject to substantial constitutional question. Those dissenting insisted upholding the conviction supported an unconstitutional ordinance which the petitioners were warranted in flouting. Each petitioner was sentenced to five days in jail and a $50 fine. One of the number was the Reverend Martin Luther King, Jr.

Majority			*Dissenting*	
STEWART	CLARK	WHITE	WARREN	DOUGLAS
BLACK	HARLAN		BRENNAN	FORTAS

FREDERICK WALZ, Appellant

v.

TAX COMMISSION OF THE CITY OF NEW YORK

397 US 664   May 4, 1970

The Court sided with the state. Tax exemption did not violate the religion clause it was argued because exemptions also were granted other nonprofit organizations such as hospitals, libraries, playgrounds, and scientific, professional, historical, and patriotic groups. In addition, it was held taxing churches would involve the state with the church and thus could contribute to prohibiting free exercise of religion. Justice Douglas, the lone dissenter, objected on the basis that the decision permitted unequal treatment to the believer and nonbeliever, and that tax exemption was clearly a subsidy.

Majority			*Dissenting*
BURGER	HARLAN	STEWART	DOUGLAS
BLACK	BRENNAN	WHITE	

ROBERT WATTS, Petitioner

v.

UNITED STATES

394 US 705   April 21, 1969

The Court remanded the case with instructions for the entry of a judgment of acquittal. In a per curiam opinion expressing the view of five members of the Court, it was held that Watts' statement taken in context was political hyperbole rather than a true "threat" upon the President's life.

Majority	*Dissenting*
WARREN	FORTAS
BLACK	HARLAN
DOUGLAS	WHITE
BRENNAN	STEWART
MARSHALL	

WEST VIRGINIA STATE BOARD OF EDUCATION et al.

v.

BARNETTE et al.

319 US 649   June 14, 1943

The Court sided with Barnette, holding that a child may not be required to salute the flag when such an act is in conflict with religious beliefs, thus asserting a "right to silence."

Majority		*Dissenting*
JACKSON	DOUGLAS	FRANKFURTER
STONE	MURPHY	
ROBERTS	RUTLEDGE	
BLACK		
REED		

LOUIS ZEMEL, Appellant

v.

DEAN RUSK, Secretary of State, et al.

381 US 1   May 3, 1965

The majority of the Court sided with Rusk, holding that the Passport Act of 1926 justly granted authority to the Executive to impose area restrictions and that Rusk's restriction was sound. However, in a similar case decided two years later, United States v. Lamb, 1967, the Court unanimously upheld the right of Lamb, who had recruited and arranged travel to Cuba of 58 persons with valid passports, but which were not specifically validated for travel to that country.

Majority		*Dissenting*
WARREN	BRENNAN	BLACK
CLARK	STEWART	DOUGLAS
HARLAN	WHITE	GOLDBERG

References to Additional Supreme Court Cases Concerned with or Related to Free Speech and Free Press

Academic Freedom

State law prohibiting integration
> *Berea College v. Kentucky 211 US 45 (1908)*

Compulsory attendance in public schools
> *Pierce v. Society of Sisters 268 US 510 (1925)*

Religious objection to military training
> *Hamilton v. Regents 293 US 245 (1934)*

Flag salute
> *Minersville School District v. Gobitis 310 US 586 (1940)*

Bus fares for parochial school pupils
> *Everson v. Board of Education 330 US 1 (1947)*

Release time for religious instruction
> *McCollum v. Board of Education 333 US 203 (1948)*

Release time limited
> *Zorach v. Clausen 343 US 306 (1952)*

Membership in certain organizations made ineligible to teach
> *Adler v. Board of Education 342 US 485 (1952)*

Taking Fifth Amendment resulted in discharge
> *Slochower v. Board of Higher Education 350 US 551 (1956)*

Loyalty of University speaker
> *Sweezy v. New Hampshire 354 US 234 (1957)*

Congressional investigations of professors
> *Barenblatt v. United States 360 US 109 (1959)*

Freedom of association
> *Shelton v. Tucker 364 US 479 (1960)*

Prayer in public schools
> *Engle v. Vitale 370 US 421 (1962)*

Loyalty oath
> *Baggett v. Bullitt 377 US 360 (1964)*

Book lending to parochial schools
> *Board of Education v. Allen 392 US 236 (1968)*

Teaching evolution
> *Epperson v. Arkansas 393 US 97 (1968)*

Censorship

Deposit of obscene letter in mails
> *United States v. Chase 135 US 255 (1890)*

Obscene letter in mails
> *Andrews v. United States 162 US 420 (1896)*

Taxing to control press
> *Grosjean v. American Press Company 297 US 233 (1936)*

Contempt by publication; fair trial–free press
   Bridges v. California 314 US 252 (1941)

Obscene periodical in mails
   Hannagan v. Esquire, Inc. 327 US 146 (1946)

Possession with intent to sell
   Winters v. New York 333 US 507 (1948)

State statute making it unlawful to disseminate any communication tending to incite minors to violent or immoral acts
   Butler v. Michigan 352 US 380 (1957)

Seizure of obscene literature by injunction
   Kingsley Books Inc., v. Brown 354 US 436 (1957)
   Alberts v. California 354 US 476 (1957)

Censorship of homosexual magazines
   One Inc. v. Oleson 355 US 371 (1958)

Censorship of nudist magazine
   Sunshine Book Co. v. Summerfield 355 US 372 (1958)

Seizure of obscene literature
   Marcus v. Search Warrant 367 US 717 (1961)
   Bantam Books, Inc. v. Sullivan 372 US 767 (1963)

Censorship of obscene books
   Tralins v. Gerstein 378 US 567 (1964)
   Grove Press, Inc. v. Gerstein 378 US 577 (1964)
   A Quantity of Copies of Books v. Kansas 378 US 205 (1964)
   A Quantity of Copies of Books v. Kansas 388 US 452 (1967)

Mailing of undeveloped film of nude poses
   Redmond v. United States 384 US 264 (1966)

Censorship of literature for deviant group
   Mishkin v. New York 383 US 503 (1966)

An obscene telephone call by a juvenile–rights of
   In Re Gault 387 US 1 (1966)

Obscene periodicals
   Redrup v. New York, Austin v. Kentucky, Gent v. Arkansas 386 US 767 (1967)
   Aday v. United States 388 US 477 (1967)
   Potomac News Co. v. United States 389 US 47 (1967)
   Conner v. Hammond 389 US 48 (1967)

Censorship of nudist magazine
   Rosenbloom v. Virginia 388 US 450 (1967)

Seizure of obscene literature from house maintained for lewd purposes
   Monique Von Cleef v. New Jersey 395 US 814 (1969)

Defamation and Libel

Press in contempt for comments on pending litigation–fair trial
   Bridges v. California 314 US 252 (1941)

Press in contempt for criticism of the court
 Pennekamp v. Florida 328 US 331 (1946)

Criminal libel law tested
 Ashton v. Kentucky 384 US 195 (1966)

Defamation of a public official
 Rosenblatt v. Baer 383 US 75 (1966)

Publication invading privacy
 Time, Inc. v. Hill 385 US 374 (1966)

Libel of a public official by the press
 Beckley Newspapers v. Hanks 389 US 81 (1967)

Political Dissent

Use of flag for commercial purposes
 Halter v. Nebraska 205 US 34 (1907)

Speech critical of WWI policies
 Debs v. United States 249 US 211 (1919)

Publication of materials critical of WWI policies
 Abrams v. United States 250 US 616 (1919)
 Frohewerk v. United States 249 US 204 (1919)

Congressional investigation committee
 McGrain v. Daugherty 273 US 135 (1927)

Syndicalism
 Whitney v. California 274 US 357 (1927)
 Fiske v. Kansas 274 US 380 (1927)

Disclosure of KKK membership lists
 Bryant v. Zimmerman 278 US 63 (1928)

Red flag laws
 Stromberg v. California 283 US 359 (1931)

Possession of Communist literature
 Herndon v. Lowery 301 US 242 (1937)

Civil v. military courts
 Duncan v. Kahanamoku 327 US 304 (1946)

Clear and present danger and the Communist Party
 Dennis v. United States 341 US 494 (1951)

Advocacy of overthrow
 Yates v. United States 354 US 298 (1957)

Contempt for refusal to cooperate with congressional investigation
 Watkins v. United States 354 US 178 (1957)

Disclosure of membership and records
 Garner v. Board of Public Works 341 US 716 (1951)
 NAACP v. Alabama 357 US 449 (1958)
 Bates v. Little Rock 361 US 516 (1960)
 Louisiana v. NAACP 366 US 293 (1961)

Religious test for holding public office
  Torcaso v. Watkins 367 US 488 (1961)

Passports revoked for failure to register as a Communist organization
  Aptheker v. Secretary of State 378 US 500 (1964)

Seizure of "Communist" literature
  Stanford v. Texas 379 US 476 (1965)

Conscientious objection
  United States v. Seeger 380 US 163 (1965)

Denial of seat in state legislature for political statements
  Bond v. Floyd 385 US 116 (1966)

Travel to a restricted area
  United States v. Laub 385 US 475 (1967)

Conscientious objector's protest by turning in registration cards
  Oestereich v. Selective Service Board 393 US 233 (1968)
  Gutknecht v. United States 396 US 295 (1970)

Nonreligious conscientious objection
  Welsch v. United States 398 US 333 (1970)

Privacy

Freedom of Movement
  Edwards v. California 314 US 160 (1941)

Intercepted telephone communication
  Goldstein v. United States 316 US 114 (1942)

Curfew
  Hirabayashi v. United States 320 US 81 (1943)

Detention
  Ex Parte Endo 323 US 283 (1944)

Door-to-door selling
  Breard v. City of Alexandria 341 US 622 (1951)

Use of contraceptives
  Poe v. Ullman 367 US 497 (1961)

Wiretapping
  Schwartz v. Texas 344 US 199 (1953)
  Silverman v. United States 365 US 505 (1961)

Eavesdropping by a paid informer
  Hoffa v. United States 385 US 293 (1966)
  Katz v. United States 389 US 347 (1967)

Surveillance
  Mancusi v. DeForte 392 US 364 (1968)

Illegal eavesdropping on murderous threats
  Alderman v. United States 394 US 165 (1969)

Provocation and Demonstration

Permits to speak on public property
Davis v. Massachusetts 167 US 43 (1897)

Breaking an injunction which limited disclosure of information
Gompers v. United States 233 US 604 (1914)

Speaker incitement to riot
De Jonge v. State of Oregon 299 US 353 (1937)

Ordinance restricting distribution of circulars, etc.
Lovell v. Griffin 303 US 444 (1938)

Dissemination of information in labor dispute
Thornhill v. Alabama 310 US 88 (1940)

Soliciting religious contributions in residential area
Cantwell v. Connecticut 310 US 296 (1940)

Discretion in granting permits for parades, etc.
Cox v. New Hampshire 312 US 569 (1941)

Peaceful picketing and abusive language
Cafeteria Union v. Angeles 320 US 293 (1943)

Sale of religious literature by minors
Prince v. Massachusetts 321 US 158 (1944)

Loudspeakers
Saia v. New York 334 US 558 (1948)

Speech connected with an illegal act
Giboney v. Empire Storage and Ice Company 336 US 490 (1949)

Potential riot outside private hall rented by racist speaker
Terminiello v. Chicago 337 US 1 (1949)

Conducting a religious street service without a permit
Kunz v. New York 340 US 290 (1951)

Door-to-door selling
Breard v. City of Alexandria 341 US 622 (1951)

Permit to speak in public park
Poulos v. New Hampshire 345 US 395 (1953)

Labor picketing
Garner v. Teamsters Union 347 US 485 (1953)

Intimidation and Threats in Labor dispute
United Automobile Workers v. Russell 356 US 634 (1958)

Loitering
Tompson v. City of Louisville 362 US 199 (1960)

Blue laws
McGowan v. Maryland 366 US 420 (1961)
Braufeld v. Brown 366 US 599 (1961)

Demonstrations on state capitol grounds
   Edwards v. *South Carolina 372 US 229 (1963)*

Sit-ins in a restaurant
   Bell v. *Maryland 378 US 226 (1964)*

Use of public library by Negroes
   Brown v. *Louisiana 383 US 131 (1966)*

Parading when denied a permit
   Shuttlesworth v. *City of Birmingham 394 US 147 (1969)*

Employer's right to free speech
   National Labor Relations Board v. *Gessel Packing 395 US 575 (1969)*

Antiwar demonstration and sit-in in recruiting station
   Bachellar v. *Maryland 397 US 564 (1970)*

Disturbing the peace at a political rally
   Gunn v. *University Committee to End the War in Viet Nam 399 US 383 (1970)*

Format for Developing New Cases

Name _____

_____

v.

_____

_____ US _____ , _____ , 19 _____

SUMMARY:

Justices:

_____1   _____2

_____ 3

_____ 4

_____ 5

_____ 6

Name _____

_____ **7**

_____ **8**

_____ **9**

_____ **10**

Decision

_____

v.

_____

_____ US _____   _____ , 19____

The Court held that

_____

_____

_____

_____

_____

Majority   *Dissenting*

Name _____

_____

v.

_____

_____ US _____ , _____ , 19 _____

SUMMARY:

Justices:

_____|1   _____|2

_____ 3   _____ 4

_____ 5   _____ 6

Name _____

_____ **7**

_____ **8**

_____ **9**

_____ **10**

Decision

_____

v.

_____

_____ US _____   _____ , 19____

The Court held that

_____

_____

_____

_____

_____

Majority   _Dissenting_

Name _____

_____

v.

_____

_____ US _____ , _____ , 19 _____

SUMMARY:

Justices:

_____ 1   _____ 2

_____ 3

_____ 4

_____ 5

_____ 6

Name _____

_____ 7   _____ 8

_____ 9   _____ 10

Decision

_____

v.

_____

_____ US _____   _____ , 19___

The Court held that

_____

_____

_____

_____

_____

Majority   *Dissenting*

Name _____

_____

v.

_____

_____ US _____ , _____ , 19 _____

SUMMARY:

Justices:

_____1   _____2

_____ 3

_____ 4

_____ 5

_____ 6

Name _____

_____ **7**

_____ **8**

_____ **9**

_____ **10**

Decision

_____

v.

_____

_____ US _____   _____ , 19 _____

The Court held that

_____

_____

_____

_____

_____

Majority   _Dissenting_

Name _____

_____

v.

_____

_____ US _____ , _____ , 19 _____

SUMMARY:

Justices:

_____1   _____2

_____ 3

_____ 4

_____ 5

_____ 6

Name _____

_____ 7

_____ 8

_____ 9

_____ 10

Decision

_____

v.

_____

_____ US _____   _____ , 19____

The Court held that

_____

_____

_____

_____

_____

Majority   *Dissenting*

Appendix D

Ballots

Name _____

NINE MEN PLUS
An Academic Game-Simulation

Individual Score Sheet

PHASE I *Who Won*	PHASE II *Which Way Justice*	PHASE III *If I Were Justice Today*	T O T A L S
100 points if you correctly selected the party who won the case.	10 points for each justice you correctly assigned to a majority or minority opinion. Minus 10 points for any incorrect assignment.	Persuasion-Conviction Vote 100 points—if unanimous 75 points—if more than simple majority 50 points—if one vote majority 25 points—if more than one man minority* 0 points—if tie 0 points—if one man minority*	
Write in parties in the case and circle the party you think won.	Limited to two justices per case.	*If same pattern of voting in *this Phase* occurs in Case 2 or 3 as in Case 1, the minority's score should be equalized to the total of the majority.	

Case 1 _____

      versus

_____

_____ Points

Majority Dissenting   I side with

1._____ 1._____   _____

2._____ 2._____

_____ Points   _____ Points

_____

The game is more competitive when three cases are played.

Play three cases to determine your GRAND TOTAL_____

Name _____

NINE MEN PLUS
An Academic Game-Simulation

Individual Score Sheet

PHASE I	PHASE II	PHASE III	T
Who Won	*Which Way Justice*	*If I Were Justice Today*	O
100 points if you correctly selected the party who won the case.	10 points for each justice you correctly assigned to a majority or minority opinion. Minus 10 points for any incorrect assignment.	Persuasion-Conviction Vote 100 points—if unanimous 75 points—if more than simple majority 50 points—if one vote majority 25 points—if more than one man minority* 0 points—if tie 0 points—if one man minority*	T A L
Write in parties in the case and circle the party you think won.	Limited to two justices per case.	*If same pattern of voting in *this Phase* occurs in Case 2 or 3 as in Case 1, the minority's score should be equalized to the total of the majority.	S

Case 1 _____   Majority   Dissenting   I side with

      versus   1._____ 1._____   _____

_____   2._____ 2._____

_____ Points   _____ Points   _____ Points   _____

The game is more competitive when three cases are played.

Play three cases to determine your GRAND TOTAL_____

Name _____

NINE MEN PLUS
An Academic Game-Simulation

Individual Score Sheet

PHASE I *Who Won*	PHASE II *Which Way Justice*	PHASE III *If I Were Justice Today*	T O T A L S
100 points if you correctly selected the party who won the case.	10 points for each justice you correctly assigned to a majority or minority opinion. Minus 10 points for any incorrect assignment.	Persuasion-Conviction Vote 100 points—if unanimous 75 points—if more than simple majority 50 points—if one vote majority 25 points—if more than one man minority* 0 points—if tie 0 points—if one man minority*	
Write in parties in the case and circle the party you think won.	Limited to two justices per case.	*If same pattern of voting in *this Phase* occurs in Case 2 or 3 as in Case 1, the minority's score should be equalized to the total of the majority.	

Case 1 _____   Majority Dissenting   I side with

        versus   1._____ 1._____   _____

_____   2._____ 2._____

_____ Points   _____ Points   _____ Points   _____

The game is more competitive when three cases are played.

Play three cases to determine your GRAND TOTAL _____

Name _____

NINE MEN PLUS
An Academic Game-Simulation

Individual Score Sheet

PHASE I *Who Won*	PHASE II *Which Way Justice*	PHASE III *If I Were Justice Today*	T O T A L S
100 points if you correctly selected the party who won the case.	10 points for each justice you correctly assigned to a majority or minority opinion. Minus 10 points for any incorrect assignment.	Persuasion-Conviction Vote 100 points—if unanimous 75 points—if more than simple majority 50 points—if one vote majority 25 points—if more than one man minority* 0 points—if tie 0 points—if one man minority*	
Write in parties in the case and circle the party you think won.	Limited to two justices per case.	*If same pattern of voting in *this Phase* occurs in Case 2 or 3 as in Case 1, the minority's score should be equalized to the total of the majority.	

Case 1 _____   Majority   Dissenting   I side with

       versus   1._____   1._____   _____

_____   2._____   2._____

_____ Points   _____ Points   _____ Points   _____

The game is more competitive when three cases are played.

Play three cases to determine your GRAND TOTAL_____

Name _____

NINE MEN PLUS
An Academic Game-Simulation

Individual Score Sheet

PHASE I *Who Won*	PHASE II *Which Way Justice*	PHASE III *If I Were Justice Today*	T O T A L S
100 points if you correctly selected the party who won the case.	10 points for each justice you correctly assigned to a majority or minority opinion. Minus 10 points for any incorrect assignment.	Persuasion-Conviction Vote 100 points—if unanimous 75 points—if more than simple majority 50 points—if one vote majority 25 points—if more than one man minority* 0 points—if tie 0 points—if one man minority*	
Write in parties in the case and circle the party you think won.	Limited to two justices per case.	*If same pattern of voting in *this Phase* occurs in Case 2 or 3 as in Case 1, the minority's score should be equalized to the total of the majority.	

Case 1 _____   Majority   Dissenting   I side with

versus   1._____ 1._____   _____

_____   2._____ 2._____

_____ Points   _____ Points   _____ Points   _____

The game is more competitive when three cases are played.

Play three cases to determine your GRAND TOTAL_____

Name _____

NINE MEN PLUS
An Academic Game-Simulation

Individual Score Sheet

PHASE I *Who Won*	PHASE II *Which Way Justice*	PHASE III *If I Were Justice Today*	T O T A L S
100 points if you correctly selected the party who won the case.	10 points for each justice you correctly assigned to a majority or minority opinion. Minus 10 points for any incorrect assignment.	Persuasion-Conviction Vote 100 points—if unanimous 75 points—if more than simple majority 50 points—if one vote majority 25 points—if more than one man minority* 0 points—if tie 0 points—if one man minority*	
Write in parties in the case and circle the party you think won.	Limited to two justices per case.	*If same pattern of voting in *this Phase* occurs in Case 2 or 3 as in Case 1, the minority's score should be equalized to the total of the majority.	

Case 1 _____   Majority   Dissenting   I side with

versus   1. _____   1. _____   _____

_____   2. _____   2. _____

_____ Points   _____ Points   _____ Points   _____

The game is more competitive when three cases are played.

Play three cases to determine your GRAND TOTAL _____

Name _____

NINE MEN PLUS
An Academic Game-Simulation

Individual Score Sheet

PHASE I	PHASE II	PHASE III	
Who Won	*Which Way Justice*	*If I Were Justice Today*	**T O T A L S**

PHASE I — Who Won

100 points if you correctly selected the party who won the case.

Write in parties in the case and circle the party you think won.

PHASE II — Which Way Justice

10 points for each justice you correctly assigned to a majority or minority opinion. Minus 10 points for any incorrect assignment.

Limited to two justices per case.

PHASE III — If I Were Justice Today

Persuasion-Conviction Vote

100 points—if unanimous
75 points—if more than simple majority
50 points—if one vote majority
25 points—if more than one man minority*
0 points—if tie
0 points—if one man minority*

*If same pattern of voting in *this Phase* occurs in Case 2 or 3 as in Case 1, the minority's score should be equalized to the total of the majority.

Case 1 _____

      versus

_____

_____ Points

Majority Dissenting

1. _____ 1. _____

2. _____ 2. _____

_____ Points

I side with

_____

_____ Points

_____

The game is more competitive when three cases are played.

Play three cases to determine your GRAND TOTAL _____

Name _____

NINE MEN PLUS
An Academic Game-Simulation

Individual Score Sheet

PHASE I *Who Won*	PHASE II *Which Way Justice*	PHASE III *If I Were Justice Today*	T O T A L S
100 points if you correctly selected the party who won the case.	10 points for each justice you correctly assigned to a majority or minority opinion. Minus 10 points for any incorrect assignment.	Persuasion-Conviction Vote 100 points—if unanimous 75 points—if more than simple majority 50 points—if one vote majority 25 points—if more than one man minority* 0 points—if tie 0 points—if one man minority*	
Write in parties in the case and circle the party you think won.	Limited to two justices per case.	*If same pattern of voting in *this Phase* occurs in Case 2 or 3 as in Case 1, the minority's score should be equalized to the total of the majority.	

Case 1 _____

        versus

_____

_____ Points

Majority Dissenting   I side with

1._____ 1._____   _____

2._____ 2._____

_____ Points   _____ Points

_____

The game is more competitive when three cases are played.

Play three cases to determine your GRAND TOTAL_____

Name _____

NINE MEN PLUS
An Academic Game-Simulation

Individual Score Sheet

PHASE I **Who Won**	PHASE II **Which Way Justice**	PHASE III **If I Were Justice Today**	T O T A L S
100 points if you correctly selected the party who won the case.	10 points for each justice you correctly assigned to a majority or minority opinion. Minus 10 points for any incorrect assignment.	Persuasion-Conviction Vote 100 points—if unanimous 75 points—if more than simple majority 50 points—if one vote majority 25 points—if more than one man minority* 0 points—if tie 0 points—if one man minority*	
Write in parties in the case and circle the party you think won.	Limited to two justices per case.	*If same pattern of voting in *this Phase* occurs in Case 2 or 3 as in Case 1, the minority's score should be equalized to the total of the majority.	

Case 1 _____

      versus

_____

_____ Points

Majority Dissenting   I side with

1._____ 1._____   _____

2._____ 2._____

_____ Points   _____ Points

_____

The game is more competitive when three cases are played.

Play three cases to determine your GRAND TOTAL.____

Name _____

NINE MEN PLUS
An Academic Game-Simulation

Individual Score Sheet

PHASE I *Who Won*	PHASE II *Which Way Justice*	PHASE III *If I Were Justice Today*	T O T A L S
100 points if you correctly selected the party who won the case.	10 points for each justice you correctly assigned to a majority or minority opinion. Minus 10 points for any incorrect assignment.	Persuasion-Conviction Vote 100 points—if unanimous 75 points—if more than simple majority 50 points—if one vote majority 25 points—if more than one man minority* 0 points—if tie 0 points—if one man minority*	
Write in parties in the case and circle the party you think won.	Limited to two justices per case.	*If same pattern of voting in *this Phase* occurs in Case 2 or 3 as in Case 1, the minority's score should be equalized to the total of the majority.	

Case 1 _____

       versus

_____

_____ Points

Majority Dissenting   I side with

1. _____ 1. _____   _____

2. _____ 2. _____

_____ Points   _____ Points

_____

The game is more competitive when three cases are played.

Play three cases to determine your GRAND TOTAL _____

Name _____

NINE MEN PLUS
An Academic Game-Simulation

Individual Score Sheet

PHASE I *Who Won*	PHASE II *Which Way Justice*	PHASE III *If I Were Justice Today*	T O T A L S
100 points if you correctly selected the party who won the case.	10 points for each justice you correctly assigned to a majority or minority opinion. Minus 10 points for any incorrect assignment.	Persuasion-Conviction Vote 100 points—if unanimous 75 points—if more than simple majority 50 points—if one vote majority 25 points—if more than one man minority* 0 points—if tie 0 points—if one man minority*	
Write in parties in the case and circle the party you think won.	Limited to two justices per case.	*If same pattern of voting in *this Phase* occurs in Case 2 or 3 as in Case 1, the minority's score should be equalized to the total of the majority.	

Case 1 _____   Majority Dissenting   I side with

versus   1._____ 1._____   _____

_____   2._____ 2._____

_____ Points   _____ Points   _____ Points   _____

The game is more competitive when three cases are played.

Play three cases to determine your GRAND TOTAL_____

Name _____

NINE MEN PLUS
An Academic Game-Simulation

Individual Score Sheet

PHASE I *Who Won*	PHASE II *Which Way Justice*	PHASE III *If I Were Justice Today*	T O T A L S
100 points if you correctly selected the party who won the case.	10 points for each justice you correctly assigned to a majority or minority opinion. Minus 10 points for any incorrect assignment.	Persuasion-Conviction Vote 100 points—if unanimous 75 points—if more than simple majority 50 points—if one vote majority 25 points—if more than one man minority* 0 points—if tie 0 points—if one man minority*	
Write in parties in the case and circle the party you think won.	Limited to two justices per case.	*If same pattern of voting in *this Phase* occurs in Case 2 or 3 as in Case 1, the minority's score should be equalized to the total of the majority.	

Case 1 _____

       versus

_____

_____ Points

Majority   Dissenting   I side with

1. _____ 1. _____   _____

2. _____ 2. _____

_____ Points   _____ Points

_____

The game is more competitive when three cases are played.

Play three cases to determine your GRAND TOTAL _____

Name _____

NINE MEN PLUS
An Academic Game-Simulation

Individual Score Sheet

PHASE I *Who Won*	PHASE II *Which Way Justice*	PHASE III *If I Were Justice Today*	T O T A L S
100 points if you correctly selected the party who won the case.	10 points for each justice you correctly assigned to a majority or minority opinion. Minus 10 points for any incorrect assignment.	Persuasion-Conviction Vote 100 points—if unanimous 75 points—if more than simple majority 50 points—if one vote majority 25 points—if more than one man minority* 0 points—if tie 0 points—if one man minority*	
Write in parties in the case and circle the party you think won.	Limited to two justices per case.	*If same pattern of voting in *this Phase* occurs in Case 2 or 3 as in Case 1, the minority's score should be equalized to the total of the majority.	

Case 1 _____   Majority   Dissenting   I side with

        versus   1._____   1._____   _____

_____   2._____   2._____

_____ Points   _____ Points   _____ Points   _____

The game is more competitive when three cases are played.

Play three cases to determine your GRAND TOTAL _____

Name _____

NINE MEN PLUS
An Academic Game-Simulation

Individual Score Sheet

PHASE I *Who Won*	PHASE II *Which Way Justice*	PHASE III *If I Were Justice Today*	T O T A L S
100 points if you correctly selected the party who won the case.	10 points for each justice you correctly assigned to a majority or minority opinion. Minus 10 points for any incorrect assignment.	Persuasion-Conviction Vote 100 points—if unanimous 75 points—if more than simple majority 50 points—if one vote majority 25 points—if more than one man minority* 0 points—if tie 0 points—if one man minority*	
Write in parties in the case and circle the party you think won.	Limited to two justices per case.	*If same pattern of voting in *this Phase* occurs in Case 2 or 3 as in Case 1, the minority's score should be equalized to the total of the majority.	

Case 1 _____   Majority   Dissenting   I side with

       versus   1._____ 1._____   _____

_____   2._____ 2._____

_____ Points   _____ Points   _____ Points   _____

The game is more competitive when three cases are played.

Play three cases to determine your GRAND TOTAL _____

Name _____

NINE MEN PLUS
An Academic Game-Simulation

Individual Score Sheet

PHASE I *Who Won*	PHASE II *Which Way Justice*	PHASE III *If I Were Justice Today*	T O T A L S
100 points if you correctly selected the party who won the case.	10 points for each justice you correctly assigned to a majority or minority opinion. Minus 10 points for any incorrect assignment.	Persuasion-Conviction Vote 100 points—if unanimous 75 points—if more than simple majority 50 points—if one vote majority 25 points—if more than one man minority* 0 points—if tie 0 points—if one man minority*	
Write in parties in the case and circle the party you think won.	Limited to two justices per case.	*If same pattern of voting in *this Phase* occurs in Case 2 or 3 as in Case 1, the minority's score should be equalized to the total of the majority.	

Case 1 _____   Majority Dissenting   I side with

       versus   1._____ 1._____   _____

_____

                            2._____ 2._____

_____ Points   _____ Points   _____ Points   _____

The game is more competitive when three cases are played.

Play three cases to determine your GRAND TOTAL_____

Name _____

NINE MEN PLUS
An Academic Game-Simulation

Individual Score Sheet

PHASE I *Who Won*	PHASE II *Which Way Justice*	PHASE III *If I Were Justice Today*	T O T A L S
100 points if you correctly selected the party who won the case.	10 points for each justice you correctly assigned to a majority or minority opinion. Minus 10 points for any incorrect assignment.	Persuasion-Conviction Vote 100 points—if unanimous 75 points—if large majority 50 points—if one vote majority 25 points—if more than one man minority* 0 points—if tie 0 points—if one man minority*	
Write in parties in the case and circle the party you think won.	Limited to two justices per case.	*If same pattern of voting in *this Phase* occurs, the minority's score will be equal to the total of the majority.	

Case 1 _____   Majority   Minority   I side with

versus   1. _____   1. _____   _____

_____   2. _____   2. _____

_____ Points   _____ Points   _____ Points   _____

Case 2 _____   Majority   Minority   I side with

versus   1. _____   1. _____   _____ *

_____   2. _____   2. _____

_____ Points   _____ Points   _____ Points   _____

Case 3 _____   Majority   Minority   I side with

versus   1. _____   1. _____   _____ *

_____   2. _____   2. _____

_____ Points   _____ Points   _____ Points   _____

The game is more competitive if three cases are played.

YOUR GRAND TOTAL _____

Name _____

NINE MEN PLUS
An Academic Game-Simulation

Individual Score Sheet

PHASE I *Who Won*	PHASE II *Which Way Justice*	PHASE III *If I Were Justice Today*	T O T A L S
100 points if you correctly selected the party who won the case.	10 points for each justice you correctly assigned to a majority or minority opinion. Minus 10 points for any incorrect assignment.	Persuasion-Conviction Vote 100 points—if unanimous 75 points—if large majority 50 points—if one vote majority 25 points—if more than one man minority* 0 points—if tie 0 points—if one man minority*	
Write in parties in the case and circle the party you think won.	Limited to two justices per case.	*If same pattern of voting in *this Phase* occurs, the minority's score will be equal to the total of the majority.	

Case 1 _____

versus

_____

_____ Points

Majority   Minority   I side with

1. _____   1. _____   _____

2. _____   2. _____

_____ Points   _____ Points

_____

Case 2 _____

versus

_____

_____Points

Majority   Minority   I side with

1. _____   1. _____   _____*

2. _____   2. _____

_____ Points   _____ Points

_____

Case 3 _____

versus

_____

_____ Points

Majority   Minority   I side with

1. _____   1. _____   _____*

2. _____   2. _____

_____ Points   _____ Points

_____

The game is more competitive if three cases are played.

YOUR GRAND TOTAL _____

Name _____

NINE MEN PLUS
An Academic Game-Simulation

Individual Score Sheet

PHASE I *Who Won*	PHASE II *Which Way Justice*	PHASE III *If I Were Justice Today*	T O T A L S
100 points if you correctly selected the party who won the case.	10 points for each justice you correctly assigned to a majority or minority opinion. Minus 10 points for any incorrect assignment.	Persuasion-Conviction Vote 100 points—if unanimous 75 points—if large majority 50 points—if one vote majority 25 points—if more than one man minority* 0 points—if tie 0 points—if one man minority*	
Write in parties in the case and circle the party you think won.	Limited to two justices per case.	*If same pattern of voting in *this Phase* occurs, the minority's score will be equal to the total of the majority.	

Case 1 _____   Majority   Minority   I side with

versus   1. _____ 1. _____   _____

_____   2. _____ 2. _____

_____ Points   _____ Points   _____ Points   _____

Case 2 _____   Majority   Minority   I side with

versus   1. _____ 1. _____   _____ *

_____   2. _____ 2. _____

_____ Points   _____ Points   _____ Points   _____

Case 3 _____   Majority   Minority   I side with

versus   1. _____ 1. _____   _____ *

_____   2. _____ 2. _____

_____ Points   _____ Points   _____ Points   _____

The game is more competitive if
three cases are played.

YOUR GRAND TOTAL _____

Name _____

NINE MEN PLUS
An Academic Game-Simulation

Individual Score Sheet

			T
PHASE I *Who Won*	**PHASE II** *Which Way Justice*	**PHASE III** *If I Were Justice Today*	O
100 points if you correctly selected the party who won the case.	10 points for each justice you correctly assigned to a majority or minority opinion. Minus 10 points for any incorrect assignment.	Persuasion-Conviction Vote 100 points—if unanimous 75 points—if large majority 50 points—if one vote majority 25 points—if more than one man minority* 0 points—if tie 0 points—if one man minority*	T A L
Write in parties in the case and circle the party you think won.	Limited to two justices per case.	*If same pattern of voting in *this Phase* occurs, the minority's score will be equal to the total of the majority.	S

Case 1 _____

versus

_____

_____ Points

Majority   Minority   I side with

1. _____ 1. _____ _____

2. _____ 2. _____

_____ Points   _____ Points

_____

Case 2 _____

versus

_____

_____Points

Majority   Minority   I side with

1. _____ 1. _____ _____*

2. _____ 2. _____

_____ Points   _____ Points

_____

Case 3 _____

versus

_____

_____ Points

Majority   Minority   I side with

1._____ 1. _____ _____*

2._____ 2. _____

_____ Points   _____ Points

_____

The game is more competitive if three cases are played.

YOUR GRAND TOTAL _____

Name _____

NINE MEN PLUS
An Academic Game-Simulation

Individual Score Sheet

PHASE I — *Who Won*	PHASE II — *Which Way Justice*	PHASE III — *If I Were Justice Today*	T O T A L S
100 points if you correctly selected the party who won the case.	10 points for each justice you correctly assigned to a majority or minority opinion. Minus 10 points for any incorrect assignment.	Persuasion-Conviction Vote 100 points—if unanimous 75 points—if large majority 50 points—if one vote majority 25 points—if more than one man minority* 0 points—if tie 0 points—if one man minority*	
Write in parties in the case and circle the party you think won.	Limited to two justices per case.	*If same pattern of voting in *this Phase* occurs, the minority's score will be equal to the total of the majority.	

Case 1 _____

versus

_____

____ Points

Majority   Minority   I side with

1. _____   1. _____   _____

'2. _____   2. _____

_____ Points   _____ Points

Case 2 _____

versus

_____

_____ Points

Majority   Minority   I side with

1. _____   1. _____   _____ *

2. _____   2. _____

_____ Points   _____ Points

Case 3 _____

versus

_____

_____ Points

Majority   Minority   I side with

1. _____   1. _____   _____ *

2. _____   2. _____

_____ Points   _____ Points

The game is more competitive if three cases are played.

YOUR GRAND TOTAL ____

Name _____

NINE MEN PLUS
An Academic Game-Simulation

Individual Score Sheet

PHASE I _Who Won_	PHASE II _Which Way Justice_	PHASE III _If I Were Justice Today_	T O T A L S
100 points if you correctly selected the party who won the case.	10 points for each justice you correctly assigned to a majority or minority opinion. Minus 10 points for any incorrect assignment.	Persuasion-Conviction Vote 100 points—if unanimous 75 points—if large majority 50 points—if one vote majority 25 points—if more than one man minority* 0 points—if tie 0 points—if one man minority*	
Write in parties in the case and circle the party you think won.	Limited to two justices per case.	*If same pattern of voting in _this Phase_ occurs, the minority's score will be equal to the total of the majority.	

Case 1 _____

versus

_____

_____ Points

Majority   Minority   I side with

1. _____   1. _____   _____

'2. _____   2. _____

_____ Points   _____ Points

_____

Case 2 _____

versus

_____

_____ Points

Majority   Minority   I side with

1. _____   1. _____   _____ *

2. _____   2. _____

_____ Points   _____ Points

_____

Case 3 _____

versus

_____

_____ Points

Majority   Minority   I side with

1. _____   1. _____   _____ *

2. _____   2. _____

_____ Points   _____ Points

_____

The game is more competitive if three cases are played.

YOUR GRAND TOTAL _____

Name _____

NINE MEN PLUS
An Academic Game-Simulation

Individual Score Sheet

PHASE I *Who Won*	PHASE II *Which Way Justice*	PHASE III *If I Were Justice Today*	T O T A L S
100 points if you correctly selected the party who won the case.	10 points for each justice you correctly assigned to a majority or minority opinion. Minus 10 points for any incorrect assignment.	Persuasion-Conviction Vote 100 points—if unanimous 75 points—if large majority 50 points—if one vote majority 25 points—if more than one man minority* 0 points—if tie 0 points—if one man minority*	
Write in parties in the case and circle the party you think won.	Limited to two justices per case.	*If same pattern of voting in *this Phase* occurs, the minority's score will be equal to the total of the majority.	

Case 1 _____

      versus

_____

_____ Points

Majority Minority I side with

1. _____ 1. _____ _____

2. _____ 2. _____

_____ Points   _____ Points

_____

Case 2 _____

      versus

_____

_____ Points

Majority Minority I side with

1. _____ 1. _____ _____*

2. _____ 2. _____

_____ Points   _____ Points

_____

Case 3 _____

      versus

_____

_____ Points

Majority Minority I side with

1. _____ 1. _____ _____*

2. _____ 2. _____

_____ Points   _____ Points

_____

The game is more competitive if three cases are played.

YOUR GRAND TOTAL _____

Name _____

NINE MEN PLUS
An Academic Game-Simulation

Individual Score Sheet

			T
PHASE I *Who Won*	**PHASE II** *Which Way Justice*	**PHASE III** *If I Were Justice Today*	O
100 points if you correctly selected the party who won the case.	10 points for each justice you correctly assigned to a majority or minority opinion. Minus 10 points for any incorrect assignment.	Persuasion-Conviction Vote 100 points—if unanimous 75 points—if large majority 50 points—if one vote majority 25 points—if more than one man minority* 0 points—if tie 0 points—if one man minority*	T A L
Write in parties in the case and circle the party you think won.	Limited to two justices per case.	*If same pattern of voting in *this Phase* occurs, the minority's score will be equal to the total of the majority.	S

Case 1 _____   Majority   Minority   I side with

        versus   1. _____ 1. _____   _____

_____   2. _____ 2. _____

_____ Points   _____ Points   _____ Points   _____

Case 2 _____   Majority   Minority   I side with

        versus   1. _____ 1. _____   _____*

_____   2. _____ 2. _____

_____ Points   _____ Points   _____ Points   _____

Case 3 _____   Majority   Minority   I side with

        versus   1. _____ 1. _____   _____*

_____   2. _____ 2. _____

_____ Points   _____ Points   _____ Points   _____

The game is more competitive if three cases are played.

YOUR GRAND TOTAL _____

Name _____

NINE MEN PLUS
An Academic Game-Simulation

Individual Score Sheet

PHASE I *Who Won*	PHASE II *Which Way Justice*	PHASE III *If I Were Justice Today*	T O T A L S
100 points if you correctly selected the party who won the case.	10 points for each justice you correctly assigned to a majority or minority opinion. Minus 10 points for any incorrect assignment.	Persuasion-Conviction Vote 100 points—if unanimous 75 points—if large majority 50 points—if one vote majority 25 points—if more than one man minority* 0 points—if tie 0 points—if one man minority*	
Write in parties in the case and circle the party you think won.	Limited to two justices per case.	*If same pattern of voting in *this Phase* occurs, the minority's score will be equal to the total of the majority.	

Case 1 _____

versus

_____

_____ Points

Majority   Minority   I side with

1. _____   1. _____   _____

2. _____   2. _____

_____ Points   _____ Points

_____

Case 2 _____

versus

_____

_____ Points

Majority   Minority   I side with

1. _____   1. _____   _____ *

2. _____   2. _____

_____ Points   _____ Points

_____

Case 3 _____

versus

_____

_____ Points

Majority   Minority   I side with

1. _____   1. _____   _____ *

2. _____   2. _____

_____ Points   _____ Points

_____

The game is more competitive if three cases are played.

YOUR GRAND TOTAL _____

Name _____

NINE MEN PLUS
An Academic Game-Simulation

Individual Score Sheet

PHASE I *Who Won*	PHASE II *Which Way Justice*	PHASE III *If I Were Justice Today*	T O T A L S
100 points if you correctly selected the party who won the case. Write in parties in the case and circle the party you think won.	10 points for each justice you correctly assigned to a majority or minority opinion. Minus 10 points for any incorrect assignment. Limited to two justices per case.	Persuasion-Conviction Vote 100 points—if unanimous 75 points—if large majority 50 points—if one vote majority 25 points—if more than one man minority* 0 points—if tie 0 points—if one man minority* *If same pattern of voting in *this Phase* occurs, the minority's score will be equal to the total of the majority.	

Case 1 _____

       versus

_____

_____ Points

Majority   Minority   I side with

1. _____ 1. _____ _____

2. _____ 2. _____

_____ Points   _____ Points

_____

Case 2 _____

       versus

_____

_____ Points

Majority   Minority   I side with

1. _____ 1. _____ _____ *

2. _____ 2. _____

_____ Points   _____ Points

_____

Case 3 _____

       versus

_____

_____ Points

Majority   Minority   I side with

1. _____ 1. _____ _____ *

2. _____ 2. _____

_____ Points   _____ Points

_____

The game is more competitive if three cases are played.

YOUR GRAND TOTAL _____

Name _____

NINE MEN PLUS
An Academic Game-Simulation

Individual Score Sheet

PHASE I *Who Won*	PHASE II *Which Way Justice*	PHASE III *If I Were Justice Today*	T O T A L S
100 points if you correctly selected the party who won the case.	10 points for each justice you correctly assigned to a majority or minority opinion. Minus 10 points for any incorrect assignment.	Persuasion-Conviction Vote 100 points—if unanimous 75 points—if large majority 50 points—if one vote majority 25 points—if more than one man minority* 0 points—if tie 0 points—if one man minority*	
Write in parties in the case and circle the party you think won.	Limited to two justices per case.	*If same pattern of voting in *this Phase* occurs, the minority's score will be equal to the total of the majority.	

Case 1 _____   Majority   Minority   I side with

versus   1. _____ 1. _____   _____

_____   2. _____ 2. _____

_____ Points   _____ Points   _____ Points   _____

Case 2 _____   Majority   Minority   I side with

versus   1. _____ 1. _____   _____*

_____   2. _____ 2. _____

_____ Points   _____ Points   _____ Points   _____

Case 3 _____   Majority   Minority   I side with

versus   1. _____ 1. _____   _____*

_____   2. _____ 2. _____

_____ Points   _____ Points   _____ Points   _____

The game is more competitive if three cases are played.

YOUR GRAND TOTAL _____

Name _____

NINE MEN PLUS
An Academic Game-Simulation

Individual Score Sheet

PHASE I *Who Won*	PHASE II *Which Way Justice*	PHASE III *If I Were Justice Today*	T O T A L S
100 points if you correctly selected the party who won the case.	10 points for each justice you correctly assigned to a majority or minority opinion. Minus 10 points for any incorrect assignment.	Persuasion-Conviction Vote 100 points—if unanimous 75 points—if large majority 50 points—if one vote majority 25 points—if more than one man minority* 0 points—if tie 0 points—if one man minority*	
Write in parties in the case and circle the party you think won.	Limited to two justices per case.	*If same pattern of voting in *this Phase* occurs, the minority's score will be equal to the total of the majority.	

Case 1 _____   Majority   Minority   I side with

       versus   1. _____   1. _____   _____

_____   2. _____   2. _____

_____ Points   _____ Points   _____ Points |_____

Case 2 _____   Majority   Minority   I side with

       versus   1. _____   1. _____   _____*

_____   2. _____   2. _____

_____ Points   _____ Points   _____ Points |_____

Case 3 _____   Majority   Minority   I side with

       versus   1. _____   1. _____   _____*

_____   2. _____   2. _____

_____ Points   _____ Points   _____ Points |_____

The game is more competitive if three cases are played.

YOUR GRAND TOTAL _____

NINE MEN PLUS
An Academic Game-Simulation

Individual Score Sheet

PHASE I *Who Won*	PHASE II *Which Way Justice*	PHASE III *If I Were Justice Today*	T O T A L S
100 points if you correctly selected the party who won the case.	10 points for each justice you correctly assigned to a majority or minority opinion. Minus 10 points for any incorrect assignment.	Persuasion-Conviction Vote 100 points—if unanimous 75 points—if large majority 50 points—if one vote majority 25 points—if more than one man minority* 0 points—if tie 0 points—if one man minority*	
Write in parties in the case and circle the party you think won.	Limited to two justices per case.	*If same pattern of voting in *this Phase* occurs, the minority's score will be equal to the total of the majority.	

Case 1 _____

     versus

_____

_____ Points

Majority   Minority   I side with

1. _____   1. _____   _____

2. _____   2. _____

_____ Points   _____ Points

_____

Case 2 _____

     versus

_____

_____ Points

Majority   Minority   I side with

1. _____   1. _____   _____ *

2. _____   2. _____

_____ Points   _____ Points

_____

Case 3 _____

     versus

_____

_____ Points

Majority   Minority   I side with

1. _____   1. _____   _____ *

2. _____   2. _____

_____ Points   _____ Points

_____

The game is more competitive if three cases are played.

YOUR GRAND TOTAL _____

Name _____

NINE MEN PLUS
An Academic Game-Simulation

Individual Score Sheet

PHASE I *Who Won*	PHASE II *Which Way Justice*	PHASE III *If I Were Justice Today*	T O T A L S
100 points if you correctly selected the party who won the case.	10 points for each justice you correctly assigned to a majority or minority opinion. Minus 10 points for any incorrect assignment.	Persuasion-Conviction Vote 100 points—if unanimous 75 points—if large majority 50 points—if one vote majority 25 points—if more than one man minority* 0 points—if tie 0 points—if one man minority*	
Write in parties in the case and circle the party you think won.	Limited to two justices per case.	*If same pattern of voting in *this Phase* occurs, the minority's score will be equal to the total of the majority.	

Case 1 _____

versus

_____

_____ Points

Majority   Minority   I side with

1. _____   1. _____   _____

2. _____   2. _____

_____ Points   _____ Points

_____

Case 2 _____

versus

_____

_____ Points

Majority   Minority   I side with

1. _____   1. _____   _____ *

2. _____   2. _____

_____ Points   _____ Points

_____

Case 3 _____

versus

_____

_____ Points

Majority   Minority   I side with

1. _____   1. _____   _____ *

2. _____   2. _____

_____ Points   _____ Points

_____

The game is more competitive if three cases are played.

YOUR GRAND TOTAL _____